MITTELEUROPA AND GERMAN POLITICS

Mitteleuropa and German Politics

1848 to the Present

Jörg Brechtefeld
Assistant Professor, Institute of Political Science
Christian-Albrechts-University, Kiel, Germany

St. Martin's Press
New York

MITTELEUROPA AND GERMAN POLITICS

For information, address:

St. Martin's Press, Scholarly and Reference Division,
175 Fifth Avenue, New York, N.Y. 10010

First published in the United States of America in 1996

Printed in Great Britain

ISBN 0-312-15841-6

Library of Congress Cataloging-in-Publication Data
Brechtefeld, Jörg.
Mitteleuropa and German politics: 1848 to the present / Jörg Brechtefeld.
p. cm.
Includes bibliographical references and index.
ISBN 0-312-15841-6
1. Europe, Central—Foreign relations—Germany. 2. Germany--Foreign relations—Europe, Central. 3. Germany—Politics and government—1848-1870. 4. Germany—Politics and government—1871-1918. 5. Germany—Politics and government—20th century. I. Title.
DAW1045.G3B74 1996
327'.0943—dc20 95-52081
CIP

Contents

Acknowledgements

First of all, I would like to thank my Doktorvater and friend Ed Keynes of the Department of Political Science at the Pennsylvania State University. I will always be grateful for all his patience and support in this project. This book is dedicated to him.

Thanks also to Vernon Aspaturian, Ron Filippelli and Simon Duke who were open to my problems, gave me good advice, and, at times, provided the necessary emotional support.

Furthermore, there are many people to be mentioned without whose help this project could not have been completed. Although I cannot mention everyone, I would like to thank the departmental staff at both of 'my universities', Kiel and Penn State, and, of course, all the librarians at various libraries in Germany and the United States. Also, thanks to all of my friends, particularly Harald Walter and Karsten Mauersberger. Last but not least, I want to thank Yvonne Kurkowski for her patience and engagement.

Finally, I thank the Institute for the Study of World Politics in Washington, whose generous support made my research and this book possible.

Acknowledgements

1 Introduction

Mitteleuropa is a concept of political will, . . . a German formulation. . . . The Germans will play their part in creating Mitteleuropa, or it will not be realized at all.

Albrecht Haushofer[1]

It [Mitteleuropa] will have a German nucleus, will obviously use the German language. . . . From the very outset . . . [Mitteleuropa] must display a spirit of compromise and flexibility in relation to all component national groups associated within it, for only thus can essential fundamental harmony develop.

Friedrich Naumann[2]

PROLOGUE

In German politics 'Mitteleuropa' was a key concept from the beginning of the nineteenth century until the Third Reich. Used and abused by various groups, organizations and individuals during this period, it always remained in the political arena as a vision, a concept, or a justification for imperialism, as in Hitler's case. As a result of Hitler's anathematization of the term and concept 'Mitteleuropa', after 1945 it disappeared in the political debate until the beginning of the 1980s, when it suddenly reappeared in Central Europe.

At the end of the 1980s, German unification and the break-up of the Soviet Empire catapulted Mitteleuropa to the centre of the Western world's attention. In the process, Germany, a Mitteleuropa advocate of long tradition, once more became the centre of Europe and, therefore, a point of political and economic reference for the Central European states of the former Soviet bloc. This work examines German Mitteleuropa policies with respect to such recent and historic developments by raising questions of continuity or renewal in German foreign policy.

The term 'Mitteleuropa' never has been merely a geographical term; it is also a political one, much as Europe, East and West, are terms that political scientists employ as synonyms for political ideas or concepts.[3] Traditionally, Mitteleuropa has been that part of Europe between East and West. As profane as this may sound, this is probably the most precise definition of Mitteleuropa available. As a term of political philosophy (Ideengeschichte), Mitteleuropa stood for the involuntary separation from the West and a conscious detachment from the East.[4] In this sense, Mitteleuropa is both anti-West and anti-East. Historically, the Germans viewed Mitteleuropa as a way to overcome their (perceived) isolation in Europe in times of political weakness as well as a means to justify hegemonic aspirations in times of political strength.[5] Mitteleuropa has an additional dimension as a mediator (Mittler) between the different ethnic and cultural groups in Europe's centre.[6] In this sense, supporters of Mitteleuropa have always stressed the cultural unity and the common traditions of the region by championing a truly multi-cultural society.

At the beginning of the twentieth century, in Germany, Mitteleuropa was *en vogue* in political and economic circles. In contrast to the terms 'Western' and 'Eastern' Europe, which are used (and sometimes abused) frequently to make a political statement, Mitteleuropa more or less vanished from political terminology after the Second World War. It was not until the early 1980s, in the states of the 'Eastern bloc', that the term reappeared in a context other than that of weather forecasts or geographical charts. It is intriguing to ask what has happened to the term and the political idea in Germany over the last forty-eight years. Did it disappear without a trace? Has the political reality of East and West been so persuasive in a normative sense that there was no intellectual space in the middle? Or was the concept of Mitteleuropa in German foreign policy submerged, merely lying dormant? These are some of the questions dealt with in this work.[7]

This book identifies the elements of a political concept, 'Mitteleuropa', as it applies to German foreign policy. Furthermore, it examines the political influence that these elements have had on foreign-policy decision-makers and, subsequently, on foreign policy itself. This work's principal hypothesis is that there has been a continuous Mitteleuropa orientation in German foreign policy from Bismarck's Reich to the unified Federal Republic. The work examines the impact that 'Mitteleuropa' concepts have had on German foreign policy since 1848.

The major purpose of this book is to develop an analytical model of Mitteleuropa for evaluating German foreign policy towards Central Europe. The current unstable situation in several South-Central European countries increasingly resembles the period immediately prior to 1914. Torn apart by civil war, ethnic conflicts, sub-national movements, increasing poverty, and, above all, the feeling of exclusion from Europe, these states are seeking solutions to their problems either within or outside the context of the European Union and NATO. Indeed, the international community's failure to stop aggression and/or civil or communal warfare in Yugoslavia is the most prominent illustration of these developments.

In the interim, large-scale migration threatens European stability as a whole. The total number of refugees seeking political asylum and better economic conditions in Germany increased daily by the hundreds, until Germany passed its new asylum law in 1993. Although Germany is being called upon to respond to these conditions, the scholarly literature is virtually silent on how German policy-makers can respond. Thus far, few scholars have articulated an empirical model of Mitteleuropa that might be useful to German foreign policy-makers casting about for a legitimate policy alternative to 'Westbindung' and the EU in dealing with the other states of Central Europe.[8]

Germany, today (1995), is economically the most important factor in Central Europe, despite its own problems resulting from unification and worldwide economic recession, as the following data illustrate. In 1990, Germany agreed to stabilize the Soviet Union (today Russia) with an overall commitment of $67.11 billion. In comparison, the United States promised only $9.24 billion. By April 1993 Germany had actually paid $40 billion, while the US had paid only $5.31 billion.[9] Furthermore, approximately 25–30 per cent of Hungary's exports and 50 per cent of Poland's foreign trade are conducted with the Federal Republic.[10] These figures speak for themselves. However, despite the fact that Germany is the biggest contributor to the international fund for economic assistance, and the most important trading partner for the Central European states, it still lacks a clear policy orientation towards the former Soviet-bloc states in Mitteleuropa.

This book seeks to fill a vacuum in the scholarly literature by examining the following major questions:

1. To what extent are today's political, economic, military and geographic conditions similar to conditions prior to 1945, before the concept of Mitteleuropa was anathematized?
2. To what extent does Germany's position as a unified country, in the current European state system, favour or postulate a leading role for Germany in shaping Central Europe?
3. Do Germany's foreign policy-makers either explicitly or implicitly employ the concept of 'Mitteleuropa' as an analytical policy-making tool or as a frame of reference?

In contrast to other works in this area, this work presents Mitteleuropa concepts as part of German nation-building. It is argued that Mitteleuropa has been domestic policy as much as foreign policy since it has been used as a means to shape the Germans' national identity. This work enhances the understanding of Germany's foreign policy as well as of the development of the European international system by examining the Mitteleuropa concept in its historical context and, thus, presenting it as one of the determining factors for German nation-building as much as for the European balance of power.

METHODOLOGY

This is a study of the domestic sources of foreign policy. However, one must acknowledge that no government conducts its foreign policy in an international vacuum. Both domestic and foreign policy are influenced by the international system which the actor confronts. To a certain extent, foreign and some domestic policies constitute responses to the international system.[11] While this work acknowledges this fact, it is more concerned about internal German developments and decision-making structures, especially because there is a broad range of literature[12] that deals with external influences on German foreign policy. By contrast, this work seeks to fill the lacuna in the literature with respect to the influence of domestic politics, society, and policy-making on German Mitteleuropa concepts.

This study employs the following general methodology. First, there is a thorough review of the literature on German foreign policy in relation to the concept of Mitteleuropa. In the era prior to 1945, the study will examine several periods in which the concept emerged or resurfaced (1848–71, 1871–1914, 1914–45, and after 1945). Special weight has been given to the statements or writings of policy-makers in order to ascertain and evaluate their perceptions of the concept's value as a policy-making tool.

In addition to the scholarly literature, a review of newspapers, periodicals, and political party publications and documents has been conducted. In the period after the Second World War, the literature review focuses on the works of Gregory Treverton,[13] Peter Merkl,[14] Edwina Campbell,[15] and others who have dealt with the concept implicitly rather than explicitly. As these works indicate, the concept of Mitteleuropa has never really vanished from the scholarly scene.

Secondly, the major archives on German policy have been examined in order to evaluate the vitality of the concept of Mitteleuropa in the foreign policy-making process. The primary archives of interest are the Bundesarchiv für deutsche Außenpolitik (Federal Archive for German Foreign Policy), the archive of the Auswärtigen Amt (German Foreign Office), the archive of the Institut für Europäische Geschichte (Institute for European History), the archive of the Gesellschaft für auswärtige Politik (Society for Foreign Policy), the archive of the Süd-Ost Europa Gesellschaft (Society for South-East Europe), and the Institut für Weltwirtschaft (Institute for World Economics). Special attention was given to the relationship between Germany and such Central European countries as Poland, Czechoslovakia (formerly), and Hungary.

Thirdly, considerable research time has been devoted to the perceptions of policy-makers and writers over time.[16] Their perceptions of the concept of Mitteleuropa (or lack thereof) and of Germany's role in Central Europe was significant in determining the degree of consciousness and/or legitimacy that the concept has had among relevant policy-makers. The theoretical core of this work is a functional, structural approach to foreign policy within the school of neorealism.[17] The structural, functional approach to international relations identifies in a given state's organization the decision-making structures for foreign policy. Furthermore, it evaluates such decisions according to their internal functions (domestic policy) and external functions (foreign policy).[18] In other words, policy-makers are identified in terms of their roles and functions within the decision-making structures of the foreign-policy establishment. Fundamental to this concept is an understanding of foreign policy as a result of two domestic factors. First, foreign policy is the result of pressures from and developments in the domestic political system. Secondly, it is the result of a decision-making process involving both individual and institutional decision-makers in response to these domestic pressures.[19] Therefore, foreign policy can be explained largely as 'sequential action'[20] within a domestic context, by focusing on identifiable individuals or groups of individuals in the decision-making process.

Domestic sources of foreign policy include perceptions of the existing national interest, the party system and political coalitions, and administrative and bureaucratic structures. National interest can be defined more concretely in terms of the economic, military, or territorial interests of a nation's foreign-policy decision-makers.[21]

The party system, administration and bureaucracy are part of the institutional framework that shapes and channels foreign policy. Obviously, in a centralized system with a monarch as head of state, as in Germany prior to the First World War, foreign policy is conducted differently from that of a pluralist, decentralized society, as in the Federal Republic. A functional, structural approach to foreign policy enables the student to trace a school of thought or a foreign-policy idea through history, despite changing political systems and structures.

In the scholarly literature, the analysis of foreign-policy decision-making has occurred on several levels. The focus has been on the 'organizational process' or on the 'intellectual process'.[22] The latter literature describes the interaction of ideas that shape decisions. The former is the more relevant level of analysis to this work, because it examines the perceptions and interactions of individuals, offices and agencies that make decisions.[23] As a tool within this analysis, the concept of 'role', as developed by Ralf Dahrendorf,[24] for example, describes the links between individuals and institutions. In most cases, individuals who play a part in the decision-making process are officials in a larger entity or organization. Their 'roles' as officials link the analysis of agencies and of individuals, since decisions are made by individuals in their role as an agency's official.[25] This functional, structural model of foreign policy affords an opportunity to analyse a country's foreign-policy orientation over time, although the constitutional and institutional settings may have changed.

As a form of applied analysis, this work enhances the understanding of decision-making in German foreign policy and the role that the particular concept of Mitteleuropa has played in it. Furthermore, it explains the effects that this policy concept has on the structure and power relations of the regional international system.

SCOPE

The scope of this work is characterized by its subject, 'Mitteleuropa'. As Henry Meyer has written:

> Writers and speakers of varying occupations in many countries endowed the term with a host of vague and different meanings. Geographers sought to give it definition; economists, politicians, and journalists manipulated it; and idealists caressed it with romantic devotion. The more current the expression became in Germany and abroad, the more vague, ambiguous, and emotional was its use.[26]

Therefore, it is critical to provide a clear and limited working definition of Mitteleuropa in geographical and political terms.

The scope of this book is confined to the German approach to Mitteleuropa. Thus the various views on Mitteleuropa expressed by Central European intellectuals and politicians, Czechoslovaks, Hungarians and Poles in particular, are disregarded, except in those cases where these views or concepts have a direct impact or influence on German thought.

For the purpose of this study, 'German' refers to all German populations both within and outside the German state. In cases where greater differentiation is useful, the respective geographic terms are employed, i.e., Reich-German, Austrian-German, Sudeten-German, and so forth. Furthermore, Austria is not considered to be part of Germany or German, aside from the period between the Anschluß in 1938 and the defeat of the Third Reich in 1945. However, there were important German and Austrian intellectuals and politicians within Austria during the inter-war period who held and articulated a Reich-German position and who are, therefore, referred to in this work.[27] Other than that, the Austrian vision of Mitteleuropa is either largely anti-German or, at least, posits Vienna as the natural heart of Mitteleuropa rather than Berlin.[28]

In addition, this work will not examine the problems of the specific German–Austrian relationship and its impact on Mitteleuropa aside from the discussion above. Even before Bismarck's decision in favour of a smaller Germany (kleindeutsche Lösung), the relationship between Austria and Germany must be considered as an intra-German problem. Until 1918 the question of Anschluß was a dynastic dispute between the Habsburg and the Hohenzollern kings about supremacy in a region that basically was understood as a cultural entity (Kulturgemeinschaft) by its political elite as well as by its inhabitants. Thus German politics towards Austria are not considered foreign policy. The fact that, despite the quarrels between the two empires, the German–Austrian military assistance pact was never truly questioned by either side before or during the First World War illustrates this point. The scope of this work, therefore, is limited to Germany's foreign policy towards the Central European countries with the exception of Austria.

Ethnic Germans are defined as those who consider themselves to be of German heritage and are considered as such by the state in which they live. The criterion of actual identification as Germans by their respective states, however, does not necessarily imply recognition as a legally protected minority. Rather, it implies recognition as a group with a different cultural background. Therefore, German Jews cannot be considered German even though it was Jewish-German culture that was the cultural base of Mitteleuropa. Some authors, such as Karl Schlögel or Martin Kutz,[29] argue that the typical Central European character was developed in a culture that resulted from centuries of German-Jewish assimilation and migration. These authors argue that the culture of Mitteleuropa cannot be separated from either its German or its Jewish component.

Therefore, the argument follows, the cultural entity of Mitteleuropa was lost after the Second World War in a twofold sense. First, many Central European Jews were exterminated by the Germans between 1935 and 1945. Secondly, the Red Army subsequently expelled the Germans from the region following Germany's defeat in 1945. Without pursuing this argument further at this point, undoubtedly Jewish culture and thought had a significant impact on German views of Mitteleuropa. However, this influence was primarily a cultural one, especially among the bourgeoisie, which did not find its way into explicit political statements or proposals regarding Mitteleuropa. Since it is virtually impossible to distinguish between the distinctly German and the distinctly Jewish within the German cultural heritage in Mitteleuropa, this work does not distinguish between German and Jewish positions or views in order to determine the influence of the Mitteleuropa concept on German foreign policy.

Furthermore, there is a clear distinction between Mitteleuropa as a political concept and as a pan-German idea. While both terms were frequently used interchangeably between 1914 and 1918, one has to separate them analytically. Pan-German ideas within Germany as well as among its neighbours have been 'equated with militarism, aggression, Prussianism, conquest, Caesarism, oppression, and annexation'.[30] For the purposes of this work, Mitteleuropa encompasses concepts that were economic and cultural rather than militaristic or imperial in nature. This is not to say that some Mitteleuropa ideas did not contain militaristic options. However, these concepts did not primarily envision an area from the North Cape to Baghdad under German hegemonic control.

The idea of Mitteleuropa encompasses three different and distinct dimensions.[31] The first dimension is cultural: that is, the idea of a cultural 'Gemeinschaft'[32] in the heart of Europe with common values, common traditions, and a common history. The second dimension is an economic one in the form of a common market or free-trade zone.[33] Finally, there is the political component, that is, a region with common political interests, primarily directed against Russia in the East and France in the West.[34]

One can also distinguish three more philosophically or theoretically oriented approaches regarding the 'mitteleuropäischen Traum':[35] the imperialistic, the romantic–political, and the cultural approaches.[36]

The imperialistic approach rests on an economic-capitalist view of Central Europe as a potential market for German manufactured goods, and on control of the area's resources.[37] At its core lies the demand for German economic hegemony in Central Europe. The 'Mitteleuropäische Wirtschaftsverein' is the most prominent example of an institutionalization of this view. This vision of Mitteleuropa posits Berlin as the ideological centre.

The romantic–political version advocates some form of revival or reconstruction of the Holy Roman Empire of the German Nation in the

Roman Catholic tradition as a bulwark against the Orthodox and Islamic religions. In contrast to the imperialistic approach, this view usually defines Vienna as the centre of Europe.[38] In its contemporary version, this view replaced the religious conflict line with the Cold War conflict between the East and West, which was useful in developing an anti-communist foreign policy. According to the romantic–political version, German hegemony usually has cultural and political-elite overtones, rather than economic ones.

Finally, there is the third version of Mitteleuropa as a narrow cultural concept that is largely non-political. The region's ethnic and nationalistic provincialism is to overcome through a notion of universalism shaped by literary traditions and the German language. Until today, German rather than English or Russian has been the *lingua franca* in large parts of Central Europe. Milan Kundera and others embody this view. The common denominator is the region's German cultural tradition.

All of these dimensions of the Mitteleuropa concept have one thing in common. They view Mitteleuropa as a quasi-framework transcending and opposing what Egbert Jahn has called the 'pseudo-universalism of social-nationalism' (pseudo-Universalismus des Sozialnationalismus).[39] In the geographically fragmented entity of Central Europe with its ethnic 'melting pot', social-nationalism has dominated the region. Before 1918, nationalism and its centrifugal force were among the major problems within the Austrian K&K (Kaiser und König, i.e., Emperor of Austria and King of Hungary) monarchy. As a result of the Versailles Treaty, in all Central European states, with the partial exception of Czechoslovakia, social-national (sozialnationale) governments were established, with the most horrifying version in Germany after 1933. As Jahn wrote, 'Mitteleuropa läßt sich nicht ohne diesen [sozialnationalistischen] gemeinsamen gesellschaftspolitischen Inhalt . . . begreifen.'[40] While advocates of this social-national tradition contributed to the development of Central Europe as an analytical concept, Mitteleuropa as a political concept extends beyond this tradition and rests on a more diversified vision of the region. If the concept of Mitteleuropa has failed in the past it is because the national political elites in the region have failed to solve problems of ethnic diversity in a humanistic or, at least, non-violent manner.

Henry C. Meyer has stated, in his pathbreaking work *Mitteleuropa in German Thought and Action*, that Mitteleuropa is one 'semantic confusion'.[41] Therefore, the geographic demarcation of the area is as difficult to determine as the intellectual, ideological identification of the term 'Mitteleuropa'. Like beauty, geographically the area of Central Europe varies according to the eye of the beholder.

Nevertheless, one can identify a maximal and a minimal version of Mitteleuropa as ideal types. Depending on the perspective applied and the global political and/or military situation, that is, especially during the First World War, the actual image of the area lies between these two extremes. The minimal version of Mitteleuropa contains the area between France and Russia, in other words, the basin between the rivers Rhine, Danube, and Vistula. It includes Germany, Austria/Hungary, Czechoslovakia, parts of Poland, and the Netherlands (see the Appendix on pp. 98–103).[42]

The maximal version of Mitteleuropa can be subsumed under the phrase 'from the North Cape to Baghdad' (vom Nordkap bis Bagdad). As early as the First World War both sides used the term as a propaganda tool. The Germans employed the concept to strengthen their troops' morale, while the Allies used it to convince their societies of an omnipresent German threat.[43] According to this concept, Mitteleuropa encompassed the vast area of Scandinavia, Europe to the Urals, France and the Benelux States, and the former Ottoman Empire to Baghdad. Evidently, Western Europe included only the British Isles and Spain. In Germany, the various visions of Central Europe oscillate between these two poles. However, middle-of-the-road versions of Mitteleuropa are usually closer to the minimal version in geographical scope.

All definitions of Mitteleuropa, geographic and political, clearly emphasize the second half of the word, 'Europa'; that is, they stress Europe in opposition to the non-European East, primarily Russia and the Central Asian countries.[44] The definitions become vague, however, in defining the middle. This book uses Mitteleuropa in its minimal definition, i.e., Germany, Austria (with the limitations expressed earlier), Hungary, Poland, the Czech Republic, Slovakia, Slovenia and Croatia. This is a definition of Mitteleuropa from the perspective of 1996. This work acknowledges that various areas and countries have changed their names and status over time, and deals with them in accordance with their contemporary status.

This definition has been chosen for two important reasons that are largely teleological. First, this work is interested in contemporary German foreign policy in Mitteleuropa. Naturally, this excludes all states within the EU or NATO. Germany has been fully integrated in these two 'Western' organizations at least since 1955, and its foreign policy towards these organizations has not been affected as greatly by the disintegration of the East as has German foreign policy towards its eastern neighbours. One can even argue that if Germany's foreign policy towards the European Union or NATO has changed significantly this may be a result of Germany's new relationship with the states of Mitteleuropa. In turn, incorporating EU or NATO states in an analysis of German Mitteleuropa policy would introduce a dimension that distorts the clarity of the analysis. Secondly, since 1990, German foreign policy towards these states has had the greatest impact on the region as well as on the larger international community. Therefore, from an analytical standpoint it is most fruitful to focus on the countries of Mitteleuropa.

In order to evaluate current German foreign policy towards its Central European neighbours, one has to trace the historic and theoretical roots of current policy to their origins. As the analysis suggests, there is a continuity in German foreign policy that can be subsumed under the phrase 'Mitteleuropa'. This work seeks to identify the continuous factors that influence Germany's current policy towards Central Europe.

2 The Intellectual and Political Precursors of 'Mitteleuropa' before the Second German Empire

INTRODUCTION

Prior to the establishment of the Second German Empire in 1871, concepts of Mitteleuropa resulted primarily from Austro-Prussian tensions. In the struggle for leadership of the German nation and the future German nation-state, Mitteleuropa was an instrument of national power. Whoever controlled the states of Mitteleuropa could also claim leadership of a future Germany. Compared with Prussia, Austria had the advantage, since the Danube monarchy controlled much of Central Europe. At the same time, Prussia was fast becoming the centre of gravity for German industry.

After the Vienna Congress of 1815, the international system inhibited both powers from employing military means to change the territorial status quo. Therefore, proponents of Mitteleuropa developed concepts that were primarily economic or cultural in nature. Depending on their particular viewpoint and the contemporaneous international political situation, advocates of Mitteleuropa argued for Prussian leadership of Germany as a counterweight to Austria, Austrian leadership of Germany as a counterweight to Prussia, or securing a greater Germany against its European neighbours. Until Bismarck's orchestration of the 'concert of nations' in 1871, the conflict between Prussia and Austria was regarded as an intra-German matter. The establishment of the Second Empire changed the nature of the international system and, therefore, the way that Germans perceived Mitteleuropa.

THE PRE-BISMARCK ERA

The concept 'Mitteleuropa' is closely related to German nation-building and national identity.[1] Understanding this linkage between Mitteleuropa and national identity is an important first step towards understanding the contemporary debate over Mitteleuropa. Since the beginning of the nineteenth century, German unification has been a major topic in intellectual and political debates. One of the reasons that it took almost three-quarters of a century before German unification finally occurred was that various German political groups could not agree on what should be incorporated into a (new) German Reich. This debate peaked after 1848, over the conflict between Austria and Prussia.

In the debate over Germany's future configuration Mitteleuropa was advanced as one possible scenario to ease the tensions between Prussia and Austria; that is, to provide a comprehensive solution to the German question.[2] This uncertainty and disagreement continues today, which partially explains why concepts of Mitteleuropa have become fashionable in Germany again, after these concepts were rediscovered by Polish, Hungarian and Czech intellectuals during the mid-1980s. The German Mitteleuropa debate has become part of the German nation-building conflict that has been going on since 1945. After all, German unification in 1990 was no less an act of nation-building than was Bismarck's *Reichsgründung* in 1871.[3]

While Mitteleuropa was prominent in German rhetoric and thought between 1914 and 1918, German history since Frederick the Great has been interpreted as a continuous drive for German domination of Central Europe. Moreover, Germany's imperial aspirations were often presented as part of its national identity. However, as depicted retrospectively at the beginning of the twentieth century, Mitteleuropa predicated a united Germany – which had not occurred until 1871. Before 1871, any type of economic or political hegemony or dominance over the vast regions between the Alps and the Urals by one or more of the small German principalities (Fürstentümer) would have been impossible. Therefore, what was interpreted during the First World War as a long, continuing German struggle for Mitteleuropa, in reality was little more than an attempt to unify the German Reich.[4] The Mitteleuropa ideas of Friedrich List, Freiherr von Bruck, and the *Großdeutsche Bewegung* represent such attempts and, therefore, are examined here analytically, in contrast to the writings of politicians, journalists and scholars during the First World War which were *post hoc* attempts to explain or justify the war.

In contrast to France and Great Britain, which began to develop a sense of nationalism following the peace of Westphalia, Germany did not develop a complete sense of nationalism until some time after 1813.[5] The Revolution of 1848 added the new dimension of a potential international role for the Germans to the 'German question' of unification. Moreover, despite the Germans' dispersal into numerous principalities, German nationalism blossomed as a result of the Revolution.[6] The wars of liberation against Napoleon underpinned the development of a national identity and the perception of a *Kulturnation*, incorporating basically all territories possessing the German language and a German cultural majority. German nationalism 'began not as political theory, but rather as a belief in a shared culture and a shared history', and it 'developed as a response to two contrasting international systems: first that of Napoleon, then that of Metternich'.[7]

The late development of German nationalism is one of the reasons why some observers describe Germany as the 'late nation' (verspätete Nation).[8] This lack of 'national sensitivity'[9] to the idea of nationalism resulted partially from the Germans' dispersal throughout Europe over centuries, making it difficult subsequently to define a clear territorial state. Aside from a relatively small number of states that were part of the Deutsche Bund, later the core of Bismarck's Reich, and, of course, the Austrian part of the Danube monarchy, most states in Central Europe were not nation-states. 'Statehood' in Mitteleuropa was primarily a question of majority and minority distribution within a given territory. The 'German nation' existed in a number of states as a cultural–ethnic minority.[10] Among these respective German minorities feelings of nationality and statehood did not correspond to one another.

Thus after 1871 both the Habsburg and Hohenzollern political elites attempted to represent the national interests of Austria, the German Reich, and the German nation. However, these claims are both confusing and misleading. The competing claims account for many of the tensions between the Hohenzollern and Habsburg dynasties, since such elusive distinctions ignored popular perceptions of a common German national identity. The claims of each elite to represent the mutually exclusive interests of the Reich or Austria would eventually separate the German nation rather than unite the Austrian or Reich Germans.

Before 1871 the Mitteleuropa debate encompassed the question of the German struggle for unification. As both J. G. Herder (1802) and Freiherr von Stein (1812), the great social reformer, observed, there was a close connection between Mitteleuropa and German nation-building. Furthermore, they perceived Austria as a natural part of a future German nation-state in Mitteleuropa. Herder wrote that;

> The western and southern parts of Europe . . . have changed! Should we then not thank providence that [Prussia] . . . now united with Austria . . . should become a part of the great Central Power which must protect the continent of all German peoples as well as the northern kingdoms from subjugation by foreign nations.[11]

Ten years later, von Stein, in a letter to a friend, wrote that 'it is my desire that Germany shall become great and strong, in order to achieve again its independence and sense of nationality, and that it asserts both of these qualities in its position between France and Russia'.[12]

Herder and von Stein clearly linked German unification or nation-building to concepts of Mitteleuropa. Furthermore, their views shed light on the subsequent conflict over who should dominate a German Reich – Austria or Prussia. This controversy eventually led to the war of 1866 and to Bismarck's smaller German Reich solution (kleindeutsche Lösung).[13] The rivalry between the Habsburg and Hohenzollern dynasties also shaped conceptions of Mitteleuropa during the First World War. It did not matter whether Vienna or Berlin was perceived as the centre of German culture and heritage; both dynasties' elites believed the concept of Mitteleuropa to be important to the development of Germany. However, political and intellectual elites continued to dispute the specific elements of Mitteleuropa.[14]

Austria's and Prussia's opposing views about Mitteleuropa were most obvious in the revolutionary period of 1848. Prussia was eager to create a central state in Europe under its leadership by establishing, as its nucleus, a coalition of the three kingdoms of Prussia, Saxony and Hannover.[15] During the revolutionary period, Prussia benefited from Habsburg's weakness, which resulted from the Hungarian rebellion. This weakness translated into a potential loss of Mitteleuropa for the Habsburg Empire. After Russia had crushed the Hungarian rebellion and Austria had regained its strength, Prussia's Mitteleuropa aspirations disintegrated. However, Austria's East-Central European hegemony could not be extended to the north-west because of Prussia's resistance, which Austria could not overcome.

As a result of this stalemate between the two powers, Mitteleuropa could only be achieved through a united Germany. On 28 October 1848, Heinrich von Gagern opted against a division of the Austrian Empire, arguing that 'the German people always had the task of being a world ruling (*weltgebietende*) nation' and that 'the Germans have a mission in the Orient to incorporate the people along the Danube . . . as satellites into our [the Germans'] planetary system'.[16] Von Gagern formulated a dream of and a demand for a (united) Germany controlling Mitteleuropa as a barrier against potential Slavic or Russian domination of the region. He noted that 'if we do not accept this mission, Russia will soon have overtaken us'. Thus, at an early stage, the German concept of Mitteleuropa was driven by two dynamic forces: nation-building and defending 'civilization' against the 'East', especially Russia.

As a consequence of Prussian–Austrian antagonism, the aspiration for a German Mitteleuropa was submerged in the process of German state-building. In this context, Bismarck's smaller German Reich represented a temporary solution that only postponed the ultimate questions of Germany's leadership and territorial borders. Even in 1871 the 'Iron Chancellor's' statement that Germany had no territorial ambitions (i.e., Germany was a 'saturated Reich') was false. The speciousness of Bismarck's statement became obvious after Wilhelm II became Emperor, dismissed his Chancellor, and embarked on an 'imperialist adventure tour'. Thus the hope for a united Germany remained interwoven with concepts of a German-dominated Mitteleuropa, whether Austrian or Prussian led.

Aside from such territorial conceptions of Mitteleuropa and disputes over dynastic control, economically there were possibilities for creating a unified German-dominated Mitteleuropa. In the economic realm, the customs union (Zollverein) offered a concrete possibility for creating such a German-dominated Mitteleuropa. The two most prominent prototypes of Mitteleuropa were put forward by Friedrich List and Karl Ludwig Freiherr von Bruck, who advocated the Zollverein.[17] As an ardent advocate of Adam Smith's principles of free markets and trade, in 1819 List founded the 'Union of German Merchants and Manufacturers'. The Union's goal was to establish a free-trade zone among the German states, which since the Congress of Vienna in 1815 had been drawn together in the German Bund. Before his major work, *The National System of Political Economy*, appeared in 1841, List's thoughts took two important turns.[18]

In 1820, he stated in a memorandum to the Austrian emperor that it was necessary to promote a free-trade zone and continued trade relations with the Levant, in the tradition of the Holy Roman Empire, through Austria's Adriatic ports.[19] However, after being accused of revolutionary activities List emigrated to the United States, where he was deeply impressed by the thriving American economy. As a result of this experience he turned to external protectionism and internal free trade, through a customs union among the German states, as the foundation for a German nation-state. In his later years, List went even further by incorporating the states of Central Europe into his customs-union vision. He advocated the whole of Central Europe as a free-trade zone for the fair and free exchange of agricultural products, raw materials and manufactured goods among the region's developing nation-states. This Central European economic area (mitteleuropäische Wirtschaftszone) was an extension of List's views on the economic limitations of the nation-state, in combination with his republican, liberal political convictions.[20]

List went further in his conceptions of an economic Mitteleuropa by looking into the possibilities and actually suggesting that increased German emigration and settlement in southern-middle Europe would be beneficial both for the region and for Germany. Inspired by American westward expansionism and an envisioned 'iron band of railroads'[21] that eventually would connect and hold Germany and Austria/Hungary together, he concluded that the Danube basin as far as the Black Sea was Germany's 'natural backwoods'.[22] He argued that Germans could settle in the region for two-thirds of the cost of migrating to the United States.

However, List failed to consider a number of countervailing factors. His plan for the expansion of the German economy and population ignored the existence of the Slavic populations on Germany's borders. List viewed these populations as 'stateless peoples'.[23] Although the Hungarians received his economic ideas favourably, his views on a customs union and German migration were viewed with increasing suspicion by the Magyars and Czechs, who feared the region's Germanization. Their anxieties were justified in as much as List viewed Mitteleuropa as genuine German territory in a broad sense. Despite these 'oversights', his ventures in the economic realm were important steps in the process of German nation-building.

Another prominent advocate of Mitteleuropa was the Austrian Karl Ludwig Freiherr von Bruck, a young contemporary of List's.[24] Much like Alexander Hamilton, von Bruck was drawn into politics by way of business. His political career peaked as Secretary of Commerce in Schwarzenberg's cabinet between 1848 and 1853. He was one of the most successful Austrian businessmen of his time and his political interest in Mitteleuropa resulted directly from his economic interest in the region. As an Austrian-German, Bruck 'desired the closest possible attachment of the Austrian Empire to the German *nation*'.[25]

In the revolutionary years before 1848, von Bruck settled in Vienna, a centre of the 'revolutionary' republican movement which had originated in Germany. Austrian advocates of republicanism, the Habsburg Empire's minorities and the advocates of Anschluß, were receptive to these revolutionary ideas. The 'Austrian revolution' crested on 22 July 1848, when the constitutional assembly, representing the multi-ethnicity of the Empire, was proclaimed and held its first meeting in Vienna.[26] On 7 September the Assembly declared an end to the ethnic minorities' subordination to the Habsburg monarchy. In the ensuing turmoil von Bruck remained loyal to the pro-Anschluß party. After Russia had crushed the Hungarian uprising and returned Hungary to Habsburg, and after Duke Windisch-Grätz had recaptured Vienna from the hands of the revolutionaries, Duke Schwarzenberg restored the Habsburg monarchy.[27]

Two important facts concerning this brief period should be stressed. First,

Windisch-Grätz's troops, who crushed the revolution in Vienna, were mostly non-German, i.e., Croats, Czechs and Poles.[28] In the multi-racial state (Vielvölkerstaat) of the Austro/Hungarian Empire, the central Europeans helped to thwart the Empire's centrifugal tendencies and to restore a dynastic form of Mitteleuropa. Secondly, behind the façade of monarchy, Schwarzenberg re-established an order in the Empire that was, in reality, a Germanized bureaucratic structure and organization. In short, the backbone of the new system was German.[29] As a result, Austrian Germans such as von Bruck held the power; and consequently, they were despised by the old Habsburg aristocracy. The 'Germanization' of the Habsburg Empire contributed to unreconcilable tensions between the Habsburg and the Hohenzollern dynasties in the second half of the nineteenth century, which eventually led to the battle of Königgrätz in 1866.

As Secretary of Commerce under von Schwarzenberg, in 1848 von Bruck had the opportunity to develop an economic version of Mitteleuropa. The core of his Mitteleuropa thinking can be found in four memoranda that he wrote between 1849 and 1859.[30] In 1848, he began to put his ideas into practice by reforming the Empire's economic structure. Under von Bruck's influence, by the end of 1848 an Austrian version of Mitteleuropa had emerged. Tariffs between Austria and Hungary were abolished and a customs union was established. The customs union was to be the nucleus of an economic Mitteleuropa stretching from the Alps to the Black Sea. Bruck's ideas were structural–functional in nature; he assumed that Austro-Hungarian tensions could be reduced and the Empire could be preserved through economic interdependence.

As a politician, von Bruck took his vision of Mitteleuropa even further by pushing for a similar arrangement with Prussia–Germany's 'Zollverein'.[31] Also inspired by Adam Smith, von Bruck believed that the gloomy problems within the Empire and the rising struggle for German leadership could be solved in an expanding 'capitalist' economy.[32] Much like his successors some fifty years later, von Bruck was consumed with the potential of such an economic union: 'By means of this commercial unification of Mitteleuropa Austria will, thanks to her central position between East and West, North and South, . . . necessarily become the centre of a great international trade movement.'[33] The influence of such a powerful economic bloc in the centre of Europe would funnel trade activities from northern Europe all the way down the Danube river and, by way of the Austrian Adriatic ports, to the Near East.

Von Bruck also anticipated the argument of the 'warmonger-economists'[34] at the turn of the century who stressed the importance of expanding markets for Germany's survival. As he observed in his third memorandum:

> That is why the stream of trade must flow freely from North German ports to Trieste, from the Mediterranean to the Baltic, from the Rhine to the Lower Danube or in reverse. The customs-united states of the mid-European continent must be armed with a united tariff policy in order to assure for themselves the essential conditions for unimpeded growth and progress.[35]

Of course, von Bruck's plans did not survive the Austro-Prussian conflict, as one of the Austrian premises was Vienna's leadership, which, in turn, Berlin continuously rejected. After France and Italy defeated Austria decisively in 1859, the balance of power tilted visibly towards Berlin, thereby making von Bruck's Mitteleuropa constellation impossible. Nevertheless, he remained faithful to his vision. In his last memorandum (1859), reflecting the dreadful position of the Empire, von Bruck urged the Emperor to press for an economic union with the German confederation and to build a confederation army.[36] Von Bruck's goal of achieving an economically unified and functionally interdependent Mitteleuropa did not change but the locus of power and the driving force shifted from Vienna to Berlin.

THE KLEINDEUTSCH–GROßDEUTSCH DEBATE BEFORE 1871

From the very beginning, the conflict between Prussia and Austria was also a quarrel about who would dominate or lead a prospective German nation-state, in short the kleindeutsch versus großdeutsch debate.[37] As a rule, one can state that Prussia's approach tended to be kleindeutsch; it wanted to establish a consolidated federation (as expressed, for example, in the Zollverein). By contrast, Austria was more großdeutsch oriented. It wanted to maintain the status quo of cooperation between independent dynasties.[38]

The revolutionary years, with their nationalist overtones, however, gave the terms 'kleindeutsch' and 'großdeutsch' a somewhat new connotation. People no longer identified themselves with certain dynasties but slowly began to think of a unified Germany in nationalist terms. This development favoured großdeutsch aspirations. In the 1840s, großdeutsch advocates not only asked for a union with Austria but also incorporated in their plans close cooperation with the Slavs of the Habsburg Empire, once again thinking in Central European dimensions. As a representative of the großdeutsch faction, Hans von Perthaler stated that

> German policy, to be effective, must fill the vacuum between Russia and Germany. The people living in this area can lead an individual national

life only under the influence of the German people. There must be but one policy in Mitteleuropa; because the German people is the only powerful nation in the area, this policy must be German.[39]

While großdeutsch ideas, at first, were prominent at the Paul's Cathedral Assembly in Frankfurt, with Heinrich von Gagern as their most prominent advocate, sentiment towards großdeutsch ideas changed in the Assembly once it became clear that the Austro-Prussian conflict over leadership in Germany could not be reconciled.[40]

Following the wars of liberation, in 1815 the Congress of Vienna confirmed the status quo ante, restoring the territorial borders of the dynastic states rather than adjusting boundaries along ethnic and nationality lines.[41] The Congress also failed to deal with the question of creating a German nation-state. As a result, the concept of Mitteleuropa remained intertwined with the continuing kleindeutsch/großdeutsch debate.[41] The fact that different ethnic and linguistic minorities existed within most European states (for example, in Switzerland, France, and the Netherlands), as Werner Conze has argued, did not prejudice their 'membership of the nation, which was, after all, a nation-state. In all these states, within the given frontiers a process of national . . . integration gradually penetrated all classes. . . . *Not so in Germany.*'[42] Nation- and state-building in Germany did not take place in the same manner as it did in the rest of Europe. Neither the old Empire nor the German Confederation (Deutsche Bund) could be considered nation-states. In Central Europe, where the frontiers were ambiguous and the ethnic mixture diffuse – with Czechs living in Bohemia and Moravia, Poles in East Prussia and Posnania, and Italians in the Tyrol, for example – the nation and state question was most unclear. Moreover, the minorities in these areas neither felt nor wanted to become German.

In the National Assembly in Frankfurt these problems were discussed *ad infinitum*, but remained unresolved.[43] One of the most serious issues, in light of events after 1871, was the conflict between Prussia and the Poles living in Prussian territory, especially in Posnania, which traditionally had been Polish.[44] The Polish minority was not merely unwilling to assimilate; on the contrary, after the 'Prussian state identity [had] merged with German national identity, the old position of a Prussian monarchy with subjects of a different tongue gave way to a struggle between the German and the Polish *nation*'.[45] This struggle remained a thorn in Germany's side that would became increasingly painful for Bismarck after 1871.[46]

At an early date, even as early as the Paul's Cathedral Assembly, it became very clear that the principle of ethnicity or ethnic identity as a basis for defining territorial borders, even where the principle could be applied easily, was a tool that the two great German powers would employ to resolve border conflicts only when it served their interests. However, the principle of ethnicity played virtually no role when it conflicted with great powers' political interests. Therefore, the concept of gathering all persons of German origin in one nation-state, which one can trace through all imperial visions of Mitteleuropa from the Alldeutsche Bund[47] to Hitler, was little more than a masquerade for territorial or economic ambitions.

In paragraph 188 of the Frankfurt Charter, the Frankfurt Assembly enunciated, in an ambiguous manner, the principle of ethnic identity as the basis for building the German nation-state.

> To the non-German-speaking peoples of Germany is granted the right to an individual development, that is equality of status of their languages, within their areas, in church matters, education, and the internal administration of justice.[48]

On the one hand, the Charter acknowledged ethnic identity as a criterion for creating the German nation-state. On the other hand, by not mentioning the *nationality* of those peoples, paragraph 188 left the existing borders untouched. Therefore, it undermined ethnicity as the primary principle for creating a nation-state. While the Frankfurt Assembly incorporated a geographic notion of Mitteleuropa in its quest for a German nation-state, it fell short of the dream that Ernst Moritz Arndt expressed in the famous revolutionary song that he composed: 'A single, united Germany must extend *as far as the German tongue is heard.*'[49]

Regarding the closely related issues of kleindeutsch versus großdeutsch and of Mitteleuropa, the Paul's Cathedral Assembly was split between two lines of thought. On one side were the advocates of the 'national route',[50] which equated German-speaking people with the German nation and ultimately with the German state. On the other side were the proponents of the territorial status quo, with guaranteed minority rights for Germans in neighbouring countries and, *vice versa*, for non-German minorities within German borders.[51]

Finally, the creation of a greater Germany, including large parts of Mitteleuropa, was deferred because Austria refused to cede its German territory to a greater Germany, while Prussia insisted on retaining it Customs Union and its position of leadership among the 'kleindeutsch states'.[52] In as much as the Frankfurt Assembly also represented an attempt to transform the Austrian Empire, it

> . . . will always remain notable in the history of the German nation as the first and last great attempt to make the Austrian Empire a bridge

between the old and a new Hapsburg emperorship, and thus both to satisfy the German nation and to make their unification in the middle of the continent acceptable to the European powers.[53]

The National Assembly of the Paul's Cathedral clarified two issues that changed the dynamics of future German politics. First, prior to the Assembly the 'German question'[54] could be muted by either of the two great powers, Austria and Prussia. This was no longer possible afterwards, since German nationalism had become too pronounced for either state to ignore. The 'German question' had to be resolved one way or the other, for or against one of the major protagonists in German politics.[55]

Secondly, the discussion of what constitutes Germany brought Mitteleuropa to the forefront of the German elites' attention. In combination with stronger nationalism, Mitteleuropa was clearly perceived as an area of German interest, or, in other words, as Germany's 'natural backwoods'.[56] Not even Bismarck's smaller German solution could mute the discussion about and aspirations to acquiring the states of Mitteleuropa. With the exclusion of Austria from the German Empire, German economic elites could openly express their ambitions to penetrate the states of Mitteleuropa economically. These elites no longer needed to display any sensitivity to Austrian interests.

After Austria's defeat in 1859 and Bismarck's rise to power, the idea of 'Mitteleuropa' as a großdeutsch concept was dead politically; Mitteleuropa as a unified territory under German nationhood was put on the back burner. For the Germans living in Posnania and the Slavic countries this was especially difficult to accept, since they perceived (correctly) that the German states' attention was diverted to other directions, namely, towards colonial expansion in Africa and world trade.

A final aspect of the Mitteleuropa debate prior to 1871 was the cultural clash between Germans and Slavs in the Frankfurt Assembly, with the Germans expressing feelings of cultural superiority, primarily, but not exclusively, towards their Slavic neighbours.[57] As early as 1848, when talking about the future and past role of German culture in Mitteleuropa, Wilhelm Jordan, a Heglian poet and originally a representative of the far left wing at the Assembly, employed language that bears a striking resemblance to Nazi German formulations. As stated before Parliament:

> The preponderance of the German race over most Slav races, possibly with the sole exception of the Russians, is a fact . . . and against history and nature decrees of political justice are of no avail. . . . Mere existence does not entitle a people to political independence: only the force to assert itself as a state among the others.[58]

In the 1850s and 1860s this understanding of cultural superiority combined with Germany's perceived need for economic expansion eastwards, which eventually culminated in Hitler's '*Drang nach Osten*'. Having survived earlier crises in 1853 and 1860,[59] the Prussian-led Customs Union now became more than an economic instrument. Its members began to perceive the Union as the core of their national identification as Germans. As a Brunswick liberal remarked: 'The customs union has become . . . in fact the nourishing ground of the idea of unity. . . . We will have to get used to foreigners believing Germany to be principally the customs union.'[60]

Although the previous quote illuminates the role that the Customs Union played in the development of German unity and Mitteleuropa, it is only a half-truth, since it ignores the continuing dissatisfaction and disillusionment of those Germans who remained outside the Zollverein and Austria. These minorities were dissatisfied with the status quo of German affairs. Their call for closer linkage to the German heartland created the basis for a pan-German (gesamtdeutsch)[61] demand that would shape concepts of Mitteleuropa before and during the First World War. Ironically, however, the war destroyed both the Habsburg Empire and plans for a Central European customs union.

The Mitteleuropa debate in the 1840s and 1850s had been somewhat eclipsed and displaced by the groß- versus kleindeutsch discussion. While there were no new plans to reorganize Central Europe during the tense decade of the 1860s, a few visible proponents of Mitteleuropa kept the vision alive. Most notable were Albert Schäffle, a South German professor of history and economics, and Lorenz von Stein, a historian at the University of Kiel. Both men advocated the großdeutsch vision, which was the premise for their concepts of Mitteleuropa. Pursuing their dream, they both emigrated to Vienna after the Austrian disaster at Königgrätz.[62]

Schäffle stressed the importance of a strong Central European customs union (including France), in close alliance with Britain, in order to restrain and contain Russia as much as to protect Europe against the emerging US economy. Therefore, Mitteleuropa was primarily a defensively oriented economic union directed against pressure from the United States and Russia.[63] Schäffle's assessment was somewhat unusual at the time. He had a much broader perception of future economic developments than most of his contemporaries, who did not consider Russia or the United States as an *economic* threat to Europe.[64] Schäffle's großdeutsch enthusiasm resulted from his dream of consolidating industrial Prussia with agrarian Austria in an autarkic Central European economic bloc.

Von Stein took just the opposite approach, suggesting to the Austrian Emperor a Mitteleuropa along the lines of the defunct Holy Roman Empire.

He wanted to establish an economic entity stretching from the North Sea to the Black Sea and the Adriatic, directed against France, Britain, and Russia alike.[65]

After Bismarck's political victory in Prussia, the Mitteleuropa debate entered a new phase, since the question of a new German Reich was resolved and the tensions between Austria and Prussia were laid to rest, at least for the time being. Under Bismarck the Mitteleuropa debate took a more geostrategic turn because Mitteleuropa for Bismarck was an instrument of his 'concert of nations'. Although Austria and Prussia had regarded Mitteleuropa as their sphere of interest until 1871, Bismarck's establishment of the Second Empire changed that perspective entirely. First, Bismarck brought the area of Mitteleuropa to international attention by making it an instrument of bargaining in his world-wide aspirations and plans for Germany. Secondly, concepts of Mitteleuropa developed an intra-European colonial dimension, in as much as calls for German economic penetration and settlement of the region became increasingly forceful.

3 The Europeanization of 'Mitteleuropa', 1848–1914

INTRODUCTION

Contemporary German debate on Mitteleuropa in the Bismarck era focuses largely on German responsibility for the First World War. Some commentators, such as Ulrich Noack and Winfried Baumgart, argue that the war could have been avoided had Bismarck entered into an effective alliance with Great Britain against Imperial Russia in order to liberate Central Europe from Russian influence. As a result, Germany could have extended its hegemony over Central Europe. Other observers argue that Bismarck was a captive of the entangling alliances that he had created, which, for Mitteleuropa, led to the geopolitical disaster of the First World War.[1] At the zenith of personal power, the Iron Chancellor's ambition exceeded Germany's political, economic, and military capabilities. In as much as there is little new in this debate, this work will focus on the intellectual discourse of the Bismarck era, exploring contemporaneous German perceptions of Mitteleuropa.

Parallel to the previous discourse, the scholarly literature acknowledges an overall Europeanization of German politics under Bismarck, first as the Prussian envoy to the German Parliament (deutsche Bundestag) in Frankfurt (1851) and, later, as German Chancellor. As the debate indicates, Bismarck's contemporaries were divided over the integration of Germany into the European state system. Among those who attacked Bismarck for his European focus was Paul Rohrbach, who (in 1903) accused Bismarck of not having been able 'to read the handwriting on the wall' regarding the necessity of globalizing German colonial policy rather than focusing exclusively on Europe.[2] Bismarck's policy, Rohrbach argued, was largely responsible for Germany's disadvantageous position in world politics, since Germany had virtually no overseas colonies.

The other side accused Bismarck of conducting European politics to the detriment of Prussia's and Germany's real interests. For example, Rudolf Virchow (1863), a representative in the Prussian Assembly, stated that, as Prussia's new Foreign Minister, Bismarck had turned the Schleswig-Holstein conflict from a German question into a European one. Bismarck's answer to Virchow's statement is somewhat characteristic of his viewpoint. 'As long as we live in Europe instead of on a remote island together only with

Denmark,' Bismarck replied, 'we have to take a European viewpoint. I accept your criticism as willingly as I accept the accusation that I would conduct too Prussian a policy.'[3]

Therefore, during Bismarck's era German foreign policy developed a European dimension rather than focusing on bilateral developments. However, one should distinguish between Bismarck's early years, when he was Prussia's envoy to the Frankfurt Assembly under Austria's presidency, and his later years as the Prussian Foreign Minister and, subsequently, as German Chancellor. In the early years Prussia was in a minority position in a confederation rather than the dominant actor in a unified German state.

THE BISMARCK ERA UNTIL 1871

Bismarck and Europe

After the German Confederation (Deutsche Bund) had been re-established in 1851, Bismarck became Prussia's envoy to the Frankfurt Assembly. At that time, Bismarck's primary objective was to give 'Prussia its own voice in the European concert of nations', independent from the Confederation and, most importantly, independent from Austria, both of which were restraining Prussia.[4] For Bismarck, 'politics' meant national politics, with the goal of creating a German nation-state under Prussian hegemony.[5] Bismarck's Europe was a 'Europe of the Fatherlands'.

Therefore, as early as March 1858, Bismarck warned Prince Wilhelm I of the dangers resulting from Prussia's close alliance with Austria.[6] During his time in Frankfurt Bismarck perceived European politics primarily in terms of Prussia's ascendancy in Central Europe. When arguing about European politics, Bismarck referred continually to Frederick the Great (of Prussia), whose policies of expansion into Posnania and Silesia were directed eastwards, into the heart of Mitteleuropa.[7] Bismarck viewed the Deutsche Bund as a timid and weak construct that offered Prussia little independent manoeuvrability in matters of European politics. He recognized that the Deutsche Bund's ability to respond to external aggression depended on the Prussian and Austrian armies. However, Austria, which dominated the Bund, did not accept Prussia as a *primus inter pares*.[8]

Therefore, according to Bismarck, Prussia had become a vassal to the confederation, which was especially nettlesome in light of the Austrian/Prussian rivalries in Mitteleuropa.[9] Bismarck categorically rejected the idea that the Deutsche Bund could or should perform an 'Ordnungsfunktion' (i.e., regulator of the balance) for Europe, as envisioned by the founders of the Confederation.[10] The Confederation's function as a surrogate Reich was unacceptable to Bismarck. His first objective was political independence for Prussia, and secondly, a unified Germany under Prussian leadership.

Bismarck's policy represented an important shift in German policy to 'realist politics' or realism (Realpolitik), as August Rochau described the post-1848 situation.[11] The national and Central European question was no longer discussed in terms of reviving the 'good old days' of the Holy Roman Empire, but rather in terms of power politics, defined in military, economic, and geopolitical categories. In his book *Principles of Realist Politics* (Grundsätze der Realpolitik),[12] Rochau distanced himself from the romantic conservatism prominent among such Catholic politicians as Joseph Maria von Radowitz,[13] as well as from the arguments for 'military autocracy',[14] as expressed by von Radowitz's successor, Minister-President Erwin von Manteuffel.

Bismarck's 'Realpolitik'[15] also resulted from the industrial revolution, which (despite the fact that it commenced in Germany somewhat later than in Great Britain) was reshaping German society and communities. In a period of mechanization, urbanization, and European-wide railway connections, the paradigm of foreign policy changed.[16] The old conservatism was doomed because it was incapable of translating rapid social and economic changes into new political institutions and behaviour.[17] As a Prussian 'Junker', Bismarck was cross-pressured between the demands of his conservative clientele of landowners in the Prussian Parliament and the new economic libertarianism of the urban middle class. Bowing to the forces of modernization, he followed Rochau's Realpolitik more than he would admit even to himself at the time.[18] He knew very well that, as Prussian Minister-President, he could not fight a long-lasting constitutional war with the liberals. His zigzag politics of army reform and 'cultural struggle' (Kulturkampf) illustrate his dilemma.[19]

However, for Bismarck, economic policy was only a tool to achieve his ultimate goal of Prussian dominance over the Bund or a Prussian Reich. As Prussian Minister of Commerce, Rudolf von Delbrück's call for free trade and customs liberation from the South German states in the Bund (especially Austria) were prerequisites for Bismarck's expansion of Prussian diplomacy and, eventually, the Prussian state.[20] As Werner Conze summarizes: 'Bismarck did not have a rigid aim. The guideline for his actions was always, and above all, the interests of the Prussian monarchy.'[21]

Bismarck perceived that the interests of 'his' monarchy and, therefore, Prussia's destiny lay in Central Europe, economically as much as culturally (as a Kulturmacht).[22] Bismarck's famous saying, 'he who is the master of Bohemia, is the master of Europe', testifies to his vision of Prussia's destiny as well as to his concept of the balance of power and the international or European system. As Theodor Schieder summarized Bismarck's views:

> Thus the European vision of the young diplomat, Bismarck, remains limited to the realization of equal conditions of existence [conditio sine qua non] and of a common geographical area of existence, as they were present for the greater powers, but yet at the same time the awareness of the special place that each of the powers occupies as a function of its *geographical position and its historical destiny*. In that sense, to look after one's national interests means to discern this function and to act upon it. For the young Bismarck that was equivalent to overcoming the passivity of Prussian politics and activating its energies. Later [after 1871] it meant [that] each great power which tries to influence and control the politics . . . of other nations elsewhere but within its own original sphere of interest is acting outside of the [geographical] area that God has given. [This power] has mistaken power politics for interest politics, such as thriving [merely] for prestige.[23]

For Prussia, this 'sphere of interest' was Mitteleuropa. Bismarck was determined to 'lead Prussian policy out of its state of inactivity'[24] and, following the tradition of Frederick the Great, create a German nation-state in the heart of Europe.

In 1848 all of the politically influential forces in the Paul's Cathedral Assembly still 'strove to unite "Mitteleuropa" in one way or another, stretching from the North Sea to the Baltic, from the Adriatic Sea to the Black Sea, under German hegemony'.[25] A decade later Bismarck subjugated that goal to the Prussian national interest, which, at the time, also meant opposition to Austria. In 1862 Bismarck demanded that Austria shift its sphere of influence to the Balkans in order to accommodate Prussian interests in Central Europe.[26] But Bismarck's vision of Europe, with Prussian dominance of Central Europe, met considerable resistance. Several influential politicians and prominent historians countered Bismarck's power politics with a confederate vision of Mitteleuropa.

Constantin Frantz: Bismarck's antagonist

The best known advocate of a confederate Mitteleuropa was Constantin Frantz, a Prussian historian and constitutional lawyer.[27] Prussian by birth, Frantz opposed Bismarck's nationalist politics from the beginning. Even though Bismarck tried to persuade Frantz to the contrary until the late 1860s, the latter remained a steadfast opponent of Bismarck's (petty) power politics.

Instead, Frantz perceived Prussia's role as one of a *primus inter pares* within a Central European confederation. Frustrated after Bismarck's victory in 1871, he argued even more openly against the nation-state, which, in turn, drove him further into political isolation. The chorus for the nation-state drowned out the opposing voices.[28] However, Frantz's writings were rediscovered and reprinted during the Weimar Republic and shortly after the Second World War.[29]

Influenced by the Paul's Cathedral Assembly and visions of Prussian dominance in German politics, Frantz laid out his principal arguments in the late 1840s.[30] Although his posture towards Prussia changed in the coming decades, his main ideas on Central European federalism remained unchanged. The starting point for Frantz's Mitteleuropa vision was a global view of politics in which he foresaw a bipolar global system between the United States and Russia.[31] Given this premise, he argued that only a federally organized Central Europe could withstand pressures from the two great powers. Furthermore, he argued, the federal principle was the only adequate form of government for a united Germany, even under Prussian leadership, since German cultural diversity would neither permit nor survive within a centralized state.[32] For the same reason, it was imperative to unite Mitteleuropa in a confederation in which the Germans would play the role of a 'cultural mediator'.[33]

Frantz suggested that Europe be divided into three federations that would cooperate closely with one another in a 'Central European peace union'.[34] As Meyer has noted, this union would include 'Prussia with Russia, Poland and the Baltic Provinces; the Austrian Empire with the Balkans; and the remaining German states. Eventually the Low Countries, Denmark and Switzerland were to join.'[35] Frantz's argument for a German-led Mitteleuropa was predicated on his analysis of Germany's delicate geographical and political position in Europe after 1848. As Renate Morell has stated: 'For Frantz, the geographic, ethnic, and constitutionally amalgamated position in which the Germans were involved, was the basis for his plea for a central European federation.'[36]

In contrast to Bismarck, who wanted to solve the 'German question' by creating a more or less homogeneous nation-state embedded in a system of treaties,[37] Frantz opted for a more globally-oriented solution. He suggested creating a strong Central European confederation that would unite the disparate and heterogeneous states of Central Europe under a single umbrella. He justified his concept historically and ideologically in terms of the Holy Roman Empire of the German Nation, which he found much more suitable for uniting the various ethnic and cultural groups than a 'modern' nation-state.[38] Thus his ideas are remarkably similar to contemporary criticisms of the nation-state.

Frantz remained the 'most unforgiving critic of the Reich's founder'.[39] He was not impressed by Bismarck's military victories of 1866 or 1871. Indeed, he rejected these victories as legitimizing Bismarck's exclusion of Austria from the Empire.[40] As Heinrich von Srbik wrote: 'This Empire was not Mitteleuropa and would never be in its understanding and shape. Without Austria, Mitteleuropa is missing the keystone.'[41]

In contrast to Frantz, Bismarck had no clear Mitteleuropa concept. Disregarding Europe as a cultural or political phenomenon,[42] Bismarck's primary goal was to secure the German national state's position in the delicate European balance of power.[43] However, some historians have interpreted Bismarck's policy incorrectly as a Mitteleuropa concept. Hermann Oncken describes Bismarck's policy as an 'understanding of the political problem of Mitteleuropa'.[44] He distinguishes between Bismarck's approach to Mitteleuropa as the 'old Mitteleuropa', and imperialist Mitteleuropa (i.e., the goal of World War One) as the 'new Mitteleuropa'.[45] Hans Rothfels also interprets Bismarck's politics as Mitteleuropa politics, claiming that Bismarck always viewed Central Europe as a distinct region in which Germany was embedded. The kleindeutsche solution was the only one possible for Bismarck that theoretically left the Empire open to the East, and thus secured a long-lasting peace for the region.[46]

For Bismarck, Mitteleuropa remained a means to ensure the German position in Europe, especially after 1871.[47] He refused 'to think of Europe as a united power, as some sort of federation'. He wanted to conduct politics 'as a German, not as a European'.[48] Viewed as a means or an instrument of German security, one can interpret Bismarck's appropriation of Mitteleuropa as the centrepiece of his policy in the late 1870s. His participation in the Berlin Congress of 1878 as an 'honest broker' between Russia and Austria marks a definite turn in Germany's foreign policy towards East-Central Europe.[49] The 'Zweibund Treaty' of 1879 between Germany and Austria–Hungary officially marked the bond between the two states, which was intended to make Mitteleuropa a joint sphere of influence.[50]

Bismarck's 'Mitteleuropa policy' was an expression of German national interest and the political realities of the current constellation of power in the international system. His goal was not to establish a Mitteleuropa, but to create tensions on the periphery of Central Europe in order to promote the young German Empire's security in the centre.[51] In fact, Bismarck's policies promoted the expansion of German power in Europe and laid the foundation for future concepts of Mitteleuropa in Wilhelm II's age of imperialism.[52]

Henry Meyer quotes Edmond Vermeil, a French historian of German politics, who summarized the period between the 1848 Revolution and Bismarck's dismissal as follows:

> What had it [the period] brought to Germany? Three new prerogatives which destiny had hitherto seemed to deny her: a territory economically united . . . ; an Empire of Prussian inspiration, limited as yet in extent but militarized and strongly administered; and finally, the vision of the future Reich, the Central Europe, which would assure the domination of the Continent to a Greater Germany embracing Austria and the Slav South-East.[53]

In other words, following Bismarck's dismissal, the political balance of power in the Reich shifted regarding Mitteleuropa. In contrast to both his contemporary opponents and his political heirs, Bismarck, acting on the basis of *raison d'état*, limited the Reich's Mitteleuropa aspirations. While his contemporary opponents favoured a federal Central Europe, his political successors advanced a colonial and imperial vision of Mitteleuropa. In the end, the vision of a greater Reich became the dominant conception under Wilhelm II until the First World War.

FROM BISMARCK'S DISMISSAL TO THE FIRST WORLD WAR

During his reign as Reich Chancellor, Bismarck was able to restrain various groups' Mitteleuropa aspirations, particularly the demands of German economic circles. Thus the 'Iron Chancellor' prevented domestic political pressures from upsetting the delicate balance of power in Europe. After Bismarck left the helm, self-restraint was replaced by a more aggressive policy. Advocates of Mitteleuropa who favoured economic integration joined forces with the proponents of German political hegemony in the region. Generally, they argued[54] that, as a result of its recent unification and late industrial development, Germany was at a disadvantage compared with France and Great Britain in the race for colonies.[55] Moreover, the proponents of this view argued that the Western powers had hampered Germany's development following the wars of liberation against Napoleon and the Revolution of 1848. In order to compensate for these disadvantages and, simultaneously, 'to push colonial imperialism farther and harder . . . Germany . . . needed to form a larger territorial unit in Europe . . . in conformity with the dictates of economic geography'.[56]

As a result of these developments in the age of imperialism,[57] views on Mitteleuropa changed dramatically. As Christian Weimer puts it:

> Whereas [Mitteleuropa] thoughts and plans . . . , until the end of the nineteenth century, were mostly hypothetical concepts opposing the German and central European constellation of power, which were verbalized by isolated theorists, irrelevant publicists or largely non-influential politicians; and whereas these ideas remained largely unechoed in the disinterested public and had practically no effect on the government, now a fundamental change occurred. The term 'Mitteleuropa' as an enlarged articulated topic was made public to large parts of society in the context of the demand for a political and economic expansion of Germany.[58]

In other words, Mitteleuropa should become the base for German overseas aspirations. While striving for their 'place in the sun',[59] German elites felt that, in its present form, Germany could not withstand international political pressure from the two peripheral powers (Flankenmächte), Russia and France. A strong Mitteleuropa under German hegemony was perceived as a prerequisite for overseas colonial expansion.[60] However, German overseas expansion created tensions with France and Britain, while German continental expansion aroused Russia's dislike.[61] Nevertheless, the one was viewed as a prerequisite for the other.

The economic elites of the Centralverband and the All-German Association (Alldeutscher Verband),[62] among others, intertwined continental Mitteleuropa politics with colonial overseas politics. The All-German Association, in particular, introduced the argument of German 'superiority' into the Mitteleuropa debate, which entangled economic programmes with cultural and/or racial perspectives.

Paul de Lagarde's 'Mitteleuropa'

During this period, the most prominent and influential advocate of Mitteleuropa was Paul de Lagarde, who was closely linked to the All-German Association. Although Lagarde was a contemporary of Constantin Frantz, his views were diametrically opposed to those of Frantz. A specialist in oriental studies, a philosopher by profession, and an ultra-conservative by conviction, by the mid-nineteenth century Lagarde had begun to develop a scheme for Mitteleuropa as a Großdeutsch Empire, incorporating Austria–Hungary and Germany.[63] At the core of his belief was his strong nationalism combined with virulent anti-semitism. As early as 1878, in his 'Deutsche Schriften', he suggested either the expulsion of Polish and German Jews to Palestine or their total assimilation, as a solution to the 'Jewish problem'.[64] In any case, there would be no room for the Jews in his 'conservative, monarchically governed German Empire comprising all the Germans in Mitteleuropa'.[65] His whole tone and vocabulary was a precursor of Hitler's Nazi language. If 'it [were] not for his conservative, dynastic, Prussophile sentiments, Lagarde could have been writing for . . . the Völkische Beobachter'.[66]

According to Lagarde, Germany's natural boundaries lay eastwards, to the point where the German people were able to feed and defend themselves.[67] He explicitly demanded the Germanization of the non-German ethnic groups within the Austrian Empire. Lagarde believed that the German problem was that the Germans had too many dynasties, while the Austrian Empire had too many peoples. Unification would solve the problem, in as much as the less important German princes could be sent south to govern the Empire's disparate peoples. The result would be a Mitteleuropa bound together by a common German heritage and a single dynasty as well as by a customs union and multi-lateral military treaties. Furthermore, Lagarde suggested a common effort to colonize Europe's East with German settlers and farmers. The federation was to be governed by a parliamentary structure, modelled after the Prussian system.[68]

In its political orientation, Lagarde's concept was directed primarily against Russia, which he perceived as the greatest threat to German civilization because Germany had no defensible natural borders with Russia. Therefore, the only way for Germany to secure its position against Russia was to expand eastwards.[69] He strongly opposed Bismarck's 'kleindeutsch' unification of the German Reich on grounds that, in his opinion, peace in Europe could only be secured if Russian expansion westwards could be rolled back, especially in the Balkans and along the Black Sea.[70] This was the purpose of Lagarde's Mitteleuropa. He was aware that his plans could not be achieved without war, but thought of it as unavoidable if the German people were to survive. With some foresight he wrote in his *Schriften*, 'the war which must create "Mitteleuropa" cannot be avoided. All that we can do, is accustom our people to the idea that it will come.'[71]

During his lifetime, Lagarde's influence remained rather limited,[72] even though he attempted to awaken public attention to his *Schriften*.[73] Lagarde's influence stems from the fact that Heinrich Claß, the second president (1908–18) of the All-German Association, adopted his way of thinking. In fact, Claß 'acclaimed Lagarde as one of his teachers'.[74]

The Political 'Mitteleuropa' Associations

Among the extra-parliamentary political groups and associations in the Germany of Wilhelm II that promoted Mitteleuropa the most important were the Colonial Association (Kolonialverein) founded in 1882, the Fleet

Association (Flottenverein) founded in 1898, the Defence Association (Wehrverein) of 1913,[75] and the All-German or Pan-German Association. The most influential and most radical among the German political groups was the All-German Association.[76] It was founded as a reaction to the Heligoland–Zanzibar agreement with Great Britain, which was perceived as disadvantageous to Germany. One of its founding members was Alfred Hugenberg, who was later a benefactor of Adolf Hitler.[77]

The most pertinent task of the Verein was to create an imperialist–colonial policy enabling Germany to fulfil its role as a world power. In 1895, the Association demanded 'the establishment of a united Central European economic area under German hegemony, in opposition to "anglo-saxonism" (Angelsachsentum) and the leading slavic power, Russia'.[78] The Association's cultural views on defending occidental culture against the 'slavic hordes', supported by the British people, overshadowed its economic programme.

In 1912 the German Emperor, Wilhelm II, supported this conception of Germany's Mitteleuropa role. In reference to the report of Ambassador Max Karl von Lichnowsky (the new envoy to London) on Great Britain's position towards Germany, Wilhelm II wrote:

> England, driven by hatred and envy, will definitely support France and Russia. The inevitable battle for their existence that the Germans in Europe [Austria, Germany] will have to wage against the Gauls, backed by the Slavs [Russia], will find the Anglo-Saxons on the side of the Slavs.[79]

Mitteleuropa, as an economic base, would enable Germany to survive this struggle.

Pan-German thinking and demands were a conglomerate of Ernst Haeckel's notion of Social-Darwinism, Paul de Lagarde's writings on German folklore (Deutschtum), and Friedrich Ratzel's geopolitical idea of 'Lebensraum'. Philosophically, a popularized version of Nietzsche's 'Übermensch', 'Herrenvolk', and 'will to power' were blended into pan-German views.[80] By the turn of the century, the economic and cultural elements of the public Mitteleuropa debate had merged with the Großdeutsch sentiments of the period, as represented and dominated by the All-German Association. As its first president (1894–1908), Ernst Hasse, a member of parliament, wrote in 1905:

> We must pursue a Weltpolitik and colonial expansions, but based only upon a successful internal policy and continental policy in Mitteleuropa. . . . In light of the entire contemporary world political situation,

> Germany has but one possibility of attaining leadership, . . . namely, by the closest possible association with Austria and a mutual alliance with Turkey. . . . *Before we seek a great Germany in the far corners of the world, we must create a greater Germany in Mitteleuropa.* We must make a virtue of the disadvantage of our geographic position. Unlike the British, we do not live on an island and we are thus not forced to find settlement colonies overseas.[81]

Even though it is impossible to evaluate the Association's influence in German politics in concrete terms, it is important to note that, despite the Association's small membership before the First World War, it included some rather influential individuals.[82] Although officially the 'Verband' was in sharp opposition to German foreign policy, even under the new Chancellor, General von Caprivi,[83] government policies were identical to the demands of the Association in several instances,[84] especially regarding Germany's relation to Austria.[85]

In addition to the All-German Association's branch in Austria, under Georg von Schönerer,[86] there were several smaller groups that actively pursued Mitteleuropa interests in Austria – notably the 'German People's Association' (Deutscher Volksverein), founded in 1867 in Vienna, and the 'Association of German Nationals' (Verein der Deutschnationalen), founded in 1869 in Graz.[87] However, compared with von Schönerer's group these interest groups remained non-influential.

The Economic 'Mitteleuropa' Organizations

Even though there had been some economic interest groups before 1871, the situation changed dramatically after unification. The number[88] as well as the influence of such groups on German politics increased significantly. Unification promoted the development of larger interest groups with a broader organizational base. During this period Germany greatly increased industrial production, which also encouraged the expansion of interest groups.[89] Finally, imperialism spawned economic demands and policies for neo-mercantilist protectionism. Therefore, separating Germany's foreign policy from domestic economic and political interests became increasingly difficult as the First World War approached. During the era of Wilhelm II, three groups were most influential: the previously mentioned Centralverband Deutscher Industrieller, the Bund der Industriellen (Confederation of Industrialists), and the Hansabund. Parallel to these groups there was also the Mid-European Economic Society (Mitteleuropäische Wirtschaftsverein), which supported the economic union of Mitteleuropa.[90]

The Centralverband, founded in 1876 as an umbrella organization, contained 102 sub-organizations and 462 individual members by 1901.[91] Over the course of the organization's history, heavy industries increasingly gained influence, resulting largely from their monopolization of this sector.[92] Reacting to heavy industry's dominance of the Centralverband, in 1895 most of the chemical and textile industries' representatives founded the Bund of Industrialists. With their departure, the Centralverband's new homogeneity increased its political influence, since the German generals' and the iron and steel producers' interests overlapped considerably. Furthermore, the Verband's interest lay in the realm of economic and social regulation. The Bund of Industrialists also demanded an expansion of German trade. But, in opposition to the Centralverband, it favoured low tariffs for raw materials, especially chemicals and minerals.

Finally, the Hansabund resulted from an attempt to form an interest group representing all economic sectors with the exception of agriculture. It was a coalition of the Centralverband, the bankers' association, and several craft associations. Politically, the Hansabund was influential in that it succeeded in putting together a coalition of the two liberal parties for the election in 1910. The Hansabund split in the aftermath of the coalition's defeat, over the question of whether or not to include the socialists.[93] In turn, the Centralverband and the farmers' association founded a common cartel in 1913.

As Fritz Blaich has pointed out, in general one can separate the imperialist and Mitteleuropa-oriented interest groups into two blocs.[94] The first was composed of membership groups that sought a wide audience in order to gain political influence through sheer numbers. The other consisted of business organizations that formed close links to the administration and, therefore, maintained close ties with the state bureaucracy. The latter was rather elitist in nature and contained many prominent members.[95] However, they all had a common goal: economic re-orientation of German politics in order to achieve a unified economic bloc in Central Europe.

The organization that most effectively advocated a swift change in German economic orientation towards Mitteleuropa was the 'Mid-European Economic Society'. The famous economic theorist Gustav Schmoller[96] provided its conceptual backbone. A neo-mercantilist at heart, Schmoller saw the need for a 'defence' in Central Europe against the pressures of the other economic world colossi, such as the United States, Russia, Great Britain, and perhaps even China.[97] In 1890, Schmoller wrote:

> There is an inexorable tendency for the establishment of larger economic areas, which are, despite their political independence, capable of

> carrying through their common economic interests against the great world economic powers. This tendency forces us in Europe to establish a new order in Europe based upon international law, which is not a confederation, nor a 'most-favoured-nation' system, but a third, something new, something in between the two.[98]

Julius Wolf, a professor of national economics, pursued Schmoller's idea. In 1904 he founded the 'Mid-European Economic Society' (Mitteleuropäischer Wirtschaftsverein) in several Central European countries as a functionalist solution to the perceived problem.[99] As he, himself, wrote about the foundation of the Verein:

> It seemed to be the logical consequence of those thoughts [Schmoller's and his own], that they take root and blossom. Publications, resolutions and newspaper articles were simply not enough. Therefore, we started to built the Verein . . . , noticing the support of the states and parties in question, under the following premises:
>
> 1. the Verein is aware that a customs union among the states involved for the time being is unrealistic and therefore
> 2. the Verein will refrain from any kind of political agitation. . . .[100]

This restriction is important to note since Berlin had become cautious regarding Central European economic integration after the Caprivi disaster of 1894. The German government also wanted to avoid any confrontation with Great Britain on this matter. Furthermore, several Central European governments, above all Hungary, were rather sensitive on the issue, because they correctly perceived economic integration as a disguised form of German Mitteleuropa imperialism.[101]

The Verein was a private economic administration that 'sought to internationalize the methods and laws of trade, transportation, and communications'.[102] Although it was a private organization, its personnel had entrée to leading civil servants in the foreign and economic ministries and among industrial elites. For example, the brother of the Emperor, the vice-president of the Parliament, the vice-president of the Prussian Senate, and the president of the Krupp empire's board of directors sat on the Verein's board of directors in 1904.[103] Influencing public opinion was of little interest to the Verein. As Meyer puts it:

> The activity of the Society was characterized by a continuous and conscientious effort to work out problems in minute detail. . . . The practical results . . . were limited to simplification of banking procedures and customs formalities between Germany and the monarchy [Austria].[104]

Theoretically, the Verein's organizational structure and personal contacts should have maximized its influence over Mitteleuropa policy. However, growing tensions in Europe and the lingering economic war prevented the Society from achieving more then marginal results. Even though it existed until the end of the First World War, it became less influential after 1914, when imperial Mitteleuropa concepts dominated the political debate.

The economic vision of Mitteleuropa eventually succumbed to imperialist forces. During Caprivi's tenure as Chancellor there was a brief moment when the economic concept of Mitteleuropa had a chance. However, with the failure of the 'Caprivi system' and Russia's entry into the customs bloc, there was virtually no opportunity politically to realize an economic Mitteleuropa.[105] In effect, the Farmers' Union, with its demands for protectionist politics, had defeated the Customs Union, with its promise of a free-trade zone in the heart of Europe. In the political vacuum that ensued, the perilous imperialist concept of Mitteleuropa prevailed.

4 The Imperial 'Mitteleuropa', 1914–45

INTRODUCTION

As the result of increasing German isolationism and an overall imperialist turn in European politics, the contemporary vision of Mitteleuropa shifted on the eve of the First World War. As the Great War approached, Mitteleuropa concepts took on a menacing imperialist tone. Whereas, previously, Mitteleuropa concepts had been oriented more towards economic cooperation, by 1914 they became predominantly hegemonic. Mitteleuropa aspirations merged with Germany's war aims and 'all-German' demands. German domination of the Central European region became an undisputed national goal.

The second important aspect of the Mitteleuropa concept after 1914 was that, for the first time in German history, the theory was put into practice instead of remaining an abstract intellectual concept.[1] In other words, Germany actively pursued the goal of Mitteleuropa. This is not to argue that Mitteleuropa became a clearly defined objective. On the contrary, political, economic and military plans reflected a great variety of Mitteleuropa concepts. The most important conflict developed over the question of a federal versus an imperial framework.[2] As Egbert Jahn phrased it, in all its inconsistency,

> Mitteleuropa seemed to be the ingenious solution to the unresolved conflict of the nineteenth century between a großdeutsch, bourgeois–democratic nation state and the preservation of the two Empires; of the antagonism between political protestantism and catholicism, between the revival of the old idea of a supranational Empire [the Holy Roman Empire] and the modern industrial and colonial world-power aspirations of the . . . nobility and the bourgeoisie.[3]

Precisely because it was perceived as a patent remedy for all the conflicts, contradictions, and rivalries in German society, Mitteleuropa never could develop as a coherent policy or programme.

With the outbreak of the First World War the evolution of the concept ended in a narrow colonial–imperialist cul-de-sac. Only after the end of the Second World War would this concept of 'Mitteleuropa' be abandoned.

The period between 1914 and 1945 is of interest to this work, in so far as approaches to Mitteleuropa during this era anathematized the concept for later generations. The present reservation among German political elites regarding Mitteleuropa is largely a result of the misuse of the concept during that thirty-year period.[4]

MILITARY AND POLITICAL 'MITTELEUROPA' PLANS DURING THE FIRST WORLD WAR

During the course of the First World War, Germany's political goals were either subservient or identical to its military objectives. By 1917, the German General Staff, and General Erich Ludendorff in particular, had installed a de facto military dictatorship. The General Staff conducted politics by military decree. Moreover, the Emperor's and the Reichstag's general lack of power reinforced the authority of the military dictatorship.[5]

Bethmann-Hollweg's September Programme

The famous 1914 war programme of Chancellor Bethmann-Hollweg was an epilogue to long-term developments in German politics. In 1914, Germany perceived its situation in the European 'concert of nations' as increasingly desperate. Its expansive operations had turned sour on all fronts. Germany's Balkan engagement, the 'Berlin–Baghdad' axis, faded, not in the least because of the growing disintegration of the Ottoman Empire.[6] Both Britain and France frustrated Germany's overseas aspirations and colonial expeditions. Finally, the plan to secure the German position in Central Europe, through a 'continental alliance' (Kontinentalbündnis), failed after the Björkö Treaty of 1905.[7] As a result, Germany, under pressure, moved closer to the second German nation in Europe, Austria. The latter, in turn, was plagued by serious internal problems, mostly as a result of unrest within the Empire, that is, within Central Europe.[8] Ironically, Germany tilted towards Austria in an attempt to secure its position in Mitteleuropa, while Austria needed Germany to secure its dominance in the region.[9]

The Military Pressures

Shortly before the war, the continental Mitteleuropa option was favoured by conservative German circles, such as the Pan-Germans and the 'Prussia-first' faction.[10] At the same time, the Alldeutsche Verband published two widely read brochures, also urging continental expansion and integration in order to strengthen the German position in light of the approaching 'inevitable' war.[11] Some voices even hailed the Triple Alliance as the basis for and predecessor of a German Mitteleuropa.[12] This dominant reactionary and imperialist nationalism of the years 1913–14 set the tone of debates on Mitteleuropa throughout the Weimar Republic and the Third Reich. In 1913 Ernst Jäckh expressed his astonishment and concern in a letter to Friedrich Naumann:[13]

> Have you ever heard the expression 'to evacuate'? I had never known of it until I heard it today . . . [W]hen we discussed German foreign policy and I maintained . . . that Germany does not need war because it can derive no benefit from it. . . . [A]nd when I pointed to the obvious impossibility of annexing non-German portions of neighboring nations, . . . I always got the . . . answer, we will just have to 'evacuate' them. I learned that this meant 'expropriation' and 'transfer' of non-German elements and retention and settlement of the 'evacuated' area. This is how simply and easily these individuals perceive . . . [foreign policy].[14]

Such sentiments and conceptions of German foreign policy were widespread among the public as well as in military and economic circles. Consequently, German political advocates of a more moderate foreign policy faced increasing pressure.[15]

By instinct, Chancellor Theobald von Bethmann-Hollweg was one of the more moderate German politicians. But he lacked a certain determination and drive, which made him an easy target for pressure groups, that subsequently exerted influence on the government.[16] Given these pressures and previous foreign-policy failures, the German General Staff's military plans heavily influenced Bethmann-Hollweg's Mitteleuropa conception. Since 1897, the Schlieffen Plan had been the heart of Germany's strategic orientation for the next war.[17] And, since the era of Bismarck's successor, Chancellor Chlodwig von Hohenlohe, the Schlieffen Plan had not been questioned by the government or any subsequent chancellor. Bethmann-Hollweg was no exception to this rule.[18] In as much as the Schlieffen Plan was an offensive attack plan, the political leadership's failure to object, in effect, supported the General Staff's imperial military aspirations.

With the change in military leadership during the war, from von Falckenhayn to Ludendorff,[19] military Mitteleuropa plans changed as well. For Falckenhayn, Mitteleuropa was a means to end the war victoriously. He assumed that, after a swift victory on the western front, England would enter into a systematic war of attrition. Mitteleuropa, as a loose confederation among Germany, Austria, Bulgaria and Turkey, would help to break the British blockade and destroy England's hopes of winning such a war.[20]

The Allied Somme offensive of 1916 marked a turning point in the war, which altered the domestic situation in Germany dramatically since German society was subsequently subjugated to the necessities of war. Ludendorff became a rather omnipotent dictator who in the summer of 1916 issued the 'Hindenburg Programme',[21] which called for switching civilian industry to arms production, more rapid transport of resources, and, most important, much tighter control over industry and society.[22] Furthermore, the government was forced to increase the national debt in order to finance the programme. In 1916 Hindenburg formulated a much harsher war programme than Bethmann-Hollweg had in the same year. The Hindenburg Programme shifted the locus of Mitteleuropa westwards[23] in order to make a separate peace with Russia possible.

The Economic Pressures

In addition to such factors as the power of the General Staff and the impotence of German politicians, another driving force behind the imperialist vision of Mitteleuropa was Germany's economic, industrial, and banking circles. Through its close contracts to the government, the industrial–commercial elite was able to manipulate public opinion. This elite was able to persuade the broad public that Germany had a 'just demand for expansion' because of its disadvantageous position in world politics.[24] Mitteleuropa was portrayed as a counterweight to such world empires as Russia, Great Britain and the United States. This view remained influential until the end of the Second World War.

In the spring of 1914, the Alldeutsche Verband, under Heinrich Claß, joined forces with the Hansabund and the 'Young Liberals' (an economic organization) to demand a united German Mitteleuropa. In the autumn of 1914, prior to the announcement of Bethmann-Hollweg's government programme, Claß formulated a pan-German programme for Mitteleuropa as an economic union of the two German Empires, Scandinavia, Bulgaria, Romania and Italy. In the west, Belgium and parts of France were to fall under German hegemony.[25] In 1914 the heavy industrialists Gustav Krupp von Bohlen und Halbach and Hugo Stinnes supported Claß and the Verband in their demands.

Furthermore, Matthias Erzberger, a member of the Paliamentary Centre Party, but more importantly a representative of the influential Disconto-Society and the powerful Thyssen Group, issued a memorandum (Denkschrift) regarding German war aims in September 1914.[26] Here, Erzberger demanded immediate control over Belgium and the annexation of the industrial centre of Longwy-Briey in order to secure the supply of steel and coal for German industrial war production. Furthermore, he called for the establishment of the Kingdom of Poland under German overlordship, as well as a partial expansion of Austria–Hungary into the Ukraine, Romania, and Besarabia. He also demanded that Russia be rolled back eastward and that all non-Russian ethnic groups be 'freed' under German domination.

August Thyssen, who delivered his memorandum to the German government on 9 September 1914, had even more far-reaching plans.[27] He wanted to incorporate the Baltic states as well as some Russian territory, including parts of the Don Region, the Crimea, and the Caucasus. Thyssen also justified these demands in terms of the scarcity of German resources and the need for economic expansion in general. Arthur von Gwinner, First President of the German Bank, however, warned against such a rigid policy of annexation and argued for more subtle but none the less effective measures to increase Germany's economic hegemony in Mitteleuropa. He suggested using Germany's political influence instead of military means to achieve the nation's goals there.[28] These partially contradictory suggestions were all more or less combined in the government's September Programme.

The September Programme

Given the pressures and demands of the military and industry in 1914, Bethmann-Hollweg's September Programme appears rather moderate.[29] It was formulated at General Headquarters in Koblenz (Großes Hauptquartier) in cooperation with Karl Helffrich, President of the German Bank.[30] At that time, Helffrich had no official function; eventually, he would become the Under-secretary for the Treasury in January 1915. Industry's influence on the programme, through Helffrich, is apparent.

The basic idea of the programme was similar to the demands of the Alldeutsche Verband and industrial circles: first, German expansion as a world power, and secondly, securing the German position in Central Europe in order to achieve the main goal.[31] The 'overall goal' of the war, as Bethmann-Hollweg formulated it, was

> securing the German Empire to the East and the West for a long time. In order to achieve that, France has to be weakened to the extent that it cannot come back as a 'Großmacht'; Russia should be pushed back from Germany's frontier and its rule over the non-Russian vassal peoples shall be broken.[32]

Influenced by the leading banking and industrial circles surrounding Helffrich and Walter Rathenau,[33] Bethmann-Hollweg proposed a Mitteleuropa under German hegemony. Compared with the pan-German programme, it was designed to be a moderate conquest that was, simultaneously, economically necessary. Concretely, the programme demanded the following:[34] the annexation of Longwy-Briey from France, as well as terms of trade that would make France dependent upon Germany (as an Exportland); the preservation of Belgium, which would become a vassal state of Germany (as a military base against England), and the establishment of a Central European economic area under German rule that would include Austria–Hungary, Poland, Denmark, Italy and Scandinavia.

The programme was written according to two premises: first, the belief that France would be beaten within a short period of time, and secondly, that peace on the western front would occur within weeks. Since both premises turned out to be false,[35] the demanding tone of the programme became burdensome to future German politicians. The Chancellor's deputy, Clemens von Delbrück, Under-secretary in the State Department, clearly perceived this only days later, after the loss of the Battle of the Marne. He stated that the programme was not formulated 'on the basis of communication about mutual interests . . . but on the basis of the anticipation of a victorious German peace (Siegfrieden)'.[36]

Since the programme represented the joint interests of Germany's military and economic circles, neither Bethmann-Hollweg nor his successors could alter it significantly during the war. Until the war's end the Bethmann-Hollweg Programme, with some insignificant tactical changes, remained the guideline for German politics. As laid out in 1914, the programme was partially realized between 1917 (after the Brest–Litovsk Treaty) and the capitulation of 1918 and Versailles.[37] In the Treaty, Soviet Russia lost Lithuania, Poland, Kurland and, de facto, Estonia and Latvia. Thus Germany's goals regarding Russia, as formulated in 1914, were implemented successfully in 1917.

Naumann's 'Mitteleuropa'

In 1914–15 the German public was living in triumphant euphoria, which, after the Marne battle was not necessarily supported by military reality. Aware of the situation since November 1914, the political and military leadership had entered into cautious negotiations with England and Russia regarding peace settlements. When rumours about this surfaced among the general public there was considerable outrage. Almost immediately, a 'war-aim movement' (Kriegszielbewegung) was established to force the government to reject a 'soft peace' that would be easy on Germany's enemies.[38]

A little later, the 'war committee of German industry' (Kriegsausschuß der deutschen Industrie) joined forces with the 'war-aim movement'.[39]

The core of the movement was comprised of representatives of heavy industry and the two most influential commercial societies, the Centralverband and the Bund of Industrialists.[40] In October 1914, Alfred Hugenberg, then director of Krupp, organized a meeting of all economic societies in Berlin, at which Claß gave a speech regarding German war goals. The representatives were so impressed that they ordered Hugenberg to formulate what became the petition of March 1915.[41] In large part, it reiterated the September Programme with its demand for annexation of the industrial centres in France and Belgium and the Channel coast. As a 'counterweight' to industrial gains in the west, the petition argued for agrarian territory in the east. The only truly new element was the suggestion of securing the Ukraine for Germany, which in fact became part of the Brest–Litovsk Treaty.[42]

In the middle of this politically and militarily precarious situation, Friedrich Naumann's book *Mitteleuropa* was published in October 1915.[43] It became a best-seller and was translated into French and English during the war; today, it remains the most cited book concerning the issue of Mitteleuropa.[44] His 'political thoughts . . . were a typical product of such times, full of inner tensions',[45] as Wolfgang Schieder has observed. At first glance, Naumann's work seems to be yet another imperialist publication, but in reality his ideas and suggestions run counter to mainstream imperialist arguments.

On the surface, Naumann argues for a Central European union in order to secure resources. But his argumentation reaches beyond the immediate needs of the war; he states that, after the war, the world will be divided into two economic super-regions (wirtschaftliche Großräume): an Anglo-American and a Russo-Asiatic one.[46] The subsequent development of Mitteleuropa was, for Naumann, the next logical step on the path towards larger economic entities, something that Germany had been pursuing since the Zollverein and the subsequent creation of the Reich.[47] His views on economic cooperation are oriented towards a customs union between the two German Empires plus Romania. However, as Meyer wrote, 'committed though he was to a constructive approach, Naumann was wary of making a specific blueprint. . . . [H]e continually emphasized a spirit of unifying in searching for solutions.'[48]

In sharp contrast to the advocates of an imperialist Mitteleuropa, Naumann, with his Christian-socialist roots,[49] did not suggest large-scale annexations or 'evacuation' of ethnic groups. Rather, he favoured a confederate system in which all nationalities would be independent and protected.

In Naumann's view, the German nation naturally would dominate the confederation culturally and economically. Nevertheless, Naumann was far from advocating the 'Germanization' of the region. Aware of the nationality problem in Mitteleuropa, he wrote:

> Since it is my special task to visualize the idea of Mitteleuropa, not just for the Germans in Austria but for all the various component peoples of the Austro-Hungarian monarchy, . . . I desire to develop a milder and friendlier understanding among the Reich-Germans for the Magyars and West Slavs.[50]

Furthermore, he perceived Mitteleuropa as a tool that could be used to improve the Empire's domestic situation. Since the 1890s, Naumann had concentrated on the Empire's social problems, the tension between democracy and dynasty, and the discrepancy between the Emperor and the working class.[51] Naumann thought that, as the leading power in Mitteleuropa, Germany could overcome these tensions and unite the German people behind the goal of a German Mitteleuropa.[52]

Despite their positive and widespread public reception, Naumann's moderate suggestions had hardly any effect on the official German political position.[53] However, because of Naumann, the concept of 'Mitteleuropa' reached a broad public and sparked the interests of intellectuals. His ideas reached well beyond the Weimar Republic and continue to have influence today.[54]

The remnants of 'Mitteleuropa'

The last relatively coherent conception of Mitteleuropa during the war was formulated in 1916. After Bethmann-Hollweg's dismissal in 1917, the German Empire's political leadership was replaced by a quasi-dictatorship of the General Staff. Therefore, Mitteleuropa became a vague and unstable tactical goal that shifted with the fortunes of war. In 1916, the General Staff was reorganized for the third time since the beginning of the war and Falckenhayn was replaced by the 'dynamic duo', Hindenburg and Ludendorff.[55] In November 1916, Bethmann-Hollweg formulated a relatively moderate programme that was designed to pave the way for peace negotiations. It suggested withdrawal from France, except from Longwy-Briey, guarantees for Belgium, and a general recognition of Poland.[56]

Hindenburg responded almost immediately, changing the programme significantly by insisting on the subjugation of Poland and the annexation of Kurland and Lithuania. Securing a strong German position in Mitteleuropa remained one of the dominant objectives for the General Staff, which, in turn, would lead to increasing tensions in the political realm. Ultimately, this conflict resulted in the dismissal of the Chancellor in 1917. As a result of the peace treaty of Brest–Litovsk, for a brief period a German Mitteleuropa became a possibility. The Treaty of Versailles, though, did away with all chances of realizing Mitteleuropa as a German war goal. However, during the peace negotiations at Versailles and in the Weimar Republic, Mitteleuropa remained an important factor in German politics, primarily as a facet of the 'peace-dictate' legacy.[57]

'MITTELEUROPA' DURING THE WEIMAR REPUBLIC

The First World War created a mid-European awareness among the German people in Austria and Germany. As Meyer stated:

> The years of economic blockade and ideological isolation; the vast military–geographic panorama opening the East and Southeast; the discovering of kinsmen in remote parts of the mid-European area, personally experienced by at least a million men: these were events that made a permanent impression on the thinking and attitudes of Germans at a time of acutely aggravated sensitivity.[58]

German war aims ceased to exist on 29 September 1918, when the General Staff urged the government to propose a peace settlement. Simultaneously, ambitious German Mitteleuropa concepts also ceased to exist. From that time on, Germany was fighting for its existence as a European power. The German leadership hoped to re-establish the status quo ante, which it failed to do at Versailles.

When his two Generals, Hindenburg and Ludendorff, reported that the war was lost, Wilhelm II responded with the famous words, 'the war is over, admittedly very differently from how we expected. . . . Our politicians have failed wretchedly.'[59] With this statement the 'backstabbing legend' (Dolchstoß Legende) was born in Germany, a legend that would plague the Weimar Republic until its end. Versailles shattered all hopes for a reasonable settlement, establishing instead a harsh 'dictated-peace' (Diktatfrieden).[60] Both factors contributed to the political predicament that enabled the rise of Hitler; but both also helped 'Mitteleuropa' to survive.[61]

'Mitteleuropa' Continuity

Despite the Versailles Treaty, Germany remained a strong state in the centre of Europe. Soon after the war, it initiated political and economic manoeuvres designed to overcome the limitations of Versailles. Germany's revisionist foreign policy followed the expansionist Mitteleuropa tradition by attempting to undermine the new European system of nation-states in Central Europe.[62] In the Weimar Republic, imperialist concepts of Mitteleuropa began to function as a counter concept to the democratic values represented by the West, for example, by the United States and England. Thus for many Germans, pursuing imperial Mitteleuropa concepts became a symbol of dissatisfaction with and anger over the 'dictated peace'.

'Großdeutsch' and 'gesamtdeutsch' plans

The geopolitical situation in 1918 looked similar to the situation prior to 1871. Reich Germany had to accept large territorial losses and, even worse, the Austrian Empire was reduced to rump Austria. The result was that four new states appeared in Central Europe on Germany's borders, with at least twelve million Germans living outside the Reich. As a result, großdeutsch as well as gesamtdeutsch sentiments gained acceptance during the Weimar years. The discussion in 1918, concerning 'Anschluß' or a pan-German Empire, resembled the period between 1848 and 1871, when Germany and Central Europe were also in flux geopolitically.[63] Towards the end of the Weimar Republic, Hitler and his party managed to merge the großdeutsch idea with the gesamtdeutsch vision, so that Anschluß in 1938 was perceived only as the first step in the 'natural' development of a pan-German Empire, i.e., the Third Reich.

With the collapse of the Bismarck and Habsburg European system in 1918, großdeutsch sentiments of the pre-Bismarck period surfaced once more. As Friedrich Meinecke wrote: 'In the face of impending dissolution and woe, the grossdeutsch tradition was the last bulwark of confidence.'[64] The politicians Hermann Ullmann and Theodor Heuss stated in the journal *Deutsche Arbeit* that, among German Mitteleuropa aspirations, only the großdeutsch idea could be saved.[65] Even the *Sozialistische Monatshefte* urged an incorporation of rump Austria into a workers' republic.[66] In other words, writers, politicians, and academicians of all political orientations, whether conservative, liberal or socialist, supported what even then was called the 'Anschluß' in the Mitteleuropa Empire.

The three most prominent supporters of Mitteleuropa during the war, Friedrich Naumann, Ernst Jäckh and Paul Rohrbach, also favoured 'Anschluß'. In general, the argument was that Anschluß was not a renewal of a pan-German Mitteleuropa plan, but rather the result of the two German states' economically desperate situation.[67] But, owing primarily to the victors' firm opposition and Reich German indecisiveness,[68] Anschluß could not be achieved in 1920. By then the political situation in Germany had stabilized so that Anschluß became increasingly unlikely. By 1926, after Germany's admission to the League of Nations, the plan was politically dead[69] and remained quite literally an academic issue.[70]

In retrospect, it is clear that the Anschluß demand was only the first element in a broader conception of a gesamtdeutsch Empire and Mitteleuropa.[71] As early as 1918, the future German Foreign Minister (1923–9) Gustav Stresemann formulated the demand for Anschluß as a lever to alter Germany's geopolitical situation and to revise the Paris treaties. He stated:

> If we succeed in . . . tying the Austrian Germans to us, we will overcome the losses that we suffered in another direction [eastward]; then we will have a large block of seventy million Germans in the centre of Europe . . . which no one can pass by, that everyone must recognize. If we succeed in this, then there will be other times, there will be other political constellations to improve our situation.[72]

Later, as Foreign Minister, he would pursue a traditional foreign policy of establishing a regional power with hegemonic tendencies and a manageable economy through bilateral treaties between Germany and its neighbours. Germany's European policy of cooperation,[73] similar to its programme during the Bismarck era, continued to be a tool of German national policy. This, in turn, would require the revision of the Versailles and Paris Treaties, among other desiderata.[74]

Beginning in 1920, several organizations were established to advance the gesamtdeutsch cause.[75] However, by 1922, as a result of the events following the Ruhr-occupation and the emerging economic crisis of the 1920s, the Reich-Germans' enthusiasm for a gesamtdeutsch solution became less intense. In this period, the works of Paul de Lagarde, a gesamtdeutsch advocate, experienced a renaissance. Furthermore, Paul Rohrbach, previously an economic Mitteleuropa advocate, became a gesamtdeutsch advocate, and subsequently revised his works in light of the new development.[76] The Gesamtdeutsch solution also became a basic goal of the German government. Although all pre-Nazi governments agreed that force was not an acceptable method for changing the status quo, they had a common concern for German minorities in other states and absolutely rejected Poland's post-war border.[77]

In the academic community, Mitteleuropa was linked to a new Reich idea, with all its romantic and sentimental overtones, which had been part of this concept as early as 1848.[78] The First World War and the destruction of Austria–Hungary were perceived as an opportunity to create a new Reich and to reshape the region's contours. Between 1848 and 1918, the term 'gesamtdeutsch' had hindered Reich-German plans for the area, given the dual monarchy's opposition to the concept as well as its interests in the region. Now, with the monarchy reduced to rump Austria, there were no restrictions on Germany's gesamtdeutsch Mitteleuropa aspiration. As the historian Martin Spahn stated in 1925:

> For the first time in a thousand years our entire Volk is full of life and on the march. Only a goal is needed. We must become imbued with the conviction, the belief that a mission has also been allotted to our Volk. This mission is: Mitteleuropa. . . . [I]f . . . we can give Mitteleuropa form and function, then we shall again become the leading nation of Europe.[79]

Early in the Weimar period, German periodicals such as *Volk und Reich*, *Deutsches Archiv für Landes- und Volks-forschung*, and *Deutsche Rundschau* echoed the call for a new Mitteleuropa. These periodicals created a forum for such people as Martin Spahn, Wilhelm Schüssler, Hans Rothfels, Paul Rohrbach, and the influential Heinrich von Srbik. Representatives of German minorities, especially in Poland and the Sudetenland, also contributed to the transition from the Mitteleuropa to the gesamtdeutsch concept. They did so by demanding that the Reich-Germans take up the cause and improve their situation.[80]

Paul Sweet summed up the academic writings on Mitteleuropa in the inter-war years as follows: first, there was 'a tendency to regard Mitteleuropa as the region where the culture . . . has been largely influenced by the Germans'; secondly, 'the [gesamtdeutsch] idea was much stronger than the federal idea'; thirdly, 'there was a marked disinclination to deal with the fact . . . that Mitteleuropa was not merely a German problem, but a problem of world politics'; fourthly, there was an extreme reluctance 'to accept the fact that the Germans . . . were a decided minority, numerically, in [Mitteleuropa]'.[81] In general, as a coherent concept, Mitteleuropa was kept alive largely by geographers and economists, with only moderate success among the economists.

Economic 'Mitteleuropa' plans

Economic Mitteleuropa plans also articulated a demand for Anschluß.[82] The necessity of war had forced Germany and Austria–Hungary into a close alliance, which, in any event, would have resulted from a customs union. However, the Reich's initiatives to establish the customs union at the beginning of the war were inhibited by the domestic contradictions that existed within the dual monarchy. Only in 1918 did the Salzburg Protocols establish the framework for a customs union. The Central Powers and the subsequent Allied prohibition resulted in an early abolition of the union.[83] But the Salzburg example remained the point of departure for economic conceptions in the mid-1920s.

Parallel to thinking about the creation of an economic Mitteleuropa, German industrialists also proposed a pan-European union, as suggested, for example, by Count Richard Coudenhove-Kalergi.[84] However, as the public debate increasingly centred on the gesamtdeutsch concept, so too did German industrial circles. Coudenhove himself pointed out that

> most German economic leaders were . . . nationalists. They fought the Versailles Treaty, the politics of reparations. . . . They did not have much sympathy for the political aspect of Pan-Europe. But what they were interested in was the . . . European customs union.[85]

Only the Langnam Society[86] supported the Franco-German talks concerning heavy industrial production between 1924 and 1927. In 1926, these talks resulted in the International Raw Steel Union (Internationale Rohstahlgemeinschaft).[87] In 1931, when the economic crisis had worsened, the Langnam Society still hoped for a more complete integration of the Central European region.

Of greater significance was the establishment of the Mitteleuropäische Wirtschaftstag (Central European Commerce Group), founded in 1924–5. From its perspective, the term 'Mitteleuropa' was a much more open-ended concept geographically than Germany's wartime conception of Mitteleuropa. Aside from Germany, the countries invited to its first meeting in September 1925 included Austria, Hungary, Czechoslovakia, England and France.[88] Thereafter, the Wirtschaftstag met annually. From this movement, the Mitteleuropa Institutes were founded in 1929 and 1930. The Institutes, with branches in Vienna (1929), Brünn (1929), Budapest (1930) and Dresden, were created to track economic developments in the region. The long-term goal was to develop a plan to coordinate the region's economies.[89] The personnel for the institutes was recruited largely from industrial sectors.[90]

Whereas the Wirtschaftstag originally favoured free trade, in opposition to the increasing tendency in Europe to establish protective tariffs, over time its German section became an advocate of 'fortress Europe', returning to pre-war Mitteleuropa concepts. In the beginning the Wirtschaftstag resembled the pre-war Wirtschaftsverein[91] in organization and structure, but by the early 1930s it resembled the latter ideologically as well.[92] In 1929, in preparation for its fifth meeting, the German section released the following statement:

> Emphasis on a Central European economic union certainly exists in [Germany], and Germany's interests primarily lie in attaining in

Mitteleuropa an equivalent to the lost markets in the East, to its lost colonies, and, also, as a compensation for the increasing tariff barriers of the large economic empires, England, the United States, and other relevant states.[93]

In the same year, the directors of the German section suggested in a confidential memorandum that the complete economic Anschluß of Austria would create the necessary economic 'Lebens-Großraum', as a first step in establishing the future German 'Großreich'.[94] This all-too-familiar statement exemplifies the extent to which German commercial elites had returned to pre-war imperial positions by 1930. In light of this, the averment in 1931 that the demand for an Austrian–German customs union had only economic dimensions sounds rather hollow.[95]

In 1931, the board of directors of the German section included representatives from all important branches of German industry.[96] As a result of the growing world economic crisis in the early 1930s, the German section's influence on the Wirtschaftstag had expanded greatly by 1933.[97] The world economic crisis and the subsequent worsening of German economic and social conditions also drove the commercial elites into imperialist Mitteleuropa positions. These elites were driven by the belief that better markets lay in Central Europe. By 1933, Mitteleuropa had become a synonym for gesamtdeutsch policy on the economic level, a fact that Hitler exploited most effectively. The Weimar Republic's so-called 'indirect or covert aggression' towards Central Europe was now replaced by the Nazi regime's direct aggression.[98]

'MITTELEUROPA' UNDER HITLER

If Hitler had a clear conception of politics at all, which is debatable, it was a conception of world politics. In *Mein Kampf* he laid out the plan for a new world order in which Europe was only a part of the grand design. According to Hitler, Germany was to achieve a new and dominant role in world politics. Thus it was not really correct to speak of a 'Mitteleuropa' concept of Hitler since it was a means, at best, but never an end. Nevertheless, it is important to examine briefly the development of 'traditional' Mitteleuropa concepts in the Nazi period in order to understand post-war revulsion at the revival of Mitteleuropa in Germany foreign policy.

The final phase of the Weimar Republic was dominated and characterized by political and economic crises. As these crises intensified, nationalist discussions of a self-sufficient Germany through a new policy of 'Lebensraum' also intensified. From the perspective of military defeat and economic depression, the most promising new political force to fulfil this goal was the National Socialist Party. Therefore, large sections of Germany's economic elite supported Hitler. The National Socialist vision of German hegemony over Mitteleuropa and the creation of an economic 'Großraum' were portrayed as a realistic means of ending the Great Depression and its attendant hardships. Throughout this era, 'Mitteleuropa' concepts included Poland, Czechoslovakia, the Ukraine, and the Baltic states.

During the Weimar Republic, Germany's 'official' policy, with Stresemann's Rapallo and Locarno Treaties, followed Bismarck's approach to Mitteleuropa. Germany should be independent from the peripheral powers and, as a 'saturated' Reich without expansionist desires, should play the role of a mediator or a bridge in Central Europe. However, post-Stresemann governments changed this foreign-policy orientation, once again stressing the 'egoistic state'[99] elements in German foreign policy. '[F]rom the beginning [the Brünning government (1930–2)] subjected its politics to the primat of foreign policy, in the form of great power politics, similar to the . . . politics under Wilhelm II'.[100] Thus, Hitler's predecessors laid the imperialist base for his aggressive Mitteleuropa politics.

'Mitteleuropa' in Hitler's Ideology

Two terms that are central to Hitler's ideology, that is, 'Lebensraum' and 'Volk', played a large role in the Nazis' Mitteleuropa concept.[101] Furthermore, two of the social sciences, history and geopolitics, made important contributions to Hitler's Mitteleuropa concepts of Lebensraum and Volk.[102] The German Volk was at the centre of Hitler's ideology; one of its major problems was a lack of Lebensraum. Moreover, the Volk had to fulfil a historic task, namely, to cultivate and populate Eastern Europe. Some of these arguments, which had been developed previously by historians and geopoliticians, were cast in concrete form by the Nazis.[103]

Several conservative and nationalist historians in the 1920s developed the idea of the German people's historic mission.[104] The circle around Arthur Moeller van den Bruck, for example, emphasized the notion of Volk in German history.[105] His student May Hildebert Boehm argued that the Volk was the only constant in history and that, therefore, history had to be understood from the perspective of the Volk's interest. According to Boehm, the German Volk was to be consolidated in Mitteleuropa.[106] Many writers perceived 'Mitteleuropa' not as a theoretical concept, but rather as an 'historical and living reality'.[107] The road to German self-fulfilment led to Mitteleuropa, or as Wilhelm Schüssler formulated the proposition:

> Mitteleuropa is the only historic area where the pan-German fate occurred and still is occurring. Mitteleuropa is the stage for the pan-German fate. And thus, Mitteleuropa is German, i.e., the pan-German reality.[108]

The even more radical Heinrich von Srbik used the idea of 'Volk' to defend his imperialist Mitteleuropa concept. The survival of the Volk, he argued, was the ultimate task of a state, which, in turn, presupposed a geographically defined area. In 1937 he wrote that Mitteleuropa was German and

> as a basis for the requisite equilibrium of the community of states and nations, the centre of the continent [Mitteleuropa] has the exceptional task of saving the precious genotype [the German] from the ideology of Western constitutional theorems as much as from the despotic absolutism of the East.[109]

Many writers who shared the Nazi ideology gave almost biblical dimensions to the notion of Germany's mission and destiny in 'Mitteleuropa'. Simultaneously, 'Mitteleuropa' became a means and an end; it was a substitute religion in the German quest for the 'promised land'.[110]

The geopoliticians, under Karl Haushofer, were the second group of 'scientists' who contributed to the pseudo-scientific backbone of Hitler's ideology and propaganda. German geopolitics was built upon the theories of Friedrich Ratzel and Rudolf Kjellén, who adapted Social Darwinist notions to the role of states and nations in the international system.[111] The state was seen as a living organism that had to expand in order to survive. Karl Haushofer[112] perverted the determinist components of geopolitics into an 'anti-western substitute for the teachings of international politics'.[113] The natural German 'Lebensraum', according to Haushofer, lies in Mitteleuropa.

Finally, Heinz Brauweiler, publisher of the journal *Blätter für Ständischen Aufbau*, wrote in 1925:

> If German hegemony over Mitteleuropa, the historic destiny of the German Volk, is to become reality, it has to be earned conceivably also through battle. . . . Today the crucial interests [Lebensinteressen] of the German people and the smaller nation-states in Mitteleuropa are so interwoven that German hegemony . . . is the only realistic and stable solution.[114]

Here, Lebensraum, Volk, and historic destiny fused, becoming a blueprint for the next war. With such ideas, it was easy enough for German ideologists such as Giselher Wirsing, an influential writer for *Die Tat*, to develop the National-Socialists' Großraum Doctrine.

Hitler's 'Monroe Doctrine'

What was to become known as Hitler's Monroe Doctrine[115] was a derivation of the traditional Großraum idea that List had previously developed.[116] It was based on the premise that several large (economic) empires would develop, among which would be Germany and Mitteleuropa, England, Russia, the United States and Japan.[117] Hitler tried to justify his expansionist advances to the east by employing a slightly distorted analogy to the American Monroe Doctrine.[118] Especially after 1939, this strategy was designed primarily to prevent the United States from entering the war.[119] One of the advocates who attempted to give this 'Monroe Doctrine' a legal basis was the international law scholar Carl Schmitt.[120]

Hitler explained the idea of a German Monroe Doctrine most explicitly in his speech on 28 April 1939, which was a response to President Roosevelt's demand for a German declaration that would guarantee the safety of the Central European states from further German aggression. In his speech, Hitler asked how Roosevelt would react to a similar German demand on the United States regarding South America. He then stated that

> Mr Roosevelt, in this case, would probably refer back to the Monroe Doctrine and reject such a demand as an interference in the domestic affairs of the American continent. We Germans hold exactly the same doctrine for Europe, or at least for the region and the interests of the Großdeutsche Reich.[121]

Soon afterwards, the German foreign ministry, under Joachim von Ribbentrop, attempted to employ this strategy in articulating German foreign policy.[122] In 1937 Carl Schmitt also began to develop an interpretation of international law to justify the German Monroe Doctrine, as well as the Reich's Mitteleuropa policies such as the Anschluß with Austria and annexation of the Sudetenland in 1938.

Schmitt's German Monroe Doctrine

Karl Haushofer and his school of geopolitics assumed that the international system would evolve into several regional subsystems. The American Monroe Doctrine was the best known articulation of this geopolitical concept. Haushofer's European adaptation posited a multi-national region that 'would secure the economic consolidation and political–strategic isolation of several nations'. In other words, the geopoliticians defined the area almost exclusively in geographic terms.[123] On the basis of the geographical concept of a Großraum, Schmitt, at the Institute for Politics and International Law at the University of Kiel, developed the 'Principle of the Großraum in International Law (Großraumprinzip im Völkerrecht)'.

Schmitt argued that the idea of a Großraum, as in the Monroe Doctrine, contained three dimensions. First, the region had to be a geographic area united by a specific Volk's political ideology, regardless of its particular political content.[124] Secondly, the region had to be dominated by a politically 'awakened' people. Thirdly, the concept of Großraum was defensive in nature, a barrier against foreign intervention. As Schmitt defined 'Großraum', it was a subject of international law. In order to codify the idea of a Großraum, Schmitt introduced the term 'Reich' (*sic*) into international law.[125] The Reich would have been a 'first rate subject'[126] of international law. Within his 'Großraum' the Reich constituted the hegemonical power, for example, as the carrier of the political idea. It is obvious that this argumentation was designed for the German Monroe Doctrine and that undoubtedly the 'Reich' was the 'Third Reich'. Schmitt's objective was to rewrite international law in order to inhibit international intervention in Mitteleuropa.

The German Monroe Doctrine would have encompassed all of continental Europe, including Soviet Russia.[127] According to the German Monroe Doctrine there was to be a hierarchy among the region's peoples, who, as a general rule, would all be subjugated to German law to various degrees. While the western states, such as France and Belgium, would retain some independence, the eastern states, Poland, Russia, and the Baltic nations, were to become part of the Reich in order to establish firm control over Mitteleuropa.

Since Schmitt, like the geopoliticians, perceived the development of several 'Großraums', he also suggested regulating the relations among these Großraums and their respective states. He proposed four levels of interaction: relationships among the Großraums, relationships among the Reichs, the relationship between the peoples within a Großraum, and finally that between the peoples of different Großräume.[128] In reality, these levels also constituted a ranking of the states with respect to their competencies and rights. As stated earlier, Schmitt's concept was neither acknowledged by the international community nor followed subsequently by the Hitler government. For Hitler, it was just another tactical manoeuvre in his chess game of international power politics. Schmitt's theory remained a Nazi perversion of historic German concepts of Mitteleuropa.

Until 1914, Mitteleuropa, in all its variations and permutations, was presented as a means to enlarge Germany's sphere of political influence and economic markets. Despite the imperialist and racist overtones of Mitteleuropa concepts, these aspects did not dominate the foreign policies of German politicians and statesmen such as Bismarck and Caprivi. In its more restrained form, the various nationalities of the region condoned the concept of Mitteleuropa because it suited their interests as well as those of the German states.

In the thirty years between 1914 and 1945 there was a radical transformation of the Mitteleuropa tradition. Mitteleuropa became almost synonymous with German imperialism, which shaped subsequent generations' perceptions of the concept. Then the Hitler regime completely anathematized the concept. The Second World War swept away both Nazi Germany and the opportunity for a rational, coherent discussion of Mitteleuropa. However, while Mitteleuropa ceased to exist geographically and ideologically, even during the war leaders of the German resistance did not abandon the concept. In the immediate post-war period, public and academic discussion was suppressed but the concept persisted.

5 'Mitteleuropa' in the Adenauer Era, 1944–63

INTRODUCTION

The end of Hitler's dictatorship marked a *caesura* in the continuity of German Mitteleuropa thought and policy. First, until 1948, Germany was powerless with respect to its domestic and even more so its foreign policy. Secondly, much more than after World War One, the term and concept were so anathematized that they disappeared from the political vocabulary. Nevertheless, after 1945 politicians of all political parties insisted that Germany retain its 1937 borders. Thus Mitteleuropa survived as a political entity in the form of the pre-1938 German Reich. Although 'Mitteleuropa' disappeared from the political discourse of politicians and statesmen, it survived in the popular mind. Much like the European Union, today, Mitteleuropa remained in the public consciousness.

While the war raged, within the German resistance Carl Goerdeler and his colleagues began planning what German foreign policy would be after Hitler and the Second World War. Goerdeler's plans clearly embraced the concept of Mitteleuropa. Despite the avoidance of imperialist overtones in post-war German politics, remnants of Mitteleuropa echoed in the thoughts of German politicians after the war, even though one can search in vain in Adenauer's official policies for traces of 'Mitteleuropa'. Following the division of Europe, Mitteleuropa was largely incorporated into the German question. Therefore, a solution to the German question implied an end to the partition and division in the centre of Europe and, almost necessarily, a re-establishment of Mitteleuropa.[1]

THE RESISTANCE

The two most important groups within the German resistance during the Nazi dictatorship were the group around Carl Goerdeler and the so-called Kreisau Circle (Kreisauer Kreis), who were responsible for the assassination attempt of 20 July 1944.[2] As Wolfgang Vernohr has pointed out, 'it is entirely undisputed *against* what these men fought . . . [however,] it is rather unclear *for* what they fought'.[3] There was no necessity, at that time, to choose sides between the United States and the USSR, since, in contrast to such post-war politicians as Konrad Adenauer and Jacob Kaiser, the German resistance was not yet confronted with the systemic conflict that dominated Europe during the Cold War. Therefore, the resistance leaders' spectrum for sketching German foreign policy for Mitteleuropa was broader than that of post-war politicians. At the same time, their interaction with foreign governments was very limited or virtually non-existent.[4] As a result, their proposals for future foreign policy in Central Europe were never subject to outside scrutiny.[5] This isolation allowed the leaders of the resistance to pursue traditional concepts of German foreign policy.

In general, the resistance was committed to what it perceived as Bismarck's heritage, that is, Germany as a 'mediator between East and West'.[6] Their foreign policy ideas must be assessed against the tradition of Bismarck, Caprivi, Bethmann-Hollweg, Stresemann and Brünning. Their traditional 'sense of [Germany's] incompleteness . . . also preoccupied the representatives of the German resistance'.[7] As a result, Mitteleuropa was a natural part of their political thinking and socialization. Adam von Trott zu Solz, a former diplomat and member of the resistance, wrote in May, 1944:

> Germany is the center of Europe. It must not commit itself wholly to the East or the West. Its geographical position rather demands a balanced relationship with both sides, and that it remains always aware of Germany's all-European responsibility.[8]

In concrete terms, this meant, primarily, the preservation of Bismarck's rump Reich as a 'third force' in Europe, between Great Britain and the Soviet Union.[9] As these remarks suggest, the circle around Goerdeler failed to notice the shift in power in the West from Britain to the United States. They believed that Mitteleuropa, including an independent Polish nation-state, could be established under German leadership and directed against Russia.[10] However, Goerdeler and his circle did not support military action against Russia (or any other Central European state). Instead, they followed their 'economic, liberal-capitalist faith',[11] opting for a gradual integration of the Soviet Union in Europe. As much as the Goerdeler group wanted to preserve the German Reich and its geopolitical position, it rejected the Nazi ideology. As Goerdeler wrote:

> [The Reich's] central position, numerical strength and great capacity guarantee the German people the leadership of the European bloc, if its foes do not ruin this by unreasonableness or by a mania for power. It is stupid and arrogant to speak of a German master race. It is foolish

> to demand respect for one's own national honour and independence and to deny it to others. The nation will grow into a leadership of Europe that respects even the small nations and does not attempt to guide their destinies with brutal force. The impartial viewpoint must be decisive. Legitimate interests must be balanced skilfully and farsightedly.[12]

In May 1943, he laid out his Mitteleuropa plan in a memorandum intended for the British government. It included Poland within its eastern borders of 1938, which, together with Finland and a fully independent Czechoslovakia, constituted the core of the German-led 'European community of interest and value'.[13] As a convinced Christian pacifist, Goerdeler rejected war entirely as a political means in this community.

Although sharing similar Christian views and a hatred of Hitler, the foreign-policy suggestions of the Kreisau Circle around Helmut James von Moltke had a somewhat different orientation. They perceived German nationalism and national aspirations as the basic problem in Europe and not its cure.[14] The only way to control and overcome nationalism was to form a European confederation. In a memorandum first drafted in 1941, Moltke stated:

> All solutions which followed the loss of faith as a unifying bond have proved to be so many distinguishing marks to set men against men. . . . [T]he members of one nation [have become] the natural enemies of the member of every other nation. . . . Under this development, Europe is falling to pieces; it is the historic task of this war to overcome these conflicts and . . . to reestablish a unified concept of Europe; the necessary consequence of this task is united sovereignty over Europe and the defeat of all individual claims to sovereignty.[15]

The goal of the Kreisau Circle was a Europe of equals. Within a (Central) European confederation stretching from the Atlantic to the Mediterranean and the Black Sea, border conflicts were no longer to be a subject of major conflicts or wars. Germany was to be imbedded in this confederation as a small, non-sovereign substructure among others such as the Balkans, the Baltic States, and Scandinavia.[16]

In short, the German resistance around Goerdeler largely followed Bismarck's German Mitteleuropa tradition, while the Kreisau Circle preferred functionalist pan-European solutions. Post-war politicians employed these views as a basis for the post-war debate. In fact, Kurt Schumacher's and Jacob Kaiser's suggestions regarding Central Europe and the German position were rooted in the propositions of the resistance without significant modification.

ADENAUER, SCHUMACHER AND KAISER

After the war, Germany's foreign policy was characterized by a paradox.[17] On the one hand, Germany was eager to keep things in flux in Central Europe in order to preserve the unity of the Reich, legally and territorially. On the other hand, it had to push for a stabilization of the region in order to regain 'room to manoeuvre as a subject in the sphere of international politics'.[18] Both the US and the USSR had a distinct interest in Germany, since both perceived it as a bridgehead within the quickly developing systemic conflict. Therefore, neither the Western Allies nor the USSR objected to the developing European and German division, since it was impossible for both sides to pursue a policy of 'roll-back', militarily or politically.[19] In the midst of this conflict, German post-war politicians had to develop a foreign policy concept. The Parliamentary Council (Parlamentarischer Rat) entertained three major orientations for Germany's future foreign policy, identified respectively with Konrad Adenauer, Jakob Kaiser, and Kurt Schumacher.

Adenauer's Ideas

From the very beginning, Adenauer advocated integration with the West (Westbindung). Because of his strong anti-communism and Christian conservatism, Westbindung was a must for Adenauer. There was only 'one way, to save our [the Germans'] freedom, safety, and way of life: a close alliance with the nations and states that shared the same opinions regarding the state, the individual, and freedom'.[20] Adenauer perceived world domination as the ultimate goal of Soviet communism; thus the only option for Germany was the West.[21]

Aside from his fundamental anti-communism, Adenauer also believed that only a close alliance with the US could secure peace in Europe. To Adenauer, US isolationism after World War One had been a tragedy for Europe and had contributed to the outbreak of the Second World War. In the event of a renewed US retreat, Europe in 1945 would once more lack a leading nation that could counterbalance the military potential of the Soviet Union. Adenauer wanted a stable Central Europe, even at the price of division. Consequently, he refused any temptations or attempts to revive 'Rapallo politics'.[22] As Helga Haftendorn has stated:

> Germany had to be truthful. It could not afford to concern itself with the almost criminal thought of developing a political orientation with the West today and the East tomorrow – and therefore conduct a 'Schaukelpolitik'.[23]

As a result of this almost unconditional subjugation to Western foreign policy and security, Adenauer's foreign policy towards Central Europe became somewhat amorphous. He simply lacked a Mitteleuropa conception; for Adenauer Mitteleuropa was Germany. Arnulf Baring has pointed out that Adenauer, as a citizen of the Rhineland and Cologne, never really developed a global view of the world. For Adenauer, the world east of Cologne remained alien. It was the Catholic province around Cologne that formed his political view of the world as well. 'Adenauer knows little about Eastern Europe, and often it seems that he is even less interested.'[24] His ideas regarding Central Europe were limited to two speculations. First, he hoped that some instability would develop in the Eastern bloc, which he perceived as entirely monolithic (despite the Hungarian uprising), and secondly, he expected the Soviet Union to collapse as a result of its disproportionately high defence budget. Once that happened, Germany could be united, which would solve any Mitteleuropa problems.

In May 1952, in a memorandum to President Eisenhower, Adenauer raised the question of Mitteleuropa's future, laying out his Mitteleuropa plan, while discussing Germany exclusively. He suggested to Eisenhower that free and independent elections should take place under international control in all of Germany and that, thereafter, a government under German control should be established. Furthermore, he argued that Germany should have the right to negotiate a peace settlement. In this context, he was not willing to accept the Oder–Neisse border, but suggested negotiations on that matter. Finally, he asked for German rearmament within the European Defence Union.[25] In short, Germany's unification and re-establishment within its 1937 borders was the only Mitteleuropa concept Adenauer voiced and pursued. Because of his limited foreign-policy perspective, Adenauer's adversaries, in the CDU and outside, accused him of deliberately obstructing unification and furthering tensions between East and West.[26] While the latter is a rather questionable accusation, it is undoubtedly true that Adenauer rejected any suggestions concerning a flexible and independent policy towards Mitteleuropa.

Kaiser's Ideas

In contrast to Adenauer, who remained in the Rhineland (and eventually even made Bonn the provisional German capital), Jacob Kaiser was directly affected by the situation in Eastern Germany and Central Europe as leader of the CDU in the Soviet Occupation Zone (1945–7). Consequently, Kaiser suggested a different German foreign policy. His concept, like the ideas of all Adenauer's opponents, rested on three pillars. First, the primary foreign-policy goal of Germany was unification; secondly, a solution that would integrate the two German states in the two blocs was firmly rejected; and thirdly, West Germany would not be integrated into the Western defence alliance without first resolving the German question of unification.

Following the classical Mitteleuropa tradition of Bismarck and Stresemann, Kaiser defined Germany as 'the bridge between East and West, one which, for the sake of Germany and for Europe's sake, should not be abandoned'.[27] Therefore, Germany should conduct an independent foreign policy between the two blocs. Kaiser built upon the tradition of the German resistance,[28] for which German unity was the main objective. Hans-Peter Schwarz has pointed out that Kaiser's liaison with the Goerdeler group shaped the political convictions of the young unionist.[29] Kaiser's reversion to Prussian virtues and the Prussian sense of state (Staatssinn) had its roots in his years as a member of the resistance around Goerdeler.[30]

Kaiser did not perceive the differences between East and West as a systemic conflict.[31] He was in agreement with Kurt Schumacher that the Germans could acknowledge the Russian, British or American way of life but would reject the idea of adopting it for themselves. In contrast to Schumacher, he went further in rejecting the idea of a Western cultural identity for Germany by insisting upon a 'German way' to which the nation was committed.[32] Kaiser postulated what later became known as the 'bridge theory', that is, that 'balancing socialism and freedom is the task of the world and therefore also ours [the Germans']'.[33] Germany's Mittellage (centre position) should not result in an 'either/or' foreign policy. Nor should it mean that Germany must choose between partnership with, or subordination under, the Soviet Union. Domestically, Kaiser tried to establish a united front of all parties in favour of German unity by linking the common goal of economic recovery with foreign-policy objectives.[34]

Unique in Kaiser's Mitteleuropa concept was a synthesis between socialism and the idea of a Reich.[35] He hoped to attract a broad spectrum of the population with this concept, which was especially important after the forced fusion of the Social Democrats and the Communist Party into the United Socialist Party (SED) in April 1946. As much as he opposed regional separatism in Germany (e.g., the Saarland), he tried to retain economic ties with Central Europe in order to save remnants of Mitteleuropa. Eventually, Kaiser lost the two-front war against the communists in the East and the majority of his party in the West. When he accepted the Marshall Plan for the Soviet Occupation Zone and proposed that all of

Eastern Europe do so, the tensions between Kaiser and the Soviets exploded. In December 1947, the Soviet Secret Police in the GDR dismissed Kaiser from his political post in East Berlin. By then, he had already lost control of the CDU's Western faction to Adenauer.[36]

Kaiser's Mitteleuropa policy was based on two premises: first, that a change in the status quo in Mitteleuropa could not be obtained without the Soviet Union and, secondly, that it seemed questionable that the Western Allies were even interested in such a change. Whether there ever was a chance for Germany to conduct a successful, independent Mitteleuropa policy à la Kaiser has been widely debated.[37] Nevertheless, Jakob Kaiser represented a lively Mitteleuropa tradition in post-war German politics, bridging the gap between the tradition of the resistance and Willy Brandt's Ostpolitik.

Schumacher's Ideas

In contrast to Adenauer and Kaiser, Kurt Schumacher could fall back upon an undistorted party tradition, since the SPD was the only party that survived the Nazi dictatorship and did not have to be rebuilt. Out of this tradition (which was also anti-fascist), Schumacher rejected the idea of collective German guilt and, therefore, demanded a strong Germany that would play an independent role in Europe.[38] Schumacher had a clear understanding of Mitteleuropa and its German tradition. He rejected Kaiser's 'bridge theory' as well as Adenauer's unconditional West-integration. Instead, he advocated a moderate West-integration, while at the same time demanding German unification in an all-European security system that would include the Soviet Union. The way to achieve the latter was through Western economic approaches to the East, in order to benefit from Western prosperity. According to Schumacher, the East could then voluntarily enter such a security system. Schumacher's rather mechanistic view was labelled the 'magnet theory'.[39]

He was guided by his two convictions of strict anti-communism and the primacy of German unity.[40] These were partly incompatible, since he wanted German unification without the Soviet Union. His anti-communism was exclusively directed against an imperialist Soviet Union, which he perceived as striving to become a hegemon in Central Europe.[41] However, he was also suspicious of the Western Allies' intentions. Schumacher proposed a 'third way' for Germany, since

> it was not true that there was only the alternative between becoming a satellite state of the Soviet Union or becoming a vassal state of the West.

> We Social Democrats will let our politics be guided only by the necessities and interests of the whole German nation.[42]

Schumacher's proposed policy differed from Adenauer's in that he advocated a more independent German stance, despite the demands of the East and West. Adenauer's politics were for Schumacher 'nothing more than the politics of total resignation that was destroying Germany and [Central] Europe'.[43]

Until 1952, he objected to one-sided politics, which, in his opinion, would have destroyed German as well as European unity. Schumacher also warned against permanently adopting the American social and cultural system, since it did not genuinely 'fit' Germany and, like the Sovietization of the East, would always produce resistance and opposition. Germany and Mitteleuropa had to follow their own path.[44] A division of Germany and Europe, according to Schumacher, was not only an 'abnormal' condition but would also remain a focal point of conflict. Therefore, joining a Western alliance system was detrimental and counterproductive for Germany and Europe. As Schumacher observed:

> No people can do without national unity and enter into alliances in which its responsibilities toward other peoples would be more important than its own unity and the growing together of its own nation.[45]

When it became obvious that the creation of political blocs in Europe was unavoidable, Schumacher advocated a Central European bloc including Germany. As a neutral actor, this bloc could conceivably prevent the bipolar power structure from becoming a permanent feature of the European state system. Thus, while he accepted a loose political alliance with the West, he rejected a military alliance and opted for German neutrality. Schumacher believed that such a position could guarantee German unity as well as stability in Mitteleuropa. As President of the Parliamentary Council, Schumacher was relatively successful in implementing his ideas[46] but, nevertheless, lost the power struggle to Adenauer.

With respect to Mitteleuropa, the Adenauer era was the exception to the rule. While his predecessors as much as his successors followed a Mitteleuropa concept, Adenauer deliberately did not. Adenauer constitutes a break in the Mitteleuropa tradition that stretches from Bismarck to Stresemann, from the German resistance to Kaiser and Schumacher, and eventually to the Brandt/Scheel government. However, after 1969 the ideas of the German resistance as well as those of Kaiser and Schumacher resurfaced.

'MITTELEUROPA' THOUGHTS AFTER THE ADENAUER ERA

Brandt's 'Ostpolitik'

After Konrad Adenauer had secured his position in the early 1950s, 'West-integration' (integration in the West) was more or less Germany's undisputed foreign-policy orientation.[47] Subsequently, Mitteleuropa as an area of genuine West German interest, together with other foreign-policy options, also disappeared from the political agenda for a decade. It was not until the end of the Berlin crisis, in 1962, that Mitteleuropa was slowly rediscovered as an area of interest for German foreign policy. Willy Brandt, as mayor of Berlin, and with a circle of SPD politicians around him, was the first leading politician who seriously reconsidered Germany's foreign-policy orientation.

The Berlin crisis and the subsequent construction of the wall came as a shock to many German politicians.[48] Willy Brandt, in particular, was petrified, not so much by the construction of the wall itself, but because the Allies, who had guaranteed the security of the city (and had actively done so in 1948), now were standing idly by.[49] For the first time since the war, the German relationship with the West seemed to turn sour, and German dependence on the West was painfully felt, especially by politicians in Berlin. Consequently, Brandt and his circle within the SPD, foremost Egon Bahr, began to develop concepts that would re-establish relations with the East, primarily the Central European states, independent from, but not in opposition to, the Western Allies. These ideas became known later, in the 1970s, as Ostpolitik, which constituted the first active German Mitteleuropa policy after World War Two.

The Beginnings

Near the end of his reign, Adenauer started to reconsider his Ostpolitik;[50] however, he never put his thoughts into action. In fact, by 1962 Adenauer was, intellectually, relatively close to the new Ostpolitik that his successor, Brandt, would implement seven years later.[51] In 1959, Adenauer's confidant, the leader of the CDU's parliamentary party, Heinrich Krone, quoted him as follows:

> Since we cannot expect reunification within the next few years, we should accept it now as impracticable; the zone [the GDR] will stay under the power of Pankow [East Berlin], the Federal Republic in an alliance with the West; facing the situation as it is, we have to come to talks which aim at the humanization of the affairs in the zone.[52]

In 1958–9 Adenauer's Under-secretary at the Chancellery, Hans Globke, developed a plan according to which the two German states would recognize one another and eventually would be unified.[53] In 1962, Adenauer asked Willy Brandt, as mayor of Berlin, how he should respond to a potential Soviet offer proposing a guarantee of Berlin's freedom in exchange for acceptance of the division of Germany. A little later, in 1963, Adenauer stated to Brandt, concerning the Hallstein Doctrine, 'some things must be given away as long as one gets something in return'.[54]

As these statements demonstrate, Adenauer had moved away from the hard-line position he assumed in 1949 and already realized that the German Ostpolitik had to be conducted more flexibly if Germany wanted to avoid drifting into isolation. However, Adenauer did not translate these thoughts into political action. The real turning point in Germany's post-war foreign policy did not occur prior to 1969, when the SPD finally came to power following the Grand Coalition.[55] Until then there had been no official reconsideration of the legalistic positions that the Adenauer government had established after 1945. The Hallstein Doctrine, as well as West Germany's claim to sole representation of the German state (Alleinvertretungsanspruch), were still official German policy even though, by 1960,[56] these policies were burdensome. Furthermore, Germany's ruling elite still demanded that any approach towards détente between the two superpowers should be linked to the 'German question' of unification.[57] The prevailing German Ostpolitik obviously failed when in 1961 Walter Ulbricht, the East German head of state, on the demand of or, at least, with the support of the Kremlin, built the Berlin Wall, with no subsequent Allied response.[58]

No one understood this better than the mayor of Berlin and Adenauer's challenger in the autumn election of 1961, Willy Brandt. Hence, Brandt started thinking about new ways of viewing German relations with the East. The fundamental difference between Brandt's Ostpolitik in the early 1970s and the CDU governments' post-1961 shifting of positions[59] lies in the fact that Adenauer had no conception of the East as an integral Central European region.[60] He lacked an understanding and feeling for Mitteleuropa; therefore, the adjustments in his and his successors' Ostpolitik could not amount to a re-conceptualization of Germany's foreign policy in the region. Brandt, on the other hand, had a more global perspective, in which there was room for Mitteleuropa.[61] His Ostpolitik was more holistic in so far as it was an approach to the *region*, not simply to the USSR or Poland as individual states. Brandt thought of Mitteleuropa in terms of an integral region between the West (and Germany) and the USSR.

In 1961 the SPD conducted its first federal election campaign after the adoption of the 'Godesberg Programme' (1959), in which it distanced itself from communism, transforming itself from a party of class struggle to a people's party (Volkspartei).[62] Its new leaders were Willy Brandt, Herbert Wehner and Helmut Schmidt, who matured politically after 1945 and represented a generational change in German politics. Furthermore, they were aware of the change in the political climate in the United States under the Kennedy administration. They reacted accordingly, arguing for an acceptance of the status quo in order to modify Germany's stagnant position vis-à-vis its Central European neighbours in general, and the USSR and the GDR in particular. As early as 6 December 1961, Brandt stated in a speech to Parliament that 'the current policy of reunification has failed . . . and that unification could not be achieved against the Soviet Union. Therefore, the present task is to develop a new relationship with the world power in the East.'[63]

Immediately after the construction of the Berlin Wall, Brandt gathered his closest advisers around him to discuss the future. In contrast to Adenauer's advisers, they all came from regions east of the Elbe and, therefore, were more attentive to Mitteleuropa problems. This group included Minister Heinrich Albertz, born in Silesia and Brandt's successor as mayor of Berlin; Egon Bahr, from Thuringia, formerly a journalist and the intellectual motor of the new 'Berlin line',[64] as it was later called; Klaus Schütz, the sceptic in the team and subsequently Albertz's successor; and Dieter Spangenberg from Mecklenburg, who kept in contact with East Berlin. They all wanted to abandon the legalistic views of the Adenauer government in order to improve the daily lives of Germans on both sides of the Wall.[65] Egon Bahr first formulated the basic ideas publicly in 1963. He demanded 'change through convergence/rapprochement'[66] or 'changing the status quo by way of accepting it'. Direct confrontation with Eastern European regimes was discarded as well as the Federal Republic's refusal to acknowledge a second German state.[67]

Under the Ludwig Erhard government, Ostpolitik had not changed significantly. In fact, earlier small steps of rapprochement with the Soviet Union as the key state were withdrawn. The overall situation eventually worsened in the last years of the Erhard government. This was partly a result of a change in the political climate in the Kremlin following Khrushchev's dismissal, Bonn's unfortunate discussion about the possibility of acquiring nuclear arms, and a reaction to the 'peace note' (Friedensnote).[68]

The 'peace note' of March 1966 was the first attempt by the German government to reconsider Germany's relationship with Mitteleuropa. Even though the 'peace note' was supported by the SPD opposition, it was a typical product of the Erhard administration's position. It was 'full of good will but contained nothing new. Instead, it repeated past errors mixed with diplomatic clumsiness.'[69] The note was dispatched to all Central European states except the GDR. The only new element was an offer to discard violence as a political means; otherwise, it re-stated traditional positions towards the Central European states. Regarding Prague, the note confirmed that Germany had no territorial demands, but insisted that the Munich Treaty of 1938 remained a valid treaty in international law. With respect to Poland, the 'peace note' conceded that it had suffered most under Hitler, but expressed offence at Warsaw's demand that existing borders be acknowledged. The climax was a statement claiming that Germany still existed according to its 1937 borders.[70] Naturally, the Eastern European states perceived the note more as a threat than as an improvement in relations. Erhard's fall, in 1966, was due only partially to his Ostpolitik. His government fell because 'he could not handle it all', as Adenauer once stated. Ostpolitik was merely one area that Erhard 'could not handle'.[71]

The leaders of the Grand Coalition were aware of increasing German isolation within the alliance. On 7 October 1966, President Johnson gave a speech in which he laid out a fundamental change in America's foreign-policy orientation. He stated that German reunification could only be the result of East–West détente, not its prerequisite.[72] While Erhard resented the new turn in US foreign policy, the Grand Coalition at least was willing to go along with the new policy. Chancellor Kiesinger, in June 1967, echoed Johnson's statement, remarking that:

> A reunified Germany has a critical size. It is too big to play no role in the balance of power and too small to hold in balance the powers around it. It is therefore very difficult to see how a reunited Germany could join one side or another, given the continuation of the present European political structure. Therefore, one can only envisage the growing together of the separated parts of Germany as being an organic part of the overcoming of the East–West conflict in Europe.[73]

In his inaugural speech in December 1966 Kiesinger had already re-stated a position that Kaiser formulated two decades earlier. Talking about the post-war situation in general and German relations with Poland and Czechoslovakia in particular, Kiesinger said that 'Germany, for centuries, was the bridge between Western and Eastern Europe. We should like to fulfil the mission also in our time.'[74]

The first statement clearly demonstrates that Kiesinger was aware of Germany's delicate position in the centre of Europe. However, the second statement indicates Kiesinger's lack of a contemporary Mitteleuropa conception for the region, given the international political status quo. Furthermore, his government never explained its understanding of Germany as 'a bridge'.

Brandt's selection as Foreign Minister in the Kiesinger government was pivotal to the future evolution of Germany's Ostpolitik. Brandt was able to conduct a policy that followed the doctrine that Kennedy had established in his famous speech of 10 June 1963, which both he and Herbert Wehner cited repeatedly: 'We must conduct a policy, so that it will eventually be in their own interest for the communists to agree to a true peace settlement.'[75] The SPD leadership welcomed Kennedy's statement because it echoed Schumacher's 'magnet theory'. Therefore, Brandt's demands went further than Kiesinger's. He opted for an all-European peace structure, overcoming the division of Europe as a whole, with Germany playing a central role.[76] In an interview in January 1967, Brandt stated:

> We . . . shall not shy away from contact with the authorities in the other part of Germany. . . . This means we shall take the initiative so that the people in both parts of our fatherland will not drift apart any further. . . .[77]

As Foreign Minister, Brandt used his position repeatedly as head of the SPD to pacify the CDU as a coalition partner when he 'went beyond what the government as a whole could support'.[78] He argued that he had to represent the interests of his SPD constituency as well as the government's other constituencies.

As in the nature of any grand coalition, specific foreign policies are a compromise. Short of abandoning the Hallstein Doctrine, the Grand Coalition 'was determined to overcome the impasse of Bonn's reunification policy'.[79] Subsequently, Kiesinger declared the Munich Treaty void, thus creating an opportunity to establish diplomatic relations with Czechoslovakia.[80] Without accepting the Oder–Neisse border, he assured Poland of Bonn's desire for reconciliation, and he hinted at a de facto acceptance of the East German government without dropping the Alleinvertretungsanspruch. Kiesinger even went as far as to agree to an all-European renunciation-of-force agreement signed by both German states. Finally, Germany established official diplomatic relations with Romania in 1967.[81]

The policy of this period is often called a 'policy of movement',[82] which, in terms of Germany's general Ostpolitik, is correct, especially when compared with the last Adenauer administration. However, it contained no consistent or teleological movement. Partly restrained by its own inhibitions, partly by East Germany's pressures on its allies, the foreign policy of the Grand Coalition remained an unfinished work. Much as Germany's approach to Mitteleuropa after unification in 1990, the Grand Coalition lacked a clear conception of its foreign-policy goals for Mitteleuropa. Dennis Bark has labelled the period of the Erhard administration as 'West Germany's dilemma: with the West, but in the middle'.[83] His statement also characterizes the Grand Coalition, since it went along with the West, as an important actor, but had no concept for the middle. Nevertheless, the Grand Coalition helped to change the direction of Germany's foreign policy, not least by starting to distance itself from the US and removing itself from America's shadow.[84] Germany began to catch up with the global developments in foreign relations characterized by détente rather than deterrence.

In 1967, the FDP, under the aegis of the liberal publicist Wolfgang Schollwer, established a working group to evaluate the contemporaneous Ostpolitik. The result was a paper that was more far-reaching than Brandt's and the SPD's position because it opted for a 'bracketing together'[85] of the two German states, rather than unification. Furthermore, it suggested the disarmament of both states and an acceptance of the Oder–Neisse border. Following the traditional argument of the German liberals, which had been voiced since 1848, the paper preferred freedom before unity.[86] The study was supported immediately by the FDP leadership, principally Thomas Dehler and Hildegard Hamm-Brücher, later joined by Hans Dietrich Genscher and Walter Scheel.[87] As a result of the Schollwer study, the FDP moved more towards the SPD and, thus, towards a shift in the coalition. Furthermore, the study anticipated the later position of the SPD's left wing, which, after achieving the primary goals of the new Ostpolitik in 1973, entered into a debate on détente, disarmament, and Mitteleuropa as a nuclear free zone.

The 'Ostpolitik'

Essentially, Brandt's Ostpolitik was a Mitteleuropa policy of negation. His Mitteleuropa concept was *not* a German one but a European one, which meant several things.[88] First, Brandt acknowledged and was aware of Mitteleuropa as a distinct region in the centre of Europe. He also respected the German cultural tradition and historic achievements in that region. More importantly, however, he recognized the injustice and acts of terror that Germany had committed in the region since 1938 in pursuing 'special German interests'. Therefore, he understood German Mitteleuropa politics in terms of making clear to the region that Germany would never again conduct an aggressive foreign policy. Brandt accepted Mitteleuropa by disavowing special German aspirations. While previous German governments had ignored the region entirely as a distinct part of Europe, Brandt wanted to re-establish it as such, without reintroducing a special German claim to Central Europe.

During the 1960s the political climate changed, resulting in a realignment in German politics. Public support for Adenauer's hardline politics eroded. Furthermore, the SPD gained increasing acceptance as a people's party. In foreign policy, one could distinguish among 'flexible Atlanticists, inflexible conservatives, and flexible leftists'.[89] The first and last group were primarily sophisticated German nationalists who could be found in the right wing of the FDP and the leadership of the SPD.[90] As a result of such developments, power shifted over the course of the 1960s; when the realignment was complete, the SPD/FDP government came to power in 1969. Both the times and the German public were ripe for a dramatic turn in German foreign policy.

In the preface to the German edition of his book *Dreaming of Europe*[91] (*Träumen von Europa*), Jiri Dienstbier, a former dissident and, until the country's splitting, Czechoslovakia's Foreign Minister,[92] argues that in the 1980s only Brandt's Ostpolitik fulfilled the Yalta promise of a new Europe. Willy Brandt's concept of a new Ostpolitik envisioned a Europe 'different from the one that we got used to during the Cold War'.[93] In its absolutism, Dienstbier's statement is certainly questionable. Nevertheless, it demonstrates that in Central Europe there was a political perception of Brandt's Ostpolitik similar to the perception of Mitteleuropa prior to 1933.

Brandt's Ostpolitik contained two core concepts: 'normalization' and 'European peace arrangement' (Europäische Friedensordnung). In fact, the first term had existed in German politics since the USSR's 1955 suggestion of establishing diplomatic relations with Germany. In June 1961 the parliament passed a resolution urging the government to 'take every opportunity to normalize the relations between Germany and the Central European states'.[94] But it was not until Walter Scheel's tenure as Foreign Minister that the term took on a more specific meaning. Scheel stated that Ostpolitik meant 'nothing more than the attempt to normalize politics on the basis of the realities which we find here and now'.[95] As Chancellor, Brandt later stated in 1970, 'if one wants to dismantle the boundary markers of Europe, one must cease trying to move them'.[96] Brandt meant that existing borders should not be altered. Rather, he implied that their significance for people, commerce and exchange should be modified. 'Normalization' in 1969 meant primarily accepting the status quo in Mitteleuropa, establishing diplomatic relations with all Central European states, and attempting to convert the Iron Curtain into a velvet one.[97]

The second term of central importance, a European peace arrangement, implied solving the German question within the framework of a security arrangement for all of Europe. It was first voiced in 1957 as part of the Berlin declaration of the Federal Republic and its allies. It acquired political importance in the governmental declaration of the Grand Coalition in 1966 and, thereafter, became a central idea of the Brandt government.[98] As Foreign Minister, Walter Scheel stated that it meant a system

> in which states with different value systems could be members. In order to achieve this goal there had to be no compromise between the free and the communist system, but cooperation between states, organizations and communities.[99]

Apparently, Scheel assumed a functionalist perspective towards achieving the desired goal for Central Europe, much like thinkers in the previous century.

Furthermore, Brandt made frequent reference to Stresemann (who allegedly also wanted to build Europe) and his foreign policy. But Europe for Stresemann as much as for Bismarck and, ultimately, for Brandt was a tool of national politics. To that extent, Brandt's Ostpolitik was the second step in transforming Germany from an object of post-war history to a subject. The first step was Adenauer's 'Westintegration', which secured autonomy in the West. Brandt's Ostpolitik entailed establishing Germany as a sovereign state in the East.[100] Since unification could only be achieved as a result of an all-European security arrangement, which, in turn, was only possible by way of normalization of relations through the USSR in Central Europe, Mitteleuropa policy, in its form of Ostpolitik, was a necessary part of conducting German national politics.[101]

The actual results and provisions of the 'Eastern Treaty Package'[102] can be summarized briefly. The package contained the following treaties: the treaty with the USSR, signed in August 1970; the one with Poland, signed in December 1970; the Quadripartite Agreement on Berlin, of 1971; the Basic Treaty with the GDR in 1972; and finally, the one with Czechoslovakia, signed in 1973. The main objective of these treaties was to banish the ghost of Nazi imperialism by way of bilateral treaties affecting the whole region.[103] Following the premise that any progress in Central Europe could only be made after conclusive arrangements with the USSR, Brandt first sent his long-time confidant, Egon Bahr, to a series of meetings with Gromyko in Moscow. The Moscow Treaty was more or less imposed on the other countries in the region, such as Poland, the GDR, and Czechoslovakia. As the hegemonic power in Mitteleuropa, the USSR established new rules of the game in the region.[104]

In Moscow Bahr negotiated such important questions as Poland's borders, relations with the GDR, and the nullification of the Munich Treaty.[105]

Both parties also eventually renounced the use of force. Furthermore, West Germany 'regard[ed] today and in the future the frontiers of all States in Europe as inviolable . . . including the Oder–Neisse line . . . and the frontier between the FRG and the GDR'.[106] East Berlin was not given the international recognition it desired, but it did receive equal status.[107] In exchange for the de facto acceptance of the Oder–Neisse border, Germany established full diplomatic relations with Poland, while Warsaw agreed to release Germans in order to reunite them with their families in West Germany. Prague received an *ex nunc* renunciation of the Munich Agreement, with German insistence on specific legal conditions regarding such issues as war crimes liability and reparation claims.[108] Another important aspect of the Czechoslovakia Treaty was the fact that it enabled Germany to establish diplomatic relations with Hungary and Bulgaria, both of which had made the treaty a prerequisite for direct talks with Germany.

Brandt's main achievement was to restore Germany's independence of action towards Mitteleuropa. Subsequent discussions regarding Mitteleuropa concepts in the 1970s and 1980s were only possible because of Brandt's Ostpolitik. Furthermore, and perhaps more importantly, the slight differences in tone and emphasis among the four treaties indicated that, as a result of West Germany's Ostpolitik, the Warsaw Pact countries could move slowly towards a 'more independent, bilateral diplomatic style'.[109] In other words, even within the framework of the Warsaw Pact, Mitteleuropa began to regain its independence – a development that eventually would topple these communist regimes.

'Mitteleuropa' and Détente (1973–85)

Generally, the 1970s was a decade of détente between the superpowers until the Soviet Union invaded Afghanistan in 1979. Ratification of the SALT I Treaty and the signing of the Helsinki Accords marked the highpoints of that development, but aside from signing the Helsinki Accords, the European states participated only marginally in it. Afghanistan abruptly ended this process and the second phase of the Cold War began. The stagnation of détente and the strategy of small steps increasingly frustrated a growing number of eligible voters, especially among the younger generation.[110] The result was a turning away from traditional politics and politicians.

On the domestic level, grass-roots movements stressing peace, separation from US policy, and environmental protection developed in virtually all Western European states. In Germany this movement was both pronounced and highly successful. The evolving 'new left'[111] was comprised of the left wing in the SPD,[112] the Green movement, and independent intellectuals.[113] The Greens, who developed from local protest groups, had been active in state politics since the mid-1970s, and have been represented in Parliament since 1983. The peace movement, in part identical to the Greens, was most active in the protest against the NATO double-track decision. These groups represented an element of German society that was dissatisfied with the status quo in Europe. In their effort to overcome this situation, the peace movement proposed neutralism as a form of the Mitteleuropa concept.

Neutralism and the 'New Left'

As Egbert Jahn has stated,

> Mitteleuropa is that Europe that . . . is excluded from Western Europe, and distances itself from Eastern Europe. Therefore, Mitteleuropa is primarily anti-west and anti-east. . . . [And] Mitteleuropa, first of all, is 'disengagement-Europe'.[114]

Obviously, in Germany the anti-Western aspect of the movement was dominant. As part of what Ronald Inglehart has labelled 'post-materialism',[115] universalist concepts (as represented by the two global powers and institutionalized in the systemic conflict between them) increasingly lost their legitimacy and persuasive power among the population.[116]

Consequently, most Mitteleuropa concepts in the 1970s and early 1980s centred on military-technological suggestions and disarmament.[117] In other words, Mitteleuropa was rediscovered as a region of disengagement and disarmament. Rudolf Jaworski, in his retrospective 'stock-taking' of Mitteleuropa, offers an interesting explanation of this development. During the second half of the 1970s, one could observe

> a general trend towards historic recollection, the general decrease of the superpowers' attraction, an increasing satiety of global, universalist concepts, and in contrast to that, a rediscovery of direct neighbourhood. Adding to this, is the system-bridging consternation about atomic and ecological dangers in the centre of Europe.[118]

During the late 1970s, as a result of Ostpolitik and détente, economic exchange within Mitteleuropa tripled.[119] On the political level, a perception of the adversary as a potential partner slowly developed. In 1975, after the CSCE was signed, Brandt put this slow change into perspective when he stated: 'Europe has again been transformed and has become something different and significantly more than a divided continent controlled by Russian and American spheres of influence.'[120] A 'rediscovery of a regional approach' had occurred.[121] The peoples of Mitteleuropa started to develop a self-perception independent of the superpowers and below the level of the systemic conflict. Largely excluded from any influence over the development of this systemic conflict,[122] the nations of Mitteleuropa grew increasingly concerned about becoming the objects and, eventually, the victims of this conflict. The result was an increase in tension between the Central European states and their respective hegemonic power.[123] In Germany, this debate about security policy expanded into a rediscovery of Mitteleuropa.

Some authors have labelled the demand for German neutrality, Central European disarmament, and a nuclear free Mitteleuropa as the SPD's 'second Ostpolitisk'.[124] It resulted from and went hand in hand with the peace movement. Its origins can be traced back to the last years of the SPD/FDP coalition when, in 1979, the debate about the NATO double-track decision started. This debate took place in the out-of-parliament opposition, as well as within the governing party. In 1980, Karsten Voigt, a Social Democrat from the SPD's left wing and critic of Chancellor Schmidt, demanded for the first time a 'second phase of Ostpolitik',[125] which was concerned primarily with security matters.

Once again, Egon Bahr, who was at that time head of the party committee on 'new strategies', created the SPD's second Ostpolitik. His concept was supported by members of the younger generation, including Karsten Voigt, Oskar Lafontaine, and Andreas von Bülow.[126] Although this group in the SPD was genuinely influenced by the out-of-parliament opposition and shared its concern, it attempted to reintegrate these voter into the traditional party system. Once more, Mitteleuropa politics became a vehicle for domestic politics.[127] Similar to his suggestions in 1968, Bahr's concept, which he introduced to the party caucus in 1982, called for a European Peace System beyond the two military alliances. When the SPD moved back into opposition late in 1982 it had already largely completed its shift to the left and, on matters of collective security goals, joined ranks with the peace movement and the Greens. Furthermore, several individual members engaged directly in talks with Central European politicians and intellectuals, discussing their disengagement visions of Mitteleuropa in several publications.[128] Their position was generally anti-American and stressed the 'Europeanization of Europe'.[129] In this context, 'Mitteleuropa' reappeared for the first time in a markedly political light.[130] As Peter Bender stated provocatively:

> The renaissance of Mitteleuropa, first of all, is a protest against the division of the continent, against American and Russian domination, against the totalitarianism of ideologies. In our wish for détente we have more in

> common with Belgrade and Stockholm, and also with Warsaw and East Berlin than with Paris or London.[131]

And Peter Glotz wrote,

> we have to regain Mitteleuropa; first as a concept, then as reality. . . . [Elsewhere] let us use the term 'Mitteleuropa' as an instrument for the second phase of détente.[132]

Summary

By way of Ostpolitik and détente, Mitteleuropa reappeared on the political agenda during the late 1970s and early 1980s. Ostpolitik re-established the discussion of Mitteleuropa largely in terms of security policy and centred around the systemic conflict. Even though Mitteleuropa emerged in politics once more it remained limited to defence policies and, thus, was largely thought of as a geographical deployment area. To the extent that it lacked a cultural dimension, the Ostpolitik did not constitute a Mitteleuropa concept in the traditional sense. However, when the Mitteleuropa renaissance of the second half of the 1980s reached Germany it's advocates could build on Ostpolitik, since the latter emphasized Central Europe once more as an area of profound interest for German foreign policy. In the late 1980s, Mitteleuropa was rediscovered also as a cultural and political region. The concept came full circle in the rediscovery of Central Europe as a political, cultural, and economic region that comprehended far more than military deterrence and deployment.

6 The 'Mitteleuropa' Debate in the Mid-1980s

INTRODUCTION

The Social Democratic Party's (SPD) 'Ostpolitik' not only opened the doors politically to the Warsaw Pact states in Central Europe, but also opened intellectual doors in the minds of European thinkers. This evolution culminated in the Mitteleuropa debate of the second half of the 1980s.[1] In the 1970s and during the Era of Ostpolitik, politicians and intellectuals refrained from using the term 'Mitteleuropa' in a political context other than security concepts, in order to avoid being misunderstood as fascist or imperialist. However, in the 1980s Mitteleuropa returned to the political stage.

Although there was little room for Mitteleuropa in the dichotomy of the systemic conflict between the United States and the USSR, both the decline of the East–West conflict and the disintegration of the Warsaw Pact created a new intellectual, cultural, and political climate. Such central European writers as Vazlav Havel, György Konrád, and Milan Kundera began to lay out a 'Mitteleuropa' concept that was primarily a form of inner-emigration, and protests against Soviet oppression of their own countries' state were primarily expressions of cultural identity and self-perception. However, the idea of Mitteleuropa was transformed into a broader concept when Western intellectuals picked it up in the mid-1980s. The variety of ideas ranged from intellectual–cultural approaches, to new security arrangements, to proposals concerning new forms of economic cooperation among the Central European states.[2] For German audiences, the two most prominent and influential writers were Milan Kundera and György Konrád, whose works were widely read and discussed.

THE ORIGINS OF THE 'MITTELEUROPA' DEBATE

Milan Kundera's essay 'Un Occident Kidnappé', which the Czech writer published in 1983,[3] initiated the Mitteleuropa debate. Since Kundera's provocatively formulated article centred on criticism of Soviet cultural imperialism, it focused on the smaller Eastern European states of Hungary, Czechoslovakia and Poland, to the exclusion of Germany. This region is characterized by a 'maximum of variety in the smallest area'.[4] Short of actually arguing in favour of an independent Mitteleuropa, Kundera acknowledged that the German/Austrian identity in the region functioned as a common bond. As an 'Ordnungsmacht'[5] the Dual Monarchy was a prerequisite for both a common identity and maximum diversity. Only within this 'stronghold'[6] could cultural variety flourish.

When the German-Jewish cultural bond was severed, the demise of Mitteleuropa was guaranteed. This German-Jewish community 'in the twentieth century was the main cosmopolitan and integrative element in Central Europe, i.e., its intellectual bond, the crystallization of its esprit, the founder of its intellectual unity'.[7] The expulsion of the German Jews and subsequently of the Germans from Mitteleuropa symbolizes, for Kundera, the fate of this region. In contrast to the German domination of the area prior to 1938,[8] after 1945 Mitteleuropa fell victim to complete and lasting Sovietization. Moreover, as Kundera concluded, Russia essentially is not a part of Europe, but truly a 'different civilization'.[9]

Regarding the regional Western powers (primarily Austria and Germany), Kundera addressed the criticism that these countries had forgotten their long-lasting ties to Central Europe and left the region prey to the Soviet Union.

> With its political system Mitteleuropa is part of the East, in its cultural history part of the West. But since Europe itself is losing its cultural identity, it sees in Mitteleuropa nothing but a political regime. In other words, it perceives Mitteleuropa as Eastern Europe.[10]

For Kundera, Central Europe is, as François Bondy has observed, 'a disadvantageously located part of the West'.[11]

György Konrád, a Hungarian sociologist and writer, was even more familiar to German intellectuals than Kundera. In contrast to Kundera, Konrád is less culturally oriented and more political in his approach.[12] Among the numerous publications in which Konrád presented the topic of Mitteleuropa, the best-selling and most widely read was *Antipolitik* (anti-politics).[13] His main argument there is that

> in East Europe, we do not primarily deal with the question whether a policy is good or bad, but with the fact that we are surrounded everywhere . . . by too much politics. The state draws too many matters, questions, and decisions into the realm of politics that don't belong there.[14]

The result of this 'overkill', however, need not be a condition of apolitical resignation but rather of resistance. The right amount of non-allied politics for Mitteleuropa is what Konrád calls 'Antipolitik'.

Like Kundera, Konrád returned to the tradition of the Habsburg-German monarchy as the guarantor of cultural heterogeneity. 'In our area, the homogeneous nation state is the exception. . . . The idea of Mitteleuropa means the flourishing of a variety of ideas, the identity of diversity.'[15] According to Konrád, the European peoples must have the right to self-determination, in order for every nationality to be able to cooperate with other nationalities 'in a continental association of culture and institutions'.[16] Konrád demanded a reversal of the Yalta Treaty, which he perceived as *the* European tragedy.[17] The process of (West-) European integration is, for Konrád, only a transitional stage, since this form of integration, in the long run, cannot be limited to a few Western European states. Nevertheless, the European Community (EC) functioned as a powerful magnet that eventually liberated the eastern states from the Soviet bloc. Konrád's vision, articulated in 1984, was prescient, since one of the first foreign-policy initiatives taken by the states of Central Europe after 1989 was to request EC membership. For these states, Germany became the 'transmission belt' for this request.

In 1988 Konrád published an additional work, *Stimmungsbericht*, in which he laid out a more detailed plan for a future Mitteleuropa.[18] In this work Konrád was not only chastising Soviet (cultural) imperialism, but also accused the US of instrumentalizing Europe for its interest as well. According to Konrád, the two superpowers were holding Europe hostage in their stalemate, 'threatening each other with something that they are not prepared to go through with [i.e., mutual destruction]'.[19] He concluded that Europe should unchain itself from its hegemonic powers and create a peaceful Central Europe. Germany at the centre, according to Konrád, played a major role in this development, since the major obstacle to a solution was the division of Germany, or to be more precise, the lack of a peace treaty with Germany.[20] After such a treaty a new peaceful European order would unfold automatically. However, this work was transcended by the political revolution of 1989, which brought the intellectual Mitteleuropa discussion to centre stage.

THE AUSTRIAN–GERMAN DEBATE

West of the Iron Curtain the publications of and debates among Central European writers were echoed after a certain lag, but eventually with some enthusiasm – especially in the newly flourishing nationalist-conservative circles in Austria and Germany. In Western Europe, Austrian intellectuals promoted Kundera's and Konrád's ideas and suggestions, which, in turn, stirred further intellectual ferment in the West. In the mid-1980s, for example, several conventions were held in Austria on the topic and the journal *Europäische Rundschau* created a forum for discussion.

One of the most prominent and active contemporary advocates of Mitteleuropa is Erhard Busek. In his cultural and scientific works, he has championed what he calls 'Project Mitteleuropa'.[21] From a functionalist perspective, he suggested transcending the frontier between the two blocs through a 'limited system of relations'.[22] The result would be 'a European interior realm on the level of a helpful, day-to-day neighbourhood'.[23]

Another very active proponent among the Austrian writers is Gerhard Wilfinger, who examined the failure of the nation-state among the successor states of the Austrian Dual Monarchy. Instead of hanging on to the 'obviously misguided principle' of the nation-state in Central Europe, Wilfinger suggested a transformation of the region's political entities into cultural nations organized in a Central European confederation.[24] In Germany, the writer Günther Grass voiced a similar suggestion.[25]

As in Germany, the Mitteleuropa debate in Austria was part of a wider discussion about Austria's future role in Europe. When Busek stated that 'we must use the historical relation to Mitteleuropa and our own geopolitical position to actively shape our destiny',[26] he could have been speaking for German advocates of Mitteleuropa as well. Very like the motives of Bismarck's Prussia, during the 1980s in Austria Mitteleuropa became a synonym for new manoeuvring room in foreign policy.[27] Simultaneously, a renaissance and romantic depiction of the K&K (Kaiser and König, i.e., Emperor and King) Empire played a key role in Austria's plans for Mitteleuropa. The Empire's constitution became a model for a constitution that would guarantee 'Central European independence and a model of multi-cultural co-existence.'[28]

THE 'MITTELEUROPA' DEBATE IN GERMANY

In the 1970s Mitteleuropa was viewed primarily as a military deployment zone and, ultimately, as one of military confrontation and a potential battlefield. Therefore, the study of the region concentrated on developing proposals to reduce the risk of war or, at least, to avoid potential disaster for Mitteleuropa. In the 1980s these studies developed into a broader, more politically oriented investigation of the region.[29]

Whereas most of the non-German writers excluded Germany from their Mitteleuropa proposals, in Germany Mitteleuropa represented the frontier of the systemic conflict between the superpowers and, more importantly, the frontier between the two Germanies. The Wall stood as a symbol for the division of Germany as well as for the division of Europe.[30] Furthermore, Mitteleuropa was a synonym for West Germany's troubled relations with its eastern neighbours, resulting from the Nazi occupation. Among German works that appeared in the 1980s, one can distinguish among culturally inspired schemes, politically oriented ideas, and military concepts carried over from the previous decade.

The Cultural Approach

The nationalist-conservative author Karl Schlögel was the first writer to rediscover Mitteleuropa, in his work *Die Mitte liegt ostwärts*.[31] Similarly to his Austrian colleagues, he understood Mitteleuropa primarily as a challenge to the 'monopoly of the East–West-thinking in our heads'.[32] Following Konrád's approach, Schlögel's argument for Mitteleuropa was deliberately apolitical. Moreover, he emphasized that the whole debate about the region had taken too rapid a political turn.[33] Thus he argued for focusing on the region's common cultural heritage in order to establish a Central European 'system of communication'. Schlögel's approach links him to Peter Glotz, who perceived the rediscovery of a Central European cultural identity as a prerequisite for the development of a political identity.[34] For both authors, the goal was to overcome the separation of Europe, which also implied overcoming the division of Germany, an important symbol of separation.

They both argue that Germany must play a crucial role in this process, precisely because it is an integral part of Mitteleuropa, given the cultural interdependence among the region's states since the Middle Ages.[35] This interdependence and German influence were generally fruitful for both Germany and Mitteleuropa until the middle of the nineteenth century,[36] but growing national consciousness among the nationalities of the region created new tensions, undermining positive sentiments towards German influence. Eventually the emergence of the nation-state as the dominant form of political organization vitiated the region's cultural bonds. Thus the German cultural influence and heritage turned into a burden, marked by national hatred, the transformation of Mitteleuropa into a 'death zone'[37] during the Nazi occupation, and the subsequent expulsion of the Germans from the area. German involvement became detrimental but, nevertheless, remained essential for the region. As Glotz states, the expulsion of German populations from Mitteleuropa did not end Germany's political responsibility in this region. Glotz, himself a Sudeten German, argues that one should remember 'the first 850 years of Central European history, rather than the last 150 grim years'.[38]

By pursuing Adenauer's policy of 'Westbindung' (attachment to the West), Germany cast off a substantial part of its burdensome Central European history. However, by doing so, West Germany accepted 'the loss of the East', which ruptured its cultural ties to Mitteleuropa.[39] Turning away from Mitteleuropa as a diverse political region, German political elites could easily employ rather undifferentiated concepts of the 'Eastern Bloc' as a monolithic entity.[40]

Schlögel, as much as the other advocates of Mitteleuropa, questioned the utility and legitimacy of this undifferentiated notion. For Schlögel, Mitteleuropa is defined 'by cultural homogeneity, which, however, has always been endangered by various nationalities'.[41] As a result of the systemic conflict, he argues, the 'nerves between the Central European metropols have been cut and shut down'.[42] As Schlögel emphasizes, in this situation the Germans, with their divided, problematic identity and their geopolitical position between the two blocs, are the 'paradox Central Europeans *par excellence*'.[43]

Consequently, in addition to their demand for a revived Central European identity, both Schlögel and Glotz bemoan the increasing foreign – that is, American – infiltration of the European cultures. As Glotz formulates, 'we as Europeans have increasingly lost the ability to export our own sounds, pictures, and symbols, and, in turn, have allowed the media channels to be cloaked with products manufactured elsewhere'.[44] Schlögel goes even further, observing a 'trace of self-denial'[45] among the Germans, manifested in Germany's economic growth and power combined with its political impotence and self-restraint. Along with Glotz, he calls for a 'resurrection of national identities'[46] within Europe.

In short, advocates of the cultural approach to Mitteleuropa acknowledge a common history and culture, which, they argue, should be revitalized. Schlögel, Glotz, and others argue that the cultural approach can transcend the systemic, geopolitical conflict between East and West. They also aver that Germany and German culture is the common denominator for a Central European identity. Without the German 'glue', they conclude, Mitteleuropa is impossible. Therefore, the development of a German national identity as part of Mitteleuropa, rather than as an appendage of the West, is crucial to the reformation of a Mitteleuropa identity. This cultural perspective has an important analogue in the political realm.

Political Approaches

During the mid-1980s, when Mitteleuropa resurfaced politically, it appeared as a functionalist argument – cultural ties should develop into economic linkages, which eventually would promote political interdependence. Similar to the development of the EC, the political evolution of Mitteleuropa would occur in 'small steps' leading to (according to the most optimistic premises) a neutral confederation in between the two superpower blocs.[47] While the advocates of the cultural approach followed traditional visions of Mitteleuropa, the political debate generally lacked clarity and direction. Different groups suggested different and diverse solutions, reflecting the biases or the ideological positions of various authors.[48]

One reason for a lack of coherence is that Mitteleuropa never became part of official German foreign policy, in part, because of the mutual sensibilities of Germany and its East-Central European neighbours. Mitteleuropa policy remained disguised as détente or economic cooperation on a primarily bilateral level. As a result, a wide range of scenarios emerged concerning the configuration of the Central European region and the optimal means to realize regional development. In practical terms, this implied a second phase of détente, not initiated by the superpowers, but actively pursued by the states of Mitteleuropa – not détente *for* these states but détente *by* them. As Peter Bender stated, 'Europe was divided from the periphery; if it grows back together it will be starting in the middle.'[49] Under these premises, politicians, writers and intellectuals, primarily from the left of the political spectrum, began developing concepts that dealt with reducing tension in Mitteleuropa.

The common denominator for these politically oriented writers was not the common cultural heritage. Rather, they argued that the Central European states, especially Germany, were suffering most from the systemic conflict, particularly the military conflict. These burdens were sufficient motivation to overcome the division of Europe. Pointing to the common strategic interest of the Central European states, Glotz asked rhetorically, 'What is Europe today? Merely a double glacis: the divided deployment area for two global powers. We have to regain Mitteleuropa; first as a concept, then as reality.'[50] The goal was 'to prevent Mitteleuropa from becoming a colonial football for the superpowers to play with'.[51] Similarly, Peter Bender stated that 'the states, victimized by the division, are brothers in misfortune, but what may become of them could be a community of interest (Interessengemeinschaft) to reduce the burden of division'.[52]

Although both Glotz and Bender are Social Democratic politicians who proposed a Central European initiative, neither one actually questioned the Federal Republic's ties to the West. In fact, both were aware that there was no concrete (political) opportunity for their ideas. Thinking or speculating about Mitteleuropa was mostly a sign of discontent and frustration with the status quo of Ostpolitik among the German intellectual left in the mid-1980s, especially after the advancements of the 1970s.[53]

Instead of questioning Germany's ties to the West, Glotz and Bender argued that the political status quo should be the basis for political, economic, and security initiatives (confidence-building measures) that could ease tensions and eventually transcend existing blocs. Regarding security matters, the debate followed the same lines of argumentation as the debates in the late 1970s. The debate centred on the NATO dual-track decision to modernize middle-range nuclear delivery systems by 1982, in the event that the USSR had not entered into arms control negotiations by then. Essentially, writers and politicians on the left argued for an atomic and chemical weapon-free corridor in Central Europe.

The only concrete advance in this direction was the SPD's concept of a 'security partnership' (Sicherheitspartnerschaft). Being the opposition party at the time, it was relatively easy for the SPD to conduct this kind of 'shadow foreign policy'.[54] The two controversial agreements that the Social Democrats signed with the East German Socialist Unity Party (SED) in 1985 and 1986, calling for a Mitteleuropa free of chemical and atomic weapons, marked the apogee of the SPD's détente dialogue.[55] Obviously, these agreements were never followed by any concrete action, because the SPD was in opposition. But even if it had been in power, neither the West German nor the East German state was in a position to negotiate such matters. The agreements were largely of symbolic value for the SPD's domestic constituency.[56]

Such writers and members of the Green Party as Jochen Löser and Ulrike Schilling went one step further than the Social Democratic Party.[57] They suggested 'freeing the European centre step by step from the grip of the two blocs and putting it on a new political base'.[58] This new foundation was to be a confederation of neutral states. The authors were convinced 'that all . . . Central European peoples, despite their existing ideological and political differences, have always developed and will continue to develop stronger mutual and common interests'.[59] At the core of their proposal for neutralizing Central Europe was the 'German question', which they attempted to solve as part of an omnibus plan for the 'Austrianization' (Österreichisierung)[60] of the region.

Another prominent advocate of Mitteleuropa was Otto Schily, then a member of the Green Party in the Bundestag. Like Löser and Schilling, Schily used the term 'Mitteleuropa' in political debate as a symbol of internal German resistance to the security politics of deterrence. He opposed the strategy of deterrence because inevitably Germany would be the main deployment area and battlefield in the event of a war between the two blocs. As one of the most visible figures in the 'peace movement' (Friedensbewegung),[61] Schily developed a plan for an overarching 'peace union' that would result in a reduction of armed forces in Mitteleuropa through bilateral and multilateral treaties among the Central European states.[62] Schily acknowledged the political obstacles to his plan but argued that, nevertheless, Germany should begin to engage in cultural, economic and political cooperation, which eventually would lead to the creation of a new European security order.[63] He argued that Germany would play the role of a buffer state that could promote the creation of a new Central European identity, beyond national boundaries and conceptions.

Although the discussion concerning Mitteleuropa received more publicity in the second half of the 1980s, it became more unfocused and diffuse. At the beginning of the decade the call for a new European security arrangement was dominant. By the end of the 1980s Mitteleuropa became more of a synonym for the 'German question'[64] and a German 'Sonderrolle', similar to pre-First World War plans for an economic and territorial Mitteleuropa.[65] This shift in the Mitteleuropa debate resulted from the domestic quarrel over Germany' role in international affairs. Mitteleuropa became a viable option for transforming Germany's role in the international system into a more active and independent one than Germany had played during the forty years following the Second World War.

In 1988 Bernard Willms and Paul Kleinewefers, two historians, completely transformed the Mitteleuropa idea into a vehicle for the expression of special German interests.[66] For the authors, the 'German Question (of unification) [was] identical with the call for Mitteleuropa'.[67] Along with Austria and Czechoslovakia, Willms and Kleinewefers argued, the two German states should organize a Central European confederation. At the time, they proposed that the liberal-pluralist societies of Western Europe and the socialist societies of Eastern Europe enter into a symbiotic relationship.[68] However, this far-fetched, radical suggestion appeared too late to influence the German Mitteleuropa debate prior to the epochal changes that occurred in Central and Eastern Europe. In some ways, the Willms–Kleinewefers publication marked the end of the Mitteleuropa debated in the Cold War and détente eras.

Critical Voices in the Debate

Compared with the advocates of Mitteleuropa, those critical of such a regional conception are few, but influential. With respect to the cultural approach to Mitteleuropa, the most frequent critique focuses on the problematic use of 'history', upon which this approach is based. Historical approaches often lack the requisite critical analysis to support arguments for reconstruction of Central Europe. Portrayals of the Habsburg Empire's multi-cultural history as a possible basis for contemporary plans of Mitteleuropa often disregard the constitutional, economic, cultural, social, and other disparities among the nationalities of Central Europe. They also gloss over the history of bloodshed and uprising against Vienna and the Empire. Simplifications, idealizations, and vague analogies are more often the rule then the exception.[69]

Furthermore, the various conceptions of Mitteleuropa usually have one common characteristic; they are attempts to transcend the status quo in the area. Rarely do they agree on the means of achieving such systemic change. Werner Weidenfeld, for example, stated that 'Mitteleuropa – socio-psychologically speaking – is an intellectual–political construction.'[70] Prior to unification, in Germany Mitteleuropa became a convenient tool for dealing with the 'German question'. In Austria, Mitteleuropa was recognized as a possible means for increasing national self-esteem.[71] Finally, for those states under Soviet domination, it was a symbol of their desire for cultural and political independence.

Prior to the collapse of the Soviet Empire and the Warsaw Pact, Mitteleuropa remained a utopian vision.[72] Moreover, there were no powerful political protagonists who could transform their ideas into concrete politics.[73] However, the debate stirred unrest among intellectuals and forced politicians to reconsider Mitteleuropa as an area of special interest for Germany's foreign policy.[74] By the time the Soviet Empire finally collapsed and Germany awakened to its decisive role in Central Europe, a region of geopolitical conflict and potential, the concept of Mitteleuropa had entered the consciousness of intellectuals and political élites. Both the collapse of the Soviet Union and the military disengagement of the United States from Europe created manoeuvring room for German foreign policy in the heart of the continent. In this new context, the concept of Mitteleuropa has emerged as an intellectual foundation for regional organization.

7 Epilogue

SUMMARY

As a concept, Mitteleuropa has appeared in German political discourse for some 170 years. During that period, it has appeared as an economic, political, and cultural concept. These various conceptions of Mitteleuropa mirrored the contemporary philosophy of their advocates as well as the German nation's political and social condition, some Mitteleuropa advocates placing greater emphasis on the cultural aspects, while others stressed the political and social dimensions. Although Mitteleuropa concepts addressed questions of foreign policy, they were of equal or greater importance in questions of national domestic policy.[1] A primary, common goal or denominator for advocates of Mitteleuropa has been to build a strong, secure and united Germany, or, as Eckhard Jesse has observed, a Germany that is united, neutral and pacifist in the heart of Europe.[2]

The paradox in this line of thought is that all three requirements could not be achieved simultaneously. When Germany was divided, it was safe but weak; when it was united, it was either insecure and strong or insecure and weak. Mitteleuropa advocates proposed the concept as a remedy to this paradox precisely because under German influence Mitteleuropa could guarantee the power base that Germany required in order to remain united, safe, and strong. As a result, in one way or another, all German governments since 1871 struggled to establish German influence in Mitteleuropa. The result was either a 'Schaukelpolitik', that is, a form of strong neutralism, as under Bismarck, or an imperialist policy, a form of weak unification, as under Bethmann-Hollweg.[3]

The first version, Bismarck's Schaukelpolitik, was a Mitteleuropa policy to the extent that he attempted to achieve German security in Europe through 'sophisticated neutralism'. Bismarck's attempt to create a stable Mitteleuropa failed since Germany's strong military component eventually made neutralism impossible. The second version, the imperialist concept, called for a strong military, a non-pacifist orientation, and unification. This approach eventually failed because the military component was not strong enough to guarantee Germany's safety, which, in turn, ultimately undermined German unity.

In short, the German 'Sonderweg' of nation-building in the centre of Europe took place between the two poles of Germany's perceived needs and its neighbours' perceived threats.[4] Germany's geopolitical position, size, and strength made Mitteleuropa an inherent part of German nation-building. Historically, the basic problem for German foreign policy in Europe was to balance these dimensions.

In the period between 1945 and 1990, the process of German nation-building in the international system was subordinated to the systemic conflict, which eclipsed the question of German unification. The post-World War Two international system assumed Germany's continuing division. This is not to say that unification was no longer a major political issue in German domestic politics. However, in German foreign policy unification was subordinated to the systemic conflict. With the end of the Cold War, German nation-building became the focus of German politics once more. This process did not end in 1990 with unification.[5] Rather, it gained momentum, further altering the status quo in the (European) international system. Furthermore, the process of building a German nation will not be completed until a unified Germany has become integrated domestically and, more importantly, has redefined its role in the international system.

In terms of international relations theory, Germany has always conducted Mitteleuropa policy both as domestic and foreign policy. As domestic policy, it was modified by the domestic political structures and their respective functions within Germany; as foreign policy it was modified by the international system. As Kenneth Waltz has suggested, international structures modified German Mitteleuropa concepts, while, at the same time, the Mitteleuropa concept also altered the European balance of power. Furthermore, under certain conditions in the international system, individual interest groups can exercise considerable pressure and gain influence in the foreign policy-making process. While neo-realists have difficulties in explaining changes in a state within a stable international system, structural functionalists tend to discard the external influences on internal developments of national actors. This work has shown the interdependence of both factors with respect to German Mitteleuropa concepts. Nevertheless, further research in this area is necessary to establish particular patterns of interaction and influence.

'MITTELEUROPA' AND UNITED GERMANY TODAY

While, in the late 1980s, Mitteleuropa was discussed as the 'two rims of a bipolar world system'[6] with Germany at its centre, this view has to be revised in a twofold sense.[7] First, the bipolar world as it had been known since 1945 ceased to exist in 1989; secondly, since 1990 Germany still lies in the middle of Europe, but the middle has moved eastwards. In other words, Germany has ceased to be the 'Frontstaat' (frontline state) on the East–West divide.[8] But what appears as a new situation in Europe, at least with regard to Germany, resembles the pre-First World War environment. First, Germany has common borders with more neighbours than any other European state, and these neighbours on both sides, East and West, are suspicious of the new colossus on their frontiers in the middle of Europe. Secondly, Russia once again is the unstable and crisis-shaken great power in the East.[9]

Finally, and most importantly, the process of European integration and homogenization is counterbalanced by a trend towards heterogeneity.[10] The disappearance of fascist regimes in Spain and Portugal in the 1970s, the self-assertion of the NATO partners in Europe in the 1980s, and the transformation process in the East in the late 1980s are all signs of the process of homogenization.[11] Homogenization, in general terms, means the domination of 'democracy, the rule of law, and [free] markets' in Europe.[12]

The 'Maastricht hangover'[13] and the resurfacing of old and almost forgotten nationalistic, religious, and ethnic conflicts are striking examples of the tendency towards heterogeneity. Furthermore, in virtually all European states pressure from the 'new right' and neo-nationalists now threatens the process of European integration.[14] The 'gap between growing challenges and insufficient capabilities means a crisis for planned integration'.[15] However, that does not necessarily mean the end of Europeanization.

Within this context, a unified Germany has become the most powerful and largest state in Central Europe. Furthermore, Germany is a microcosm for the countervailing trends of homogenization and heterogenization. On the one hand, unification meant homogenization by incorporating the GDR into a German state with a single basic law and legal system. On the other hand, enormous differences in the two civil societies, economies, and political systems made the nation more diverse than it previously had been.

As a result of unification, the three traditional and seemingly incompatible requirements of a 'strong, safe, and united' nation reappeared, since Germany's position in the European international system was stable only as long as it performed its function as a Frontstaat. Since that condition no longer exists, Germany has once again become a fully independent, united, and somewhat insecure state. Consequently, it must now perform a stabilizing role in Europe.[16]

In the course of unification, the former French President François Mitterand as well as the former British Prime Minister Margaret Thatcher voiced their suspicions and their resentments regarding these developments.[17] On the one hand, both great powers in the EU were afraid of losing influence to Germany within the Union. On the other hand, they feared that Germany might turn away from the process of integration completely, or at least put it on the back burner.[18] However, after the 1995 Presidential election, it seems likely that France will reorient its foreign policy and put European integration to the back of its agenda.[19]

The East shares a somewhat ambivalent feeling towards Germany for various reasons. The wounds of Nazi aggression and terror have only healed superficially, as several statements and events around the celebration of the 50th anniversary of the end of the Second World War have shown. Yet, the Central European states, especially Poland, Hungary, Croatia, Slovenia and the Czech Republic, need Germany as a leading power in the region for two reasons.[20] First, a Central European economic region, as described in the Alpe–Adria Initiative, the Central European Initiative (CEI), or by the Visegrad Group, can only be successful with German participation.[21] Secondly, if these plans fail or are abandoned these states need Germany even more as a motor for their integration into NATO and the EU. That their current goals are not necessarily compatible with their recent history does not contribute to making the situation in Central Europe any easier.

As early as 1951 Hans Morgenthau formulated the thesis that Germany, owing to its (mostly economic) characteristics, would naturally become the most powerful, and therefore the leading, state in Europe. For this reason, he argued that 'nature' had to be restrained and controlled in order to avoid such a development.[22] Lately, this thesis has received renewed attention. However, the contemporary situation presents the advocates of this argument with a different sort of problem. While Morgenthau wrote largely from the perspective of the US 'national interest' in the early stages of the Cold War, today the question is whether it is still in the US interest to restrain and control Germany.[23]

For the last 40 years, the French answer to what they perceived as an overly active German foreign policy always has been 'more integration'. If France could not stop German foreign policy initiatives – for example, German rearmament in the 1950s or the European Central Bank in the 1990s – it took the bull by the horns and headed the initiative, hoping in this way to control Germany. However, this position may currently be shifting as well, given President Chirac's recent (1995) statements on 'Maastricht II' and a possible referendum in 1997. The British answer has been largely one of denial and the threat to withdraw from the continent. From the beginning of the process of European integration, Britain either stood aside, as in the case of the EEC or the EDU, or secured 'opt-out' clauses, as in the case of the monetary union and the Maastricht Treaty.

However, in light of the changing continental balance of power, it seems doubtful that these strategies will continue to restrain Germany. The EU is still Germany's first and most important option, but it is no longer its only one.[24] Furthermore, since his visit to Germany in July 1994, President Clinton has begun to endorse a change in Germany's role in Europe. As a result, Germany's neighbours face a German nation that once again is attempting to carve out an independent role in Europe. Under the circumstances, apparently only self-restraint will determine Germany's future path in the centre of Europe.

OUTLOOK

As Vladimir Handl wrote:

> German unification is often considered as the main geopolitical outcome of the Cold War for Europe, something which will influence the continent's development at the end of this century in a fundamental way. The significance of this development is even more apparent in the regional context of Central Europe.[25]

George F. Kennan has also stated that 'if Germany had to be reunited, then she must be a part of something larger than herself. A united Germany could be tolerable only as an integral part of a united Europe.'[26] Both statements are complementary – one points to the past, the other predicts the future. Kennan made his statement at the end of the 1940s. Fifty years later unification has taken place, but a 'United States of Europe' still seems to lie in the more distant future. Has Kennan been proved wrong? Or perhaps, is a unified Germany not tolerable? The analysis of this work suggests a 'no' to both questions. A unified Germany is tolerable to its neighbours precisely because it is searching for a constructive role in a larger entity: Europe. In pointing towards the future, Handl described what that 'something larger' may look like and what Hettne labelled Europeanization.

In 1991, President George Bush offered Germany a 'partnership in leadership', anticipating an active German role in the process of transforming the former Warsaw Pact. During his first visit to Germany in July 1994, President Clinton stated in an interview that Germany had to take a leading role in Europe. He also noted that Germany had to define this role for itself.[27] These statements were made four years after unification and clearly demonstrate the discrepancy between Germany's self-perception, which still largely reflects the foreign-policy patterns of the bipolar world, and the perceptions of its partners, who demand an active role for Germany in world politics.[28] When Clinton mentioned a leading role in Europe, he meant primarily Central Europe. However, especially in this area, during the early 1990s German foreign policy has been characterized by hesitation, inconsistency and diplomatic clumsiness.

Since Mitteleuropa has been a recurring regional concept throughout German history, after unification, theoretically, in light of the rather heated debate about Mitteleuropa in the 1970s and 1980s, the concept should have gained increasing visibility. Four years after unification this assumption has proved to be wrong. Instead, Mitteleuropa as a concept of regional organization, with strong German involvement, seems as futuristic as ever. With national disintegration in Eastern Europe, the integration of East Germany into the Federal Republic, and Eastern European migration, new demands and expectations have also surfaced in Germany.[29] Several Central European states, such as Poland, the Czech Republic, Slovakia and Hungary, have turned to Germany for political leadership on questions regarding the EU, NATO, and the UN. Germany has still to meet these expectations politically in one way or another, beyond its role as an actor in these international organizations.

As the international trade figures given in Chapter 1 demonstrate, Germany is in the fast lane with regard to economic engagement,[30] but politically has not yet become the reliable partner that the Central European states demand. Instead of actively pursuing a coherent policy towards the former Warsaw Pact states, Germany, still overwhelmed with the political and economic consequences of unification, appears increasingly paralysed and incapable of coming to terms with its new role in the international system in general, and the European system in particular.

At the same time, the tectonic changes in Central and Eastern Europe have already forced Germany to respond to problems in the states of Mitteleuropa. The implementation of the new German asylum policy,[31] Germany's role in the break-up of Yugoslavia, initiatives regarding the Baltic states,[32] or rapprochement with Russia[33] are only a few examples of the steps that Germany has taken in response to quickly evolving developments. However, the German government's responses were rather clumsily implemented and diplomatically tactless. Furthermore, they did not demonstrate a clear political pattern or 'national interest'.

Regarding the asylum compromise, the domestic debate was conducted without any consideration of the effects that a change in German asylum law would have on Germany's neighbours.[34] As a result, there was considerable consternation and protest from Poland and Czechoslovakia.[35] It is obvious that the German government has an interest in stopping the flow of immigrants into the country. But Germany's rather crude management of problems with its Central European neighbours, especially following the Federal Republic's attempts to build confidence and erase the legacy of its Nazi past, was counterproductive.

Germany's single-handed recognition of Croatia and Slovenia has been the subject of numerous protests within the EU and NATO. Indeed, unilateral recognition illustrates the consequences of a German Mitteleuropa decision-making that is not integrated into or part of a clear foreign-policy conception towards the region. The US, in particular, argued that the unilateral and non-coordinated decision to recognize the two countries would have produced different results if Germany had had a clearer foreign-policy concept. In fact, Germany has been accused of being partially responsible for the escalation of the civil war in the former Yugoslavia.[36]

It is still unclear what Hans-Dietrich Genscher's motives were in forcing the EU to follow his lead.[37] On the one hand, doing so increased concerns among Germany's Western partners; on the other, it raised the expectations of Central European states that some form of German leadership would be forthcoming. However, the latter could never be fulfilled since Germany, until today (1996), is hardly prepared to translate rhetoric into action.[38]

The establishment of a cooperative relationship with Russia and Germany's attempt to be an advocate for the Baltic states[39] are also mutually incompatible. To be a spokesman for the Baltic states means primarily advocating their interests against those of Russia, which conflicts with Russo-German rapprochement. Furthermore, aside from providing advice to the Baltic states, Germany remains hesitant to take any action on the international stage. In reality, the Baltic states remain on the periphery of Germany's European interests.[40]

Obviously, Germany's interest in Russia remains paramount, since the latter is still a great regional power on the continent and, therefore, a natural partner or adversary of Germany's Mitteleuropa interests. However, 'intermittent rapprochement between the two giants makes the rest of Europe and America nervous'.[41] What may be the reappearance of a Rapallo or a Schaukelpolitik[42] at this point appears as the lack of a foreign-policy concept.[43]

Several conclusions can be drawn from these policies and actions. First, Germany is not ready to assume a more visible and leading role on the international stage – that is, beyond the EU. Secondly, developments in Central Europe will increasingly demand a coherent policy towards that region. Thirdly, without a clear and consistent foreign-policy conception regarding Central Europe, Germany will increasingly become an unreliable partner and, thus, a factor of instability for the East as well as for the West. The zigzag course that it has steered over the last four years[44] has bewildered its partners in the West and the new states in the East. For the future, there are essentially two views possible regarding European development and Germany's role in Mitteleuropa. In both scenarios Germany may play the role of a 'region state', as developed by Kenichi Ohmae.[45]

First, the concept of Mitteleuropa may be swallowed as a whole by the expanding concept of the EU. An argument in favour of this scenario is shown in the trends that are operating from both ends of the European continent. Germany is the principal advocate of the integration of the Central European states. These states have expressed the view that they would prefer to be directly integrated into Europe rather than being perceived as a subregion. Given Germany's economic size and geopolitical position, the Central European states prefer that Germany's leadership be exercised through Europe as a whole rather than through the medium of Mitteleuropa.

On the other hand, 'another expansion of the EU will re-define Europe, change the character of the community, and force a restructuring of EU institutions'[46] and procedures. The project of a federal system could become increasingly problematic, not merely because of its size, but because of its heterogeneity. Furthermore and more importantly, expansion would limit (Western) Europe's leverage towards Russia. The exclusion of Russia would provoke this great power in the east and, simultaneously, strengthen nationalistic and reactionary forces within Russia. Undoubtedly, further destabilization of Russia would affect Central Europe, which would be counterproductive to Western interests.[47]

The second scenario envisions a different form of Europeanization, that is, a gradual process that eventually would make the region a partner to the EU. The years between 1990 and 1995 demonstrate that Germany requires a clearly formulated plan towards Central Europe.[48] This means that policy goals have to be identified, resources have to be allocated, and institutional–structural changes in the region must be made, all of which require German initiative. Despite the existence of mixed feelings among Germany's Central European neighbours, these states are already one step ahead of Germany in so far as they realize that there will be no Central European initiative, no Mitteleuropa, without Germany.[49] It seems that the future development of the international system favours regional cooperation, with a somewhat reduced importance for the nation-state,[50] a development that will further strengthen regional European organizations on a subsystem level.[51] German engagement in such a scenario is crucial.

Germany's history in Mitteleuropa stretches further back than Haushofer and the Third Reich. Therefore, it may be helpful for German political elites to rediscover this fruitful tradition in order to develop a more compelling and effective foreign policy towards their Central European neighbours.

Shying away from this task not only undermines Germany's position in the international system but also contributes to the growing anarchic tendencies in the region of the former Soviet Empire.

Although Europe in 1996 resembles the period prior to 1914 in some respects, there is one crucial difference. Today, there are several functioning international organizations in Europe, such as the EU, OSCE, NATO, WEU, with a tradition that is old enough to make them factors of stability.[52] As a result of its 'national interest', Germany is deeply rooted in these institutions. Therefore, Germany cannot abandon its ties with the EU in order to promote a Central European political or economic initiative. At the same time, an enlargement of the EU eastwards seems counterproductive to the intentions of the EU and some of its member states.[53]

Germany is predominantly a Western state and will remain so for the foreseeable future.[54] Its Western priorities include integration within the EU and a close alliance with France. However, the latter is perhaps becoming more difficult under the new French President. Germany's priorities in the East, for now, are stabilization of and partnership with Russia. However, in between these two poles, Germany has an important role in Mitteleuropa of furthering stability and prosperity as cornerstones of regional democracy.[55] What Mitteleuropa requires is a political, economic and security framework to achieve these objectives. Currently, it appears that it would be useful to establish some form of a Central European economic union, a cooperation council (perhaps under the auspices of the OSCE) of the heads of state, and a more decisive form of the Partnership for Peace initiative of NATO.[56]

As a bridge, Germany today could provide the initiative and leadership for such organizations. Dual membership for Germany (and Austria for that matter) in traditional Western organizations as well as new Central European ones is not only imaginable but necessary. This means that the small states of Central Europe, along with Germany, would be part of an 'integrating organism' that could avoid the recrudescence of Germany as a regional hegemon and instead could support a whole range of pan-European and regional processes.[57]

Germany's tortuous path from Hitler's 'obsession with power' to its post-war 'amnesia about power'[58] must now develop into a 'conscience for power', that is, a responsible and restrained use of power. In other words, Germany has to define its attitude towards the concept of power while finding its role in Europe. As a first and crucial step in taking the initiative, German policymakers should re-examine the long-standing German tradition of Mitteleuropa. While researching this work in 1993, several German officials in foundations and political parties were interviewed. Almost all individuals, with few exceptions, shied away from the topic and reiterated the position that there was no alternative for German foreign policy but 'Westbindung'. This is an indication of the paralysed state of German Mitteleuropa politics and official thinking at the time. However, a shift in policy orientation may be currently occurring. On a return visit to Bonn in spring 1995, when talking to some of the same officials who were interviewed in 1993, several of those now were freely speaking about Germany as a bridge between East and West or about Germany's role as a broker of Central European interests. This shift is overdue, because

> whatever shape Central Europe takes, the pressure on German policy and the country's economy will continue as long as there is support for transformation of the former East. . . . Germany will therefore find it necessary to differentiate in its policy toward the East.[59]

This work has attempted to point out how rich and lively the concept of Mitteleuropa has been as a German foreign-policy orientation. The next decade will disclose whether German political elites will be able to live up to their new role in Mitteleuropa in particular, and Europe in general.[60] Germany's success depends on the political élites' ability to reorient foreign policy towards Mitteleuropa as a political reality rather than a vague vision.

APPENDIX: 'MITTELEUROPA' IN MAPS, 1915–54

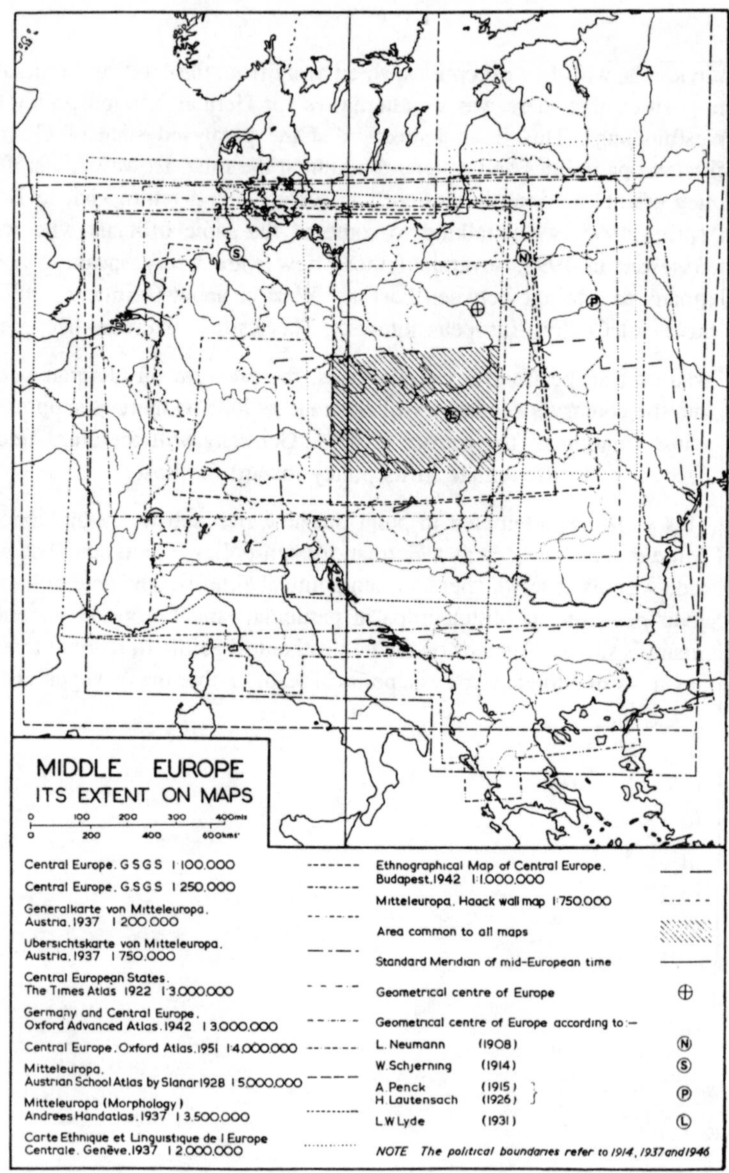

Map 1 Middle Europe: its extent on maps

The areas covered by, and the area common to, twelve maps and map series all bearing the name 'Central Europe' (or the equivalent in French and German), and their location with respect to the geometrical centre of Europe and the standard meridian of mid-European time.

(All maps are reproduced courtesy of the Royal Geographical Society)

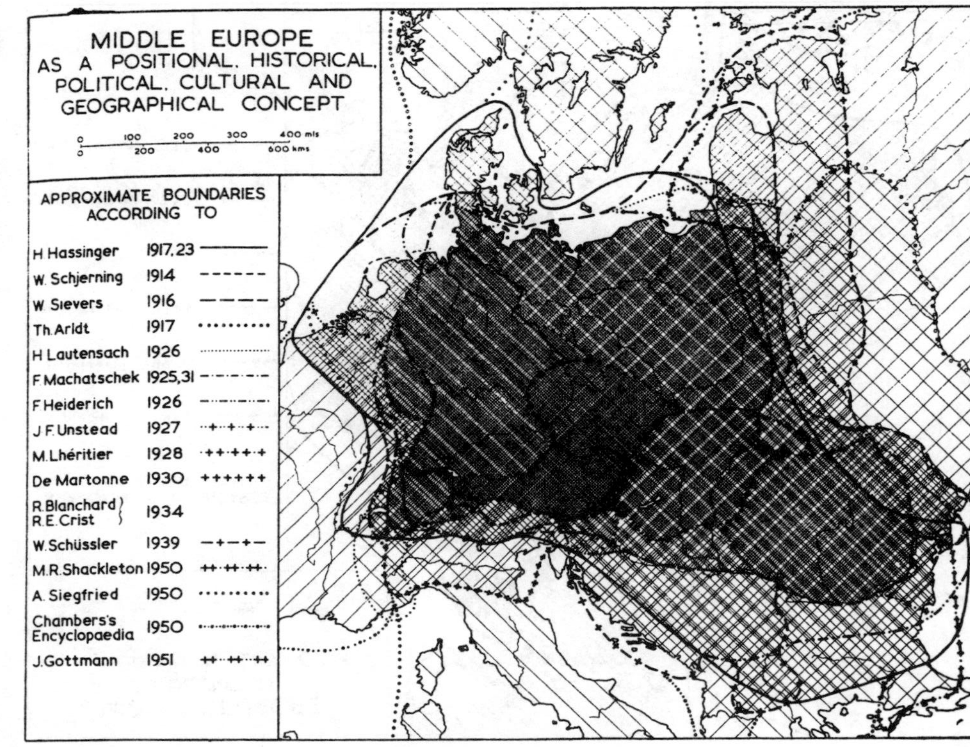

Map 2 Middle Europe as a positional, historical, political, cultural and geographical concept: a graded assessment of the degree of coincidence existing between sixteen definitions of Middle Europe

The shading density is directly proportional to the number of authorities who included a given area within Middle Europe. The various patterns are only the accidental result of the process of superimposition.

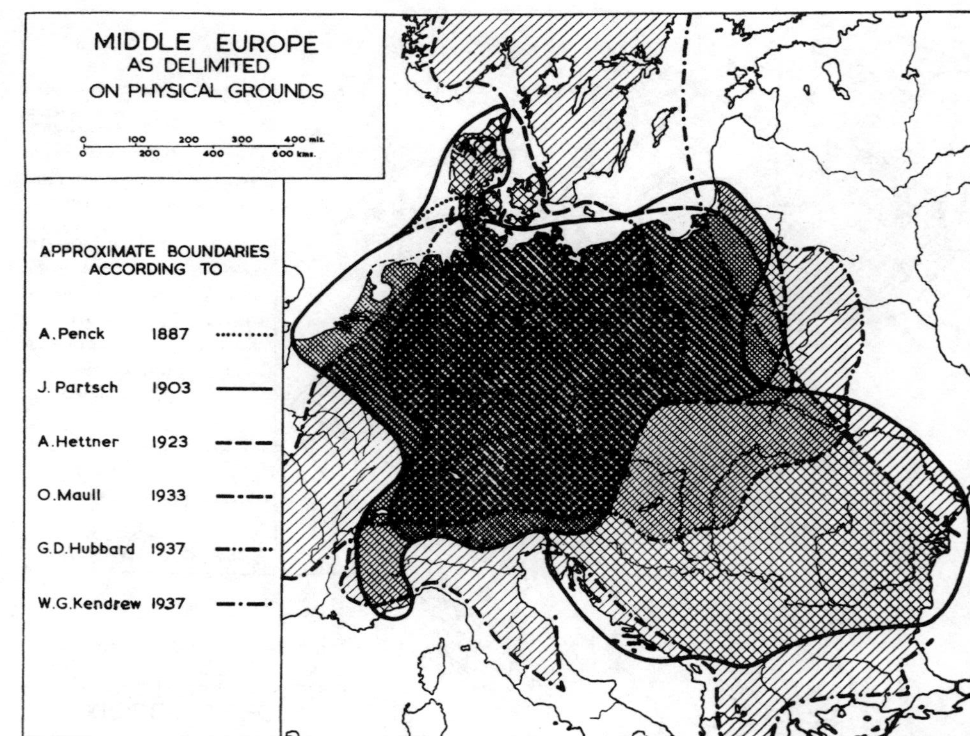

Map 3 Middle Europe as delimited on physical grounds: the amount of agreement existing about the concept of Middle Europe as a physical region

The shading density is directly proportional to the number of authorities who included a given area within Middle Europe. The various patterns are only the accidental result of the process of superimposition.

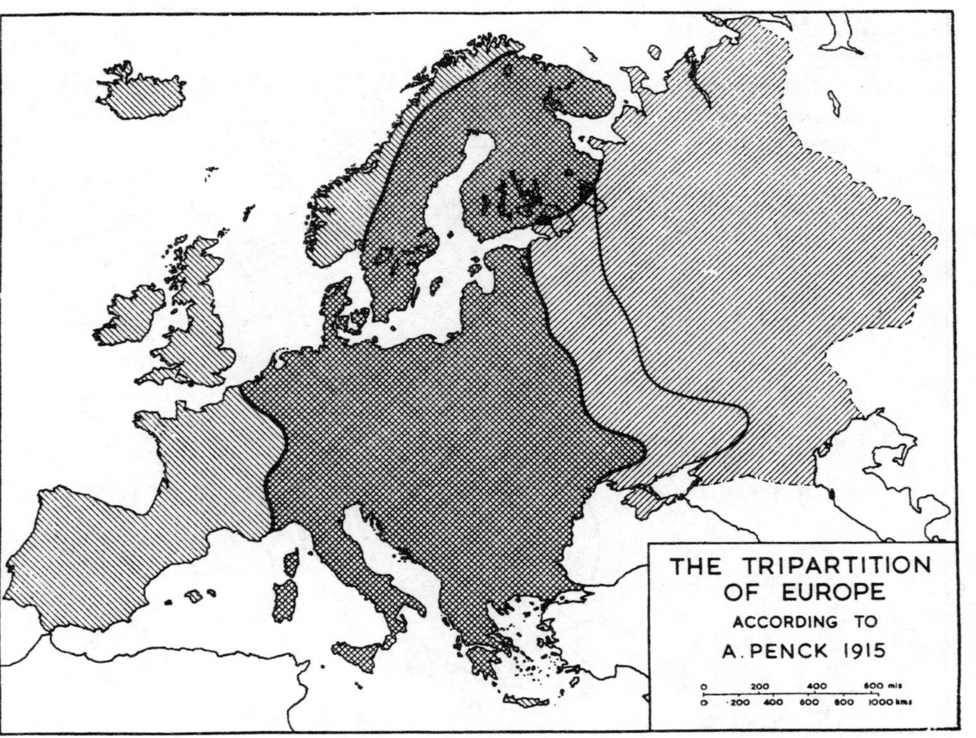

Map 4 The tripartition of Europe on the basis of space relationships into Vordereuropa, Zwischeneuropa *and* Hintereuropa *as suggested by Albrecht Penck in 1915. The zone between Karelia and the Asov Sea he termed the 'Varangian Fringe'*

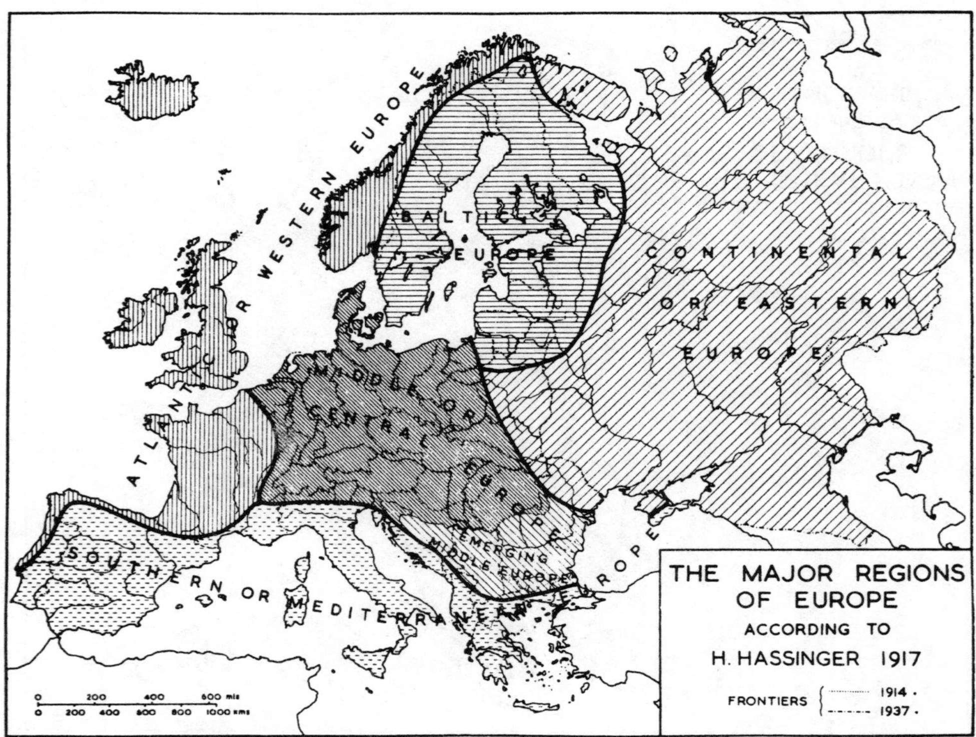

Map 5 The major regions of Europe according to Hugo Hassinger (1917), delimited on the basis of landscape character

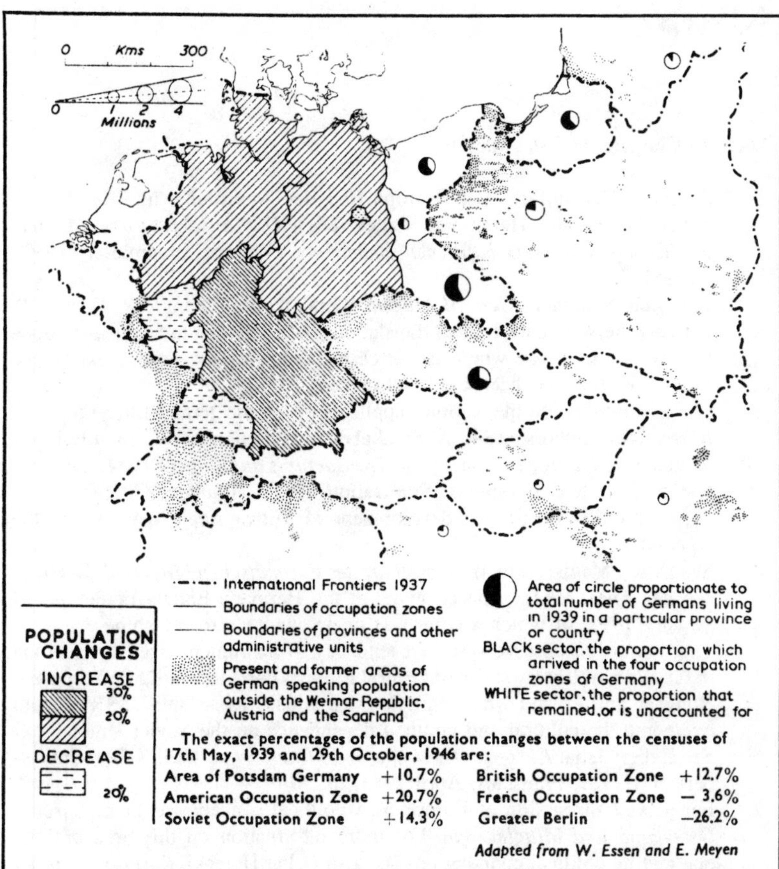

Map 6 The German Lebensraum, *its contraction from 1939 to 1946 and the overall effect of the westward migration of German nationals* (Reichsdeutsche) *and ethnic Germans* (Volksdeutsche) *on the population distribution of each occupation zone* (adapted from W. Essen and E. Meyen)

Notes

Notes to Chapter 1: Introduction

1. Albrecht Haushofer, 'Mitteleuropa und der Anschluß', in Friedrich G. Kleinwächter and Heinz von Paller (eds), *Die Anschlußfrage in ihrer politischen und wirtschaftlichen Bedeutung* (Vienna: Braumüller, 1930), pp. 151–2.
2. Friedrich Naumann, *Central Europe* (London: P. S. King, 1917), p. 100. Unless otherwise indicated all translations from German to English are done by myself. In cases where an English version of the source exists, the English edition has been used and quoted.
3. For a summary of the various applications of the term Mitteleuropa by international authors, see K. A. Sinnhuber's excellent paper 'Central Europa–Mitteleuropa–Europe Centrale', in *Transactions and Papers 1954*, the Institute of British Geographers: Publication no. 20 (London: George Philip, 1954), pp. 15–39; for the development of Mitteleuropa in maps see the Appendix.
4. See Ulrich Matthée, *Die Wiedergeburt der Europäischen Mitte und die Grenzen des Abendlandes*; speech given at the Hermann-Ehlers-Akademie, 18 January 1992, of which a copy was made available to the author.
5. Today one can observe a similar tendency to instrumentalize Mitteleuropa in the Warsaw Treaty states of Central Europe. Foremost in Czechoslovakia, Hungary and Poland where Mitteleuropa is used as an anti-USSR term to overcome the cultural and political dependence on the Soviet Union.
6. See Egbert Jahn, *Europa, Osteuropa und Mitteleuropa* (HSFK-Forschungsbericht 1/1989, Frankfurt, April 1989), p. 30.
7. For a brief discussion of Europe as a political concept see Jahn, *Europa, Osteuropa und Mitteleuropa*. For more information on this area of Europe and its political connotations see also Oskar Halecki, *Europa: Grenzen und Gliederung seiner Geschichte* (Darmstadt: Gentner, 1957); or Rolf H. Foerster, *Europa: Geschichte einer politischen Idee* (Munich: Nymphenburger Verlagshandlung, 1967).
8. Two examples illustrate this lack of conception. One is the German acknowledgement of Croatia and Slovenia in 1991; the other is the compromise on asylum (Asylkompromiß). The political debate illustrates beautifully the lack of consent or conception about Mitteleuropa in German politics, and secondly, it shows the unwillingness in the scholarly literature to deal with Mitteleuropa in a rational manner. Politicians and scholars seem to shy away from the idea that a concept of Mitteleuropa may be a useful and acceptable policy tool for German foreign policy. The asylum debate, aside from all its confusion, has made one thing very clear: in the contemporary international situation Germany cannot avoid expressing national interests outside the 'traditional' European system of EU and 'Westbindung', despite all its efforts to pursue almost exclusively European policies.

   The acknowledgement of Croatia and Slovenia illustrates the consequences of a German Mitteleuropa decision that was not integrated into or part of a clear foreign-policy conception towards Mitteleuropa. The US, especially, put forward the argument that the unilateral and non-coordinated decision to acknowledge the two countries either would have been different or would have been followed more decisively if Germany had had a clear foreign-policy concept.

9. Source: *Libération* (14 April 1993): 2. The German portion of the financial aid for Russia equals roughly two-thirds of the total amount. For reasons of space, only Germany is compared with the US as the largest Western economy. Furthermore, it is clear that large portions of the aid given are ear-marked and tied to the purchase of German goods and services. Nevertheless, the figures demonstrate that Germany is leading the economic engagement in Central Europe compared with the other Western powers.
10. Source: *Statistisches Jahrbuch*, Warsaw, 1992; *Statistische Jahrbücher zum Außenhandel*, Warsaw, 1991, 1992; *Statistisches Jahrbuch des Außenhandels Ungarns*, 1987, 1990; *Statisztikai Havi Közlemények*, no. 7/1992, p. 45. These figures are compiled for the total of the countries' foreign trade, including that with EFTA and the other Eastern European, formerly COMECON, states.
11. See the work of Kenneth N. Waltz on structural realism as well as Robert O. Keohane's and Joseph S. Nye's work in the area of neo-liberal institutionalism. In particular, see Robert O. Keohane (ed.), *Neorealism and its Critics* (New York: Columbia University Press, 1986); Robert O. Keohane, *International Institutions and State Power* (Boulder: Westview Press, 1989); Kenneth N. Waltz, *Theory of International Politics* (Reading: Addison-Wesley, 1979); Kenneth N. Waltz and Robert J. Art (eds), *The Use of Force, International Politics and Foreign Policy* (Boston: Little & Brown, 1971); K. N. Waltz and R. J. Art, 'The emerging structure of international politics', *International Security*, 2 (Autumn 1993): 44–79.
12. See the Bibliography.
13. Gregory F. Treverton, *America, Germany, and the Future of Europe* (Princeton: Princeton University Press, 1992); G. F. Treverton, *The Shape of the New Europe* (New York: Council on Foreign Relations Press, 1992). See also Hubert Ripka, *A Federation of Central Europe* (New York: Macmillan, 1953).
14. See Peter Merkl, *German Foreign Policies, West and East* (Santa Barbara: ABC-Clio, 1974).
15. See Edwina Campbell, *Germany's Past and Europe's Future* (Washington: Pergamon-Brassey, 1989).
16. Here the work followed the approach to decision-making in foreign policy as laid out by James Rosenau, Richard Snyder, and others. See James N. Rosenau, *Domestic Sources of Foreign Policy* (New York: Free Press, 1967); also James N. Rosenau, *The Scientific Study of Foreign Policy* (New York: Free Press, 1971); and James N. Rosenau, *International Politics and Foreign Policy* (New York: Free Press, 1969); Richard C. Snyder, H. W. Bruck and Burton Sapin, *Foreign Policy Decision Making* (New York: Free Press of Glencoe, 1962).
17. See the works of Kenneth N. Waltz, Robert O. Keohane and Joseph Nye cited above, note 11. See also William Olson et al. (eds), *The Theory and Practice of International Relations* (Englewood Cliffs: Prentice-Hall, 1987);

Kenneth W. Thompson et al. (eds), *World Politics* (New York: Free Press, 1976); Richard W. Mansbach and John A. Vasquez, *In Search of Theory* (New York: Columbia University Press, 1981); Morton A. Kaplan (ed.), *New Approaches to International Relations* (New York: St Martin's Press, 1968); Paul Viotti and Mark V. Kauppi, *International Relations Theory* (New York: MacMillan, 1993); and James N. Rosenau, *Turbulence in World Politics* (Princeton: Princeton University Press, 1990).

This work is largely a study of the domestic sources of a particular policy behaviour of a single nation actor. Its implications for international relations derive from the dynamics between domestic and foreign policy. With regard to these implications the work follows neo-realist theory, which relies on three fundamental assumptions: that the most important actors in international relations are states; that their behaviour is rational; and that they calculate their actions in relation to the existing international system. A regional level of analysis is applied, limited to the European international system.

18. Keohane, *International Institutions*, pp. 40–1; also Thompson, *World Politics*, p. 8.
19. As Werner Kaltefleiter has phrased it: 'Foreign policy is the result of a domestic decision-making process.' W. Kaltefleiter, 'Außenpolitische Willensbildung in der Gegenwart', *Geschichte und Gegenwart* (September 1982): 19–29.
20. Rosenau, *International Politics and Foreign Policy*, p. 167.
21. Here I follow the school of thought of logical positivism, which identifies 'national interests' as those that are subjectively identified and acted upon as such by foreign policy-makers, i.e., decision-makers. It is acknowledged that it may be possible to identify 'objective' national interests; however, for the purpose of this work the positivists' point of view is most appropriate.
22. Rosenau, *International Politics and Foreign Policy*, p. 169.
23. As in most applied works, however, this book also combines the two levels of analysis to a certain extent. It is merely noted here, since the 'idea' of Mitteleuropa is the dependent variable (with certain changes and mutations over time), the independent variable is the organizational interaction.
24. See Ralf Dahrendorf, *Homo Sociologicus: Ein Versuch zur Geschichte, Bedeutung und Kritik der Kategorie der Sozialen Rolle* (Opladen: Westdeutscher Verlag, 1972).
25. Critics of this approach usually argue that the student limits his analysis to a few people and acts as some sort of amateur psychoanalyst in order to determine what the 'true' motives of a given person were. Even though individual psychological factors may enter the analysis at one point or another (such as individual ambitions or scandals), they usually do not come first. Rather, factors such as the power structure and requirements of the individual's position, his party affiliation, traditional foreign policy values and commitments of his country, and so on, are foremost in the student's analysis of foreign-policy decision-making. This work follows this tradition, largely leaving aside individual psychological factors.
26. Henry C. Meyer, *Mitteleuropa in German Thought and Action 1815–1945* (The Hague, Netherlands: Martinus Nijhoff, 1955), p. 3. See Meyer, pp. 2–7, for a summary of the problems of defining Mitteleuropa in 'the' one way.

Meyer's analysis provides a working definition for this endeavour. As any working definition, it contains certain imperfections and is open to criticism and questioning. However, Meyer's definition is the most appropriate given the hypothesis underlying this work.

27. Most prominent among these individuals is Josef Maria Baernreither (1845–1925), an Austrian-German statesman, who was active in the Austrian Mitteleuropa movement from the late nineteenth century. His 'Nachlaß' has been published in part and is otherwise deposited in the Vienna Haus-, Hof- und Staatsarchiv. It is a valuable source for Mitteleuropa developments up to the First World War.
28. It should be mentioned here that, especially after the First World War, Austria was divided on the question of unification with Germany. While under the K&K (Kaiser und König) monarchy the question of whether Austria should join the German Empire was already virulent. It became of even greater significance after the dissolution of the Habsburg Empire at Versailles. See below, pp. 47–52.
29. See Karl Schlögel, *Die Mitte liegt ostwärts* (Berlin: Corso bei Siedler, 1986); Reinhard Frommelt, *Paneuropa oder Mitteleuropa* (Stuttgart: Deutsche Verlags Anstalt, 1977); Martin Kutz, *Die Mitte Europas-Mitteleuropa* (Hamburg: Führungsakademie der Bundeswehr, 1993); or Erhard Busek and Emil Brix, *Projekt Mitteleuropa* (Munich: Ueber-reuter, 1986).
30. Meyer, *Mitteleuropa*, p. 4.
31. See Schlögel, *Die Mitte liegt ostwärts*, p. 11.
32. For the usage of the terms *Gemeinschaft* and *Gesellschaft* see Ferdinand Tönnis, *Gemeinschaft und Gesellschaft* (Berlin: Verlag Curtious, 1922).
33. For a short summary of the economic visions regarding Mitteleuropa, especially for the inter-war period, see Frommelt, *Paneuropa oder Mitteleuropa*.
34. The role of France in the German concepts of Mitteleuropa is somewhat ambivalent, since several concepts include France, thus, attempting to weaken French–British relations. However, the more important approaches towards Mitteleuropa usually take an anti-French stand, as is shown in Chapter 3 of this work.
35. The term was coined by György Konrád in his book *Mitteleuropäische Meditationen* (Frankfurt/M.: Luchterhand, 1985). Konrád's and Kundera's writings ('Tragödie Zentraleuropa' in *Kommune, Forum für Politik und Ökonomie*, July 1984) in the early and mid-1980s are largely responsible for the renewed interest in the concepts of Mitteleuropa. The role of these authors in Central European states under communist rule is not the topic of this dissertation beyond the statement that their writings started a new Mitteleuropa discussion in the West.

    For the authors of the communist-governed states of Central Europe, of which Kundera and Konrád are only two, the vision of Mitteleuropa became a symbol of freedom and independence from Moscow. In its anti-Soviet orientation it was primarily a visionary and literary way out of their intellectual prison. It served as a focal point to redefine or redevelop a cultural and *staatsbürgerliche* identity outside the communist doctrine.

    Their idea of Mitteleuropa was a mixture of K&K monarchy romanticism and dissident writing against Moscow. As understood by its advocates in the Central European states during the 1980s, the concept of Mitteleuropa meant freedom from Soviet hegemony, without trading such hegemony for German, Austrian or any other hegemony.

However, after their writings were translated, their ideas were quickly picked up by economists advocating a Central European Wirtschaftsraum. See H. Thalberg, Zentraleuropa: Die Kunst des Möglichen', *Europäische Rundschau*, 14 (1986); R. Hrbek, 'The EC and the changes in Central and Eastern Europe', *Intereconomics*, 25 (1990); *The Economist*, 305 (December 1987): 31–2; 312 (October 1989): 27–8; 316 (August 1990): 17–19; E. Kohák, 'Can there be a Central Europe?', *Dissent*, 37 (1990). This interest, in turn, opened the way for a political Mitteleuropa discussion in the West.

36. See Kutz, *Die Mitte Europas*, p. 2.
37. One of the most prominent and more radical advocates for an economic Mitteleuropa was the German economist Friedrich List, who died in 1846. In 1841 he published his major work, *National System of Political Economy* (Philadelphia: J. B. Lippincott, 1856), outlining a vision of an economically unified area as the heart of the German nation-state. Chapter 2 of this work will discuss List's influence on the Mitteleuropa movement in more detail.
38. Kutz, *Die Mitte Europas*, p. 3.
39. Jahn, *Europa, Osteuropa und Mitteleuropa*, p. 14.
40. Ibid., p. 16.
41. Meyer, *Mitteleuropa*, p. 3.
42. For the definition see Giselher Wirsing, *Zwischeneuropa und die deutsche Zukunft* (Jena: E. Diederichs Verlag, 1932).
43. One of the main reasons that the US entered the war was the belief that the ultimate German war goal was hegemony between the North Cape and Baghdad. Today, we know that this was never the case, but France used this slogan successfully as a propaganda tool against Germany, directed particularly towards the US administration at the time. In England, for example, T. G. Masaryk and R. W. Seton-Watson started a journal, *New Europe*, as a reaction against perceived pan-German Mitteleuropa ambitions. In the US the French journalist André Chéradame was most active in popularizing the message of a menacing Mitteleuropa, under German hegemony, among government officials. See his book *The Pangerman Plot Unmasked* (London: unknown, 1916), and his paper, *Le Français Réaliste* (Paris: April 1929). A good summary of this aspect of the Mitteleuropa idea and its use before the Second World War can be found in Barbara Ward's book for the Fabian Society, *Hitler's Route to Baghdad* (London: Allen & Unwin, 1939).
44. This definition of Europe is certainly questionable, since the term Europe, much as the term Mitteleuropa, has been subject to various changes. Here Europe is defined as a cultural, Latin-Christian entity. For a summary of the definitional problems regarding Europe, see H. Münkler, 'Europa als politische Idee', *Leviathan*, 19 (1991): 521–41.

Notes to Chapter 2: The Intellectual and Political Precursors of 'Mitteleuropa' before the Second German Empire

1. The term national identity 'invariably involves idealization and a substantial amount of myth-making', as Harold James writes (Harold James, *A German*

Identity, 1770–1990 (New York: Routledge, 1989), p. 9). Acknowledging the problems of terminology, it is sufficient to state that, at times, the Mitteleuropa debate throughout German history has been perceived by writers as a question of German national identity. This statement applies to German as well as to British, American, and French writers. For example, see R. E. Turner, *Europe since 1789* (New York: Doubleday Page, 1924); Jacob S. Schapiro, *Modern and Contemporary European History 1815–1952* (Boston: Houghton Mifflin, 1953); or the *Larousse du XXe Siècle, IV* (Paris: Librairie Larousse, 1928–33). See also Ralf Dahrendorf, *Gesellschaft und Demokratie in Deutschland* (Munich: Piper, 1965), who discusses the question of national identity under the larger topic of 'the German question'.

2. The first German Reich under Karl the Great and his successors already constituted a form of Mitteleuropa, if one looks at its geographic expanse. In fact, some Mitteleuropa authors fall back upon Charlemagne's Empire to justify their Mitteleuropa aspirations. However, it should be noted that the first German Empire was not at all clearly German but rather a mixture of what later became German and French elements.
3. No revisionist politics are argued or followed here. But it is a fact that sections of the German people and politicians perceive former East Germany as 'middle' Germany. The demands of the former East Prussian Germans at their annual meetings (the one in July 1993 with the slogan 'Silesia remains ours') for some form of compensation is as much an example of this perception as Mr Stoiber's statements (at this 1993 meeting) that the Czech government should negotiate directly with the Sudeten Germans about their demands, a call that has always been denied by former Czechoslovakia and currently by the Czech Republic. (Note: the same demands were reiterated by the Association and German politicians of the CSU in 1994 and 1995). Furthermore, all German state governments have considered related questions about the final settlement of Germany's eastern borders in a final *all*-Germany peace settlement. Chancellor Kohl's hesitation regarding the acceptance of Poland's western borders in the unification negotiations are another illustration.
4. See Werner Conze, *The Shaping of the German Nation* (London: George Prior, 1979), ch. III; also Hans Rothfels, *Bismarck und der Osten* (Leipzig: Hinrichs Verlag, 1934); and Fritz Fischer, *Krieg der Illusionen* (Düsseldorf: Droste Verlag, 1969), especially his first part.
5. See Henry C. Meyer, *Mitteleuropa, in German Thought and Action 1815–1945* (The Hague: Martinus Nijhoff, 1955), p. 9.
6. See James, *German Identity*, p. 12.
7. Ibid., pp. 34–5.
8. See Helmuth Plessner, *Die verspätete Nation* (Frankfurt: Suhrkamp, TB Wissenschaft, 1974).
9. Meyer, *Mitteleuropa*, p. 9.
10. This is not a work about the minority problems within and outside of German Reich territory. However, it is clear that most Mitteleuropa conceptions also incorporated this minority/majority topic and, therefore, constituted attempts to solve such problems. The most virulent minority questions were the Danish minority in northern Schleswig, the Polish question in Danzig, and the Sudeten Germans in Czechoslovakia.

11. Bernd Suphan, *Herders sämmtliche Werke*, vol. 23, p. 462; quoted in Meyer, *Mitteleuropa*, p. 9.
12. Heinrich Friedrich Karl Freiherr vom Stein, *Briefwechsel, Denkschriften und Aufzeichnungen*, ed. Emil Botzenhart (Berlin: C. Heymann, 1933), vol. 4, p. 165; quoted in Meyer, Mitteleuropa, p. 9.
13. Bismarck's smaller German solution was to create a German Reich at the expense of Austria in as much as it would be excluded from the Reich.
14. For the importance of the Mitteleuropa plan as laid out by v. Bruck and Schwarzenberg, and Prussia's continuous rejection of this plan for the German Reich's establishment, see the path-breaking work of Helmut Böhme, *Deutschlands Weg zur Großmacht* (Cologne: Kiepenheuer & Witsch, 1966).
15. Even though the alliance was organized in 1850 at the Unionsreichstag (United National Assembly) in Erfurt, it remained of negligible influence because the southern German kingdoms (Württemberg and Bavaria) never joined and Prussia's aim to crush the revolution alone, while Austria was tied up in Hungary, failed as well.
16. Heinrich v. Gagern, 28 October 1848, in a speech before the German Assembly in the Frankfurt Paul's Cathedral, quoted in Michael Freund, *Die Deutsche Geschichte* (Berlin: Bertelsmann, 1973), p. 603.
17. Two prominent proponents of Mitteleuropa at the beginning of the twentieth century, Friedrich Naumann and Ernst Jäckh, rediscovered List's economic schemes. Naumann and Jäckh largely shaped the Mitteleuropa discourse before the First World War. List is important here because Naumann's and Jäckh's writings were influenced by List's work of some seventy years earlier. Von Bruck, who was a young contemporary of List, carried List's ideas further, adapting them to new and changing political circumstances. He also influenced Naumann's and Jäckh's path of argumentation.
18. Eduard v. Beckenrath et al. (eds), *Friedrich List, Schriften, Reden, Briefe* . . . (Berlin: R. Hobbing Verlag, 1935; 10 vols) vol. V, p. 491.
19. Ibid., p. 561.
20. Meyer, *Mitteleuropa*, p. 12.
21. Cited in Freund, *Die Deutsche Geschichte*, p. 549.
22. v. Beckenrath, *Friedrich List*, vol. V, p. 502.
23. Ibid., p. 505.
24. For a detailed account of v. Bruck's life and work see Richard Charmatz, *Minister Freiherr v. Bruck: Der Vorkämpfer Mittel-Europas* (Leipzig: D. Hirzel Verlag, 1916).
25. Quoted in F. G. Kleinwächter and Heinz von Paller, *Die Anschlußfrage in ihrer politischen und wirtschaftlichen Bedeutung* (Vienna: Braumüller, 1930), p. 15, emphasis added.
26. As Michael Freund has observed with regard to the National Assembly, 'compared with the Paul's Cathedral's Assembly this one almost looked like a farmers' parliament (Bauernparlament)'. Freund, *Die Deutsche Geschichte*, p. 605.
27. For more details on this period of German history see Freund, *Die Deutsche Geschichte*, or Bruno Gebhardt, *Handbuch der Deutschen Geschichte* (Stuttgart: Union Verlag, 1973), vol. III.
28. 'Nix deitsch' (meaning: 'not German') was used by Windisch-Grätz's foreign troops as a response when being spoken to in German. It became the

secret form of identification for the Habsburgs' reactionaries before the 'liberation' of Austria from the revolution.

29. It may be noted here that, of course, the whole dual monarchy had been established by its German elements. If it had not been for the Austrian-Germans, the Habsburg Empire would not have become a reality. Consequently, the Austrian-Germans backed up the Empire in its decay.
30. All four are reprinted in Charmatz, *Minister Freiherr von Bruck* (Leipzig, 1916). pp. 157–281.
31. Ibid., p. 163.
32. Meyer, *Mitteleuropa*, p. 17. Meyer employs the term 'capitalist' in the contemporary sense of a free-market economy.
33. Charmatz, *von Bruck*, p. 163.
34. The term 'warmonger-economists' refers to the economists at the beginning of the twentieth century who pushed for a war in order to ensure the economic growth of the German Empire. Among them were individuals such as Heinrich Claß, Alfred Krupp von Bohlen und Halbach and Arthur von Gwinner.
35. Charmatz, *von Bruck*, p. 203. One example of the re-emerging argument around the turn of the century is in Friedrich v. Bernhardi's, *Deutschland und der nächste Krieg* (Berlin: J. F. Gotta'sche Buchhandlung Nachf., 1912). Bernhardi reiterates the argument of 'unimpeded growth and progress' as a justification and, at the same time, a prerequisite for the next war, presumably against France, Britain, and Russia. This ominous mixture of premise and goal in a possible war scenario is one of the snares in German Mitteleuropa thinking, since this links Mitteleuropa with security policy considerations and establishes Mitteleuropa, *a priori*, as a defensive construct against its neighbour, rather than as a progressive tool for achieving economic and cultural goals and exchanges.
36. See Charmatz, *von Bruck*, p. 243.
37. Kleindeutsch and großdeutsch are an abbreviation of the still virulent German problem of what constitutes a German state, or who comprises the German nation. Essentially, this is another aspect of nation-building. Even today, Germany is one of the few countries in Europe that defines its nationality through bloodlines. In other words, rather than determining nationality by place of birth, as, for example, the US does (and consequently acknowledging different ethnic groups), Germany considers everyone who has a German bloodline in his family tree to be a German. Because of this definition, which was written into law in the Weimar Republic in 1923, Russian Germans or Volga-Germans, as much as Germans from the GDR, can become automatically German citizens once they are allowed or are able to emigrate to the FRG. Since this definition is still predominant in peoples' minds, Germany after unification is once more (or still) engaged in a process of nation-building by defining the former GDR as middle Germany and reclaiming East Prussia as German as well. For the development of the terms kleindeutsch and großdeutsch see Heidrun v. Möller, *Großdeutsch und Kleindeutsch. Die Entstehung der Worte in den Jahren 1848–49* (Berlin: Ebering Verlag, 1937); *Staatslexikon: Recht, Wirtschaft, Gesellschaft* (Freiburg: Görres-Gesellschaft, 1987; 5 vols).
38. For more details see Meyer, *Mitteleuropa*, p. 19, or Gebhardt, *Handbuch*, vol. III.

39. *Stenographischer Bericht der deutschen Nationalversammlung*, pp. 2894–6, quoted in Meyer, *Mitteleuropa*, p. 21.
40. For further information see also R. Pascal, 'The Frankfurt Parliament, 1848, and the Drang nach Osten', *Journal of Modern History*, 18 (1946): 108–17; and, E. Görlich, 'Großmitteleuropäisch und kleinmitteleuropäisch um die Mitte des 19. Jh.', *Welt als Geschichte*, 7 (1941): 259–66. Both authors examine the discussion in the Frankfurt Parliament regarding the territorial composition of a future German state.
41. The only exception was Belgium, which had to wait for such reconfirmation until 1831–9.
42. Conze, *Shaping of the German Nation*, p. 36, emphasis added.
43. The Frankfurt Assembly sent invitations to practically all countries and areas in which Germans were living (Hungary, Poland and Slovakia). Some representatives did come to Frankfurt to participate in the discussions concerning frontiers and minority status.
44. The situation was a little different in Silesia and East Prussia. These areas had not been part of 'larger Poland' before the partition of Poland, but had been subjects of the Prussian king. For most people in these areas it did not matter much whether they perceived themselves as Poles or Germans. The situation was quite different, however, in Posnania, which was given to Prussia as a result of the partition, and had had not only an independent ruling Polish aristocracy, but also a spreading 'national identity' among the people.
45. Conze, *Shaping of the German Nation*, p. 37, emphasis added.
46. No less difficult than Posnania was the dispute over Schleswig and Holstein, which served later as a test case for the validity of the principle of ethnic origin as a means of resolving border problems, with the well-known result of the 1848 Prussian–Danish war.
47 The Alldeutsche Bund is mentioned here as one of the best-known supporters of Mitteleuropa, even though it was established no earlier than 1890, in response to trading Heligoland with Great Britain for Zanzibar.
48. *Stenographischer Bericht der deutschen Nationalversammlung*, quoted in Conze, *Shaping the German Nation*, p. 39.
49. Ernst Moritz Arndt, *Ein ganzes, ein einig Deutschland muß es sein* (A whole, a united Germany it must be), quoted from the *Deutsche Commersbuch* (Stuttgart: Deutsche Verlagsanstalt, 11th edn, 1983), p. 72, emphasis added.
50. Conze, *Shaping the German Nation*, p. 39.
51. Of course, the biggest problem of the kleindeutsch vs großdeutsch problem was the question about the degree of independence among the individual states; for example, the dichotomy of a federal state vs. a confederate state system (Bundesstaat vs Staatenbund). If one demanded a truly federal state, one equally questioned the Habsburg Empire's existence, since, under the premise of ethnic origin, only those of the Empire's states that had already been members of the confederation (Deutsche Bund) could become part of a German federation. These tensions and problems would finally lead to Bismarck's smaller German solution. However, this development is neglected here since, as pointed out in the introduction, this work treats Austrian–German conflicts as 'internal' conflicts.

    The Assembly confronted Austria with the particular problem of its dual monarchy status in the first three paragraphs of the draft constitution, where it said: '(1) The German Empire consists of the area of the former German Confederation . . . (2) No part of the German Empire may be united with non-German countries into a state . . . (3) If a German country has the same head of state as a non-German country, then the relationship between both countries is to be arranged according to the principle of a purely personal union.' (*Stenographischer Bericht der deutschen Nationalversammlung*, p. 2587).

That this phrasing caused problems for the Habsburg Empire, with its Hungarian and Czech areas as part of the Empire, is obvious, especially until 1867, when it split into the dual monarchy. Hence, this approach to greater Germany was rejected by Austria.

52. Meyer, *Mitteleuropa*, p. 23.
53. Conze, *Shaping of the German Nation*, p. 49.
54. Again, the 'German question' in this context is meant as the question of German unification, as Ralf Dahrendorf understands it in his *Gesellschaft und Demokratie in Deutschland.*
55. In a sense, a more trenchant version of the kleindeutsch vs großdeutsch problem was presented by Paul Pfizer in his work *Correspondence of Two Germans* (P. A. Pfizer, *Briefwechsel zweier Deutschen* [Stuttgart: Cotta Verlag, 1832]), with his alternative of either freedom before unity, or the opposite. As Harold James has pointed out correctly, these two objectives correspond on the philosophical level with the old German dispute about whether the Germans were really nordic or heavily influenced by and drawn to the South – one standing for the belief in a conservative, nationalist 'revolution', the other for the belief in philosophical, liberal renewal; one represented through Prussia, the other through Austria; a dispute manifested in German literature through Goethe on the one side and Schiller on the other.

    See James, *German Identity*, pp. 50–3. The national assembly had a mixture of both 'spirits' and eventually split over them. For Mitteleuropa, the two opposing opinions meant the difference between a multinational (economic) unity or Germanization of the area.
56. v. Beckenrath, *Friedrich List . . .*, vol. V, p. 502.
57. This was also true for the Danish minority question after the Prussian/Austrian–Danish war of 1864 and for the newly developing Polish nationalism. See James, *German Identity*, p. 53. Later this perception of cultural superiority was exploited and misused by Hitler's Third Reich.
58. Landon Namier, *1848: The Revolution of the Intellectuals* (London: The Raleigh Lecture, 1946), p. 88.
59. The first crisis was induced by Austria's attempt to create a larger customs union and thus regain control over the middle and south German states under Prussian leadership. The second crisis was provoked by Prussia itself when it tried to lower the tariff levels of the union, and the southern German states in turn feared that this would ruin their mostly agriculturally oriented economy.
60. Quoted in Herbert W. Hahn, *Wirtschaftliche Integration im 19. Jhd: Die hessischen Staaten und der Deutsche Zollverein* (Göttingen: Van der Hoeck & Ruprecht, 1982), p. 246. One example of the fact that the economic

identification finally would turn into political identification is Hessen-Darmstadt, which originally wanted to affiliate itself with Austria but refrained from doing so after its influential businessmen had forecast economic disaster as a result of this affiliation. In turn, Hessen-Darmstadt became a loyal follower of the Prussian customs union. See James, *German Identity*, p. 60. For the theory that the customs union formed the basis of German unity in 1871, see Heinrich v. Treitschke, *Politik (Vorlesungen gehalten an der Universität zu Berlin*) (Leipzig: Hirzel, 1900).

61. 'Gesamtdeutsch' here means ideas or concepts based on culture and custom, demanding that a German Reich should incorporate all areas of German cultural heritage (deutsche Kulturbereiche). In Munich in 1938, Hitler partly legitimized seizure of Austria and Czechoslovakia under this gesamtdeutsch doctrine.
62. Albert Schäffle, *Aus meinem Leben* (Berlin: Hofmann, 1905; 2 vols); and Heinz Nitzschke, *Die Geschichtsphilosophie Lorenz von Steins*, Historische Zeitschrift, Beiheft 26 (Munich: Oldenbourg, 1932). Both individuals are known for their contributions to German sociology, which goes beyond their engagement with Mitteleuropa.
63. Meyer, *Mitteleuropa*, p. 25.
64. Another individual who foresaw Russia and the US as the forthcoming 'superpowers' of the world and who argued for a reorganization of Mitteleuropa in defence against these two powers was Constantin Frantz. Frantz had no influence a his times, largely because his großdeutsch vision rested heavily on a philosophical idealism influenced by Kant, which stood in opposition to Bismarck's Realpolitik (see Chapter 3, below). Mitteleuropa was to appear as a Christian federalist fortress built out of the need for peace and morality. However, Frantz's way of mixing economic with idealist notions in his Mitteleuropa thoughts had an impact on Friedrich Naumann who, in turn, was probably the most influential Mitteleuropa advocate. See Constantin Frantz, *Der Föderalismus als das leitende Prinzip für die sociale, staatliche und internationale Organisation, unter besonderer Bezugnahme auf Deutschland* (Mainz: Kirchheim, 1879); also Constantin Frantz, *Die Weltpolitik unter besonderer Bezugnahme auf Deutschland* (Chemnitz: Schmeitzner, 1882–3; 3 vols).
65. See Meyer, *Mitteleuropa*, p. 25.

Notes to Chapter 3: The Europeanization of 'Mitteleuropa', 1848–1914

1. See Ulrich Noack, *Bismarcks Friedenspolitik und das Problem des Deutschen Machtverfalls* (Leipzig: Quelle & Meyer, 1928); Joseph Vincent Fuller, *Bismarck's Diplomacy at its Zenith* (Cambridge: Harvard University Press, 1922); Winfried Baumgart, *Deutschland im Zeitalter des Imperialismus 1890–1914* (Stuttgart: Verlag W. Kohlhammer, 1986); also Winfried Baumgart, *Quellenkunde zur deutschen Geschichte der Neuzeit*: vol. 5, *Das Zeitalter des Imperialismus und des Ersten Weltkrieges (1871–1918)* (Darmstadt: Wissenschaftliche Buchgesellschaft, 1977); Great Britain, Foreign Office, *British Documents on the Origins of the War 1898–1914*, eds G. P. Gooch and Harald Temperlay (London: 1927–38; 11 vols); Eckart Kehr, *Der Primat*

der Innenpolitik, ed. Hans U. Wehler (Berlin: de Gryter Verlag, reprint 1976). In general see Fritz Fischer, *Griff nach der Weltmacht* (Düsseldorf: Droste Verlag, 1961) and the subsequent controversy as summarized in Klaus Hildebrandt, *Deutsche Aussenpolitik 1871–1918* (Munich: R. Oldenbourg Verlag, 1989), pp. 53–68.

2. Paul Rohrbach, *Deutschland unter den Weltvölkern* (Berlin-Schöneberg: 2nd edn, Buchverlag der 'Hilfe', 1908), pp. 43ff. Rohrbach writes that Bismarck was unable 'to put the greater Germany in the saddle, the Germany that belongs to a world-nation amongst world-nations' (das größere Deutschland, das Deutschland, das einem Weltvolk unter den Weltvölkern gehören sollte, in den Sattel zu setzen).
3. Quoted in T. Schieder, 'Bismarck und Europa: Ein Beitrag zum Bismarck-Problem', in Werner Conze, *Deutschland und Europa: Historische Studien zur Völker-und Staatenordnung des Abendlandes* (Düsseldorf: Droste Verlag, 1951), p. 15.
4. Ibid., p. 17.
5. See Renate Riemeck, *Mitteleuropa: Bilanz eines Jahrhunderts* (Potsdam: Edition Babelturm, 1990), p. 34.
6. See Bismarck's famous memorandum to the Prince of Prussia (1858), in which he summarizes his Frankfurt experiences, in Otto von Bismarck, *Die gesammelten Werke*, critical edition by Georg Ritter and Rainer Stadelmann (2nd edn; Berlin: Deutsche Verlagsgesellschaft, 1924–35; 15 vols), vol. 2, pp. 302ff. When Prussia's foreign ministry was handed to Alexander von Schleinitz (1859), who was a proponent of a close and good relationship with Austria, Bismarck, as a result of this memorandum, was sent into 'exile' to Russia. From Russia he observed, helplessly, the Central European crisis of 1859 – the war between France/Italy and Austria over the Kingdom of Piedmont.
7. Bismarck's most famous reference to Frederick is probably the one he made during his speech before the Prussian Parliament on 6 September 1849, in which he committed himself to a 'Stockpreußentum' and national Prussian politics (nationalen preußischen Politik). But the 1858 memorandum also contains numerous references to Frederick the Great's views on Europe. See also Bismarck's correspondence with Minister von Manteuffel, in Bismarck, *Gesammelten Werke*, vol. II.
8. See Bismarck's so-called 'Prachtbericht' to von Manteuffel on 26 April 1856, in Bismarck, *Gesammelten Werke*, vol. II. See also Schieder, 'Bismarck und Europa: Ein Beitrag zum Bismarck-Problem', p. 19.
9. For a rich and detailed account of the economic negotiations and projects among the Deutsche Bund, Austria and Prussia between 1848 and 1871, see Helmut Böhme, *Deutschlands Weg zur Großmacht* (Cologne: Kiepenhauer & Witsch, 1966).
10. For example, Wilhelm von Humboldt, in his 1816 'Denkschrift' on the confederation, wrote:

> One must not forget the true and substantial purpose of the Bund in as far as European politics are concerned. This purpose is in fact to secure peace: the whole existence of the Bund, therefore, is oriented toward keeping the balance through its inherent political weight.

Wilhelm von Humboldt, *Eine Auswahl seiner politischen Schriften*, ed. Siegfried A. Kaehler, *Klassiker der Politik* (Berlin: Hobbing, 1922), vol. VI, p. 48.

11. August Rochau, quoted in James, *A German Identity*, p. 62.
12. Ludwig August Rochau, *Grundsätze der Realpolitik angewendet auf die staatlichen Zustände Deutschlands* (Stuttgart: Göpel Verlag, 1853, 1st edn; Heidelberg: J. C. B. Mohr Verlag, 1869, 2nd edn).
13. This line of thought was also favoured by Friedrich Willhelm IV, following the 1848 Revolution.
14. Quoted in Harold James, *A German Identity 1770–1990* (New York: Routledge, 1989), p. 62.
15. Werner Conze has defined Realpolitik after the 1848 revolution as 'the implementation of liberal and national aims in conjunction with the governments [in Europe] and not against them'. (Werner Conze, *The Shaping of the German Nation* (London: George Prior, 1979), p. 50.) In that sense, Bismarck's approach can be called Realpolitik, i.e., being aware of the revolutionary and national tendencies within the German states but trying to forestall the revolution through the implementation of reform from above, while simultaneously preserving the traditional monarchy.
16. In the late nineteenth century, the first theory of international relations was formulated as the 'balance of power', a precursor of what is today labelled as 'realism' in international relations. Even though it was less a clear and coherent theory than a conglomeration of observations and experiences of European foreign policies, it greatly influenced the way in which European policymakers looked at international relations. The 'balance of power' approach is as much a brainchild of Realpolitk as of nationalism, with its focus on independent nation-states.
17. James, *A German Identity*, p. 63. The old or traditional conservatism (in decline since the enlightenment), whose core belief was, in short, that the worldly order was God-given, and that man could only interpret God's laws rather than make law, was in Germany a part of the Kulturkampf. Such conservatism is distinct from the modern or contemporary usage as normative and economic conservatism. In the nineteenth century, this understanding of conservatism was prevalent among the aristocracy in Europe as an ideological tool in its struggle to maintain the traditional social order.

    The old form of conservatism, however, became increasingly obsolete in light of changes in the political system and society. In the second half of the nineteenth century, in Great Britain, people like Thomas Carlyle, Samuel Coleridge and John Ruskin advocated a revival of conservatism. However, most European countries experienced a comeback of conservatism at the beginning of the twentieth century and shortly after the First World War, in the form of an aesthetic conservatism (which had a somewhat anti-capitalist twist). The most prominent German advocates were Hugo v. Hoffmannsthal and Oswald Spengler.
18. See Harold James, *A German Identity*, pp. 65–8.
19. Ibid., p. 65.
20. Ibid., p. 65. See also Schieder, 'Bismarck und Europa', p. 22. Bismarck's affection for determinism, a misinterpreted offspring of Hegelian philosophy, which was popular among European intellectuals, is not discussed

here. Aware of the fundamental social changes of his times, Bismarck was determined to 'observe the currents and steer [his] ship in them as best [he could]'. Hans Rothfels, *Bismarck Briefe* (Göttingen: Vandenhoek & Ruprecht, 1955), p. 345. In Bismarck's opinion, romantic nationalism, as it was expressed in the 1848 revolution, was unable to account for the rapid and fundamental social and economic changes that would mould Germany's national destiny.

21. Conze, *Shaping of the German Nation*, p. 51.
22. Schieder, 'Bismarck und Europa', p. 22.
23. Ibid., p. 22 (emphasis added). The reference to God in this quote stems from Bismarck's pietism, which was heavily influenced by his wife and her circle.
24. Conze, *Shaping of the German Nation*, p. 51.
25. Andreas Hillgruber, *Die gescheiterte Großmacht: Eine Skizze des Deutschen Reiches, 1871–1945* (Düsseldorf: Droste Verlag, 1980), p. 11.
26. The demand was part of the ongoing economic debate with Austria in connection with the German Commerce Association (Deutsche Handelstag). It was issued in a letter to Duke Aloys von Károlyi, the Austrian envoy in Berlin at the time. See Bismarck, *Gesammelte Werke*, vol. III, p. 190.
27. For a detailed description of Frantz, his personality, and his influence in German politics, see the dissertation by Paulus Lauxtermann, 'Constantin Frantz: Romantik und Realismus im Werk eines politischen Außenseiters' (Groningen: dissertation, 1979).
28. For the contemporary discussion of the nineteenth-century question of the nation-state see Renate Riemeck, *Mitteleuropa: Bilanz eines Jahrhunderts*.
29. For a summary of Frantz's reception in the twentieth century see R. Schnur, 'Mitteleuropa in preußischer Sicht: Constantin Frantz', in Universität Innsbruck, *Symposium Mitteleuropa: Spuren der Vergangenheit – Perspektiven der Zukunft* (Innsbruck: Wagner'schen Universitäts Buchhandlung, 1987), pp. 37–43.
30. See Manfred Ehmer's dissertation on Frantz's understanding of Prussia and its role in the development of the future German state. Manfred Ehmer, *Constantin Frantz: Die politische Gedankenwelt eines Klassikers des Föderalismus* (Rheinfelden: Schäuble Verlag, 1988).
31. For a list of Frantz's major works see note 64 in Chapter 2. Regarding the US and Russia, Frantz largely followed Alexis de Tocqueville's analysis, in his (de Tocqueville's) first volume of *De la démocratie en Amérique* (Brussels: L. Haumann, 1835–40).
32. Henry C. Meyer, *Mitteleuropa in German Thought and Action 1815–1945* (The Hague: Martinus Nijhoff, 1955) p. 26.
33. Ibid.
34. For a summary of Frantz's federalist suggestions for Central Europe and, especially, their contemporary application, see also R. Altmann, 'Den Kopf über dem Nebel. Constantin Frantz – vergessener deutscher Klassiker des Föderalismus', in *Frankfurter Allgemeine Zeitung*, 2 May 1991, p. N3.
35. Meyer, *Mitteleuropa in German Thought and Action*, p. 26.
36. R. Morell, 'Constantin Frantz oder die Legitimität des Konjunktivs', in Renate Morell and Hans-Albert Steger, *Ein Gespenst geht um . . . : Mitteleuropa* (Munich: Theo Eberhard Verlag, 1987), p. 43.

37. For a critique of Bismarck's smaller German solution and its consequences for the European balance of power see Heinrich von Srbik, *Mitteleuropa: Das Problem und die Versuche seiner Lösung in der deutschen Geschichte* (Weimar: Hermann Böhlau, 1937), pp. 26ff. Also Arnulf Baring, *Unser neuer Größenwahn. Deutschland zwischen Ost und West* (Stuttgart: Deutsche Verlagsanstalt, 1988); and, concerning the 'unfinished German nation-state' in Mitteleuropa, see Winfried Baumgart, *Vom Europäischen Konzert zum Völkerbund: Friedensschlüsse und Friedenssicherung von Wien bis Versailles* (Darmstadt: Wissenschaftliche Buchgesellschaft, 1974).
38. For Frantz's understanding of the Holy Roman Empire, see Theodor Schieder, 'Idee und Gestalt des übernationalen Staates seit dem 19. Jahrhundert', in *Historische Zeitschrift*, 184 (1957): 336–66.
39. Lauxtermann, *Constantin Frantz: Romantik und Realismus im Werk eines politischen Außenseiters*, p. 185.
40. See Andreas Hillgruber, *Die gescheiterte Großmacht: Eine Skizze des Deutschen Reiches von 1871–1945* (Düsseldorf: Droste Verlag, 1980); also Andreas Hillgruber, *Die Last der Nation: Fünf Beiträge über Deutschland und die Deutschen* (Düsseldorf: Droste Verlag, 1984).
41. Srbik, *Mitteleuropa: Das Problem und die Versuche seiner Lösung*, p. 26.
42. See H. Rumpf, 'Mitteleuropa: Zur Geschichte und Deutung eines politischen Begriffs', *Historische Zeitschrift*, 165 (1942): 510–27.
43. See Christian Weimer's dissertation, *Mitteleuropa als politisches Ordnungskonzept?* (Würzburg: Universität Regensburg, 1992), p. 46.
44. Hermann Oncken, *Das alte und das neue Mitteleuropa. Historisch-politische Betrachtungen über deutsche Bündnispolitik im Zeitalter Bismarcks und im Zeitalter des Weltkriegs* (Gotha: Friedrich Andreas Perthes Verlag, 1917), p. 38.
45. Ibid.
46. Hans Rothfels, *Bismarck, der Osten und das Reich* (Darmstadt: Wissenschaftliche Buchgesellschaft, 1960); also H. Rothfels, 'Bismarck und das 19. Jahrhundert', in Walther Hubatsch (ed.), *Schicksalswege deutscher Vergangenheit: Beiträge zur geschichtlichen Deutung der letzten 150 Jahre* (Düsseldorf: Droste Verlag, 1950).
47. Helmut Böhme gives a detailed account of Mitteleuropa as an economic tool in Bismarck's political manoeuvres before 1871, especially with respect to Austria, in *Deutschlands Weg zur Großmacht*.
48. Quoted in Winfried Baumgart, *Vom Europäischen Konzert zum Völkerbund*, p. 6.
49. One of the reasons for the German interest, as well as the Russian and the Austrian, in that region was the power vacuum the had developed as a result of the decline of the Ottoman Empire. For a brief account of this development and the 'oriental crisis' of 1878, see Winfried Baumgart, *Vom Europäischen Konzert zum Völkerbund*.
50. Only a year earlier, Bismarck had postured as the 'honest broker' who wanted to help solve the conflict between Russia and Austria from a neutral standpoint. Immediately after signing the Zweibund, he adopted an anti-Russian rhetoric, which was employed to convince public opinion of the 'danger of Russia' economically and militarily. As Böhme points out, Germany's economic policies after 1879 were decisively double-tracked, insisting

on absolute autonomy in tariff negotiations with regard to Austria and, at the same time, trying to establish a central European Zollunion against Russia. Under Bismarck, the 'Central Association of German Industrialists' (Centralverband Deutscher Industrieller) gained political influence. For example, the secret negotiations with Austria in the aftermath of the 1879 Congress were conducted by the Association under Bismarck's command. The Centralverband would become even more significant under Wilhelm II. See Helmut Böhme, *Deutschlands Weg zur Großmacht*, pp. 594–8.

51. See A. Hillgruber, 'Südosteuropa in Bismarcks Außenpolitik 1875–1879', in Ralph Melville and Hans-Jürgen Schröder (eds), *Der Berliner Kongreß von 1878. Die Politik der Großmächte und die Probleme der Modernisierung in Südosteuropa in der zweiten Hälfte des 19. Jahrhunderts* (Wiesbaden: Franz Steiner Verlag, 1982), pp. 179–88.
52. See A. Novotny, 'Der Berliner Kongreß und das Problem einer europäischen Politik', *Historische Zeitschrift*, 186 (1958): 285–307.
53. Edmond Vermeil, *Germany's Three Reichs* (London: Dakers, 1945), p. 184; quoted in Meyer, *Mitteleuropa in German Thought and Action*, p. 27.
54. For the development of the overarching argument regarding Germany's economic development see Paul Kennedy, *Rise and Fall of the Great Powers* (New York: Vintage Books, 1987), especially ch. 5.
55. James, *A German Identity*, p. 104.
56. Ibid.
57. Regarding the concept of imperialism, in general, see H. J. Puhle, 'Imperialismustheorien', in Wichard Woyke (ed.), *Handwörterbuch Internationale Politik* (Opladen: Leske U. Budrich, 1986; 3rd edn), pp. 184–9; for the development of German imperialism, in particular, see Winfried Baumgart, *Deutschland im Zeitalter des Imperialismus 1890–1914*, pp. 21–32.
58. Weimer, *Mitteleuropa als politisches Ordnungskonzept?*, p. 50.
59. Originally, this phrase was used by Wilhelm II in a speech before Parliament, in which he attempted to justify the Germany Navy programme. It soon became a widely used phrase, summing up Germany's imperialist politics.
60. For the discrepancy between Germany's colonial ambitions and its limited home base see Rudolf Buchner, *Geschichte im europäischen Rahmen: Darstellung und Betrachtungen* (Darmstadt: Wissenschaftliche Buchgesellschaft, 1975).
61. Bismarck also referred to the certainty of a conflict with France and Britain over German colonial-imperialism. Ironically, his brief colonial endeavour in the 1880s functioned to obstruct the goals of the future Emperor Wilhelm II to achieve a rapprochement with Britain, which in Bismarck's view would have upset the fragile balance of power.
62. The Association was originally founded in 1890 as the pan-German 'Universal German Association' (Allgemeiner Deutscher Verband) to promote German colonial policy (especially the enlargement of the Navy), while at the same time motivating Germans in all states to support that endeavour economically. It was renamed in 1894 as the 'All-German Association' (Alldeutscher Verband), and became a haven for großdeutsch advocates with a nationalist orientation towards Germany as a world power. As Renate Riemeck has observed, the Association was 'a front organization to

propagate a new . . . world order based on the superiority of the German Volkstum' (Riemeck, *Mitteleuropa: Bilanz eines Jahrhunderts*, p. 63). The phrase 'am deutschen Wesen soll die Welt genesen' summarizes the All-German Association's ambitions for this 'new world order'.

In the literature, the term 'Alldeutsch' is sometimes used synonymously with the term 'pan-German'. In this work 'Alldeutsch' is used as a generic term for the group of people with this particular bias, while 'Alldeutscher Verband' will be used when the specific association is meant.

63. Lagarde did not actually publish monographs but collected his thinking in speeches, lectures and general writings. In 1878, he published his most influential work, 'Schriften für das deutsche Volk', in which he brought together his thoughts on German folklore and the political future of Germany. See Paul de Lagarde, *Deutsche Schriften* (Stuttgart: Alfred Kröner Verlag, 1933), vol. I.
64. Ibid., pp. 34–6.
65. Meyer, *Mitteleuropa in German Thought and Action*, p. 31.
66. Ibid., p. 32. In the preface to the second edition of Lagarde's 'Schriften' (1934) he was actually hailed in the foreword as a 'forerunner of the ideology of the Third Reich'.
67. Meyer, *Mitteleuropa in German Thought and Action.*
68. Meyer, *Mitteleuropa in German Thought and Action*, p. 31. See also J. Stern, 'Mitteleuropa: Von Leibnitz bis Naumann über List und Frantz, Planck und Lagarde', in Ernst Jäckh (ed.), *Politische Flugschriften: Der deutsche Krieg*, no. 22 (Stuttgart: Deutsche Verlagsanstalt, 1917).
69. See also H. Rumpf, 'Mitteleuropa: Zur Geschichte und Deutung eines politischen Begriffs', p. 513.
70. This roll-back would fulfil the twofold purpose of suppressing Russia while at the same time creating an area for new German settlements.
71. Lagarde, *Deutsche Schriften*, p. 83.
72. For a more detailed account of Lagarde's influence see Meyer, *Mitteleuropa in German Thought and Action*, pp. 32–3.
73. For example, when the first combined edition of his 'Schriften' appeared in 1886 he sent copies to the Emperor, Bismarck, and several Prussian deputies, with no apparent effect or response.
74. Meyer, *Mitteleuropa in German Thought and Action.*
75. These three Associations did not explicitly construct their 'own' Mitteleuropa concepts but are listed here, since they advocated general imperialist ideas of which Mitteleuropa was one. In terms of continental imperialist plans, e.g., Mitteleuropa plans, they largely followed the demands voiced by the All-German Association.
76. See Baumgart, *Deutschland im Zeitalter des Imperialismus*, p. 166.
77. Ibid., p. 167.
78. Fritz Fischer, *Krieg der Illusionen* (Düsseldorf: Droste Verlag, 1969), p. 29. For a full account of the Association's 1895 programme and vision see Ernst Hasse, *Großdeutschland und Mitteleuropa um das Jahr 1950: Von einem Alldeutschen* (Berlin: Verlag Thormann et Goetsch, 1895). Hasse, a deputy in the German Parliament for the National-Liberal Party in 1895, described the hypothetical geopolitical development of Europe for the next fifty-five years.

79. Quoted in Fritz Fischer, *Griff nach der Weltmacht*, p. 47.
80. See Baumgart, *Deutschland im Zeitalter des Imperialismus*, p. 167.
81. Ernst Hasse, *Deutsche Politik, II, Deutsche Grenzpolitik* (Munich: J. F. Lehmann, 1905), pp. 8, 162–7 (emphasis added); quoted in Meyer, *Mitteleuropa in German Thought and Action*, p. 53.
82. For example, see the works of the historians Georg von Below and Karl Lamprecht, the zoologist Ernst Haeckel, and the geographer Friedrich Ratzel. Among the most prominent members was Max Weber, who soon left the Association. The famous quotation from his speech in 1895 exemplifies the extent to which young intellectuals had absorbed the imperialist notions of the time. Weber wrote: 'We have to comprehend that Germany's unification was a youthful escapade that the nation undertook in its old days. However, it should have avoided the costs, if it [unification] was the end rather than the beginning of Germany's world-power politics' (quoted in Dann: *Nation und Nationalismus in Deutschland*, p. 204). Finally, among the politicians and members of parliament, Gustav Stresemann was also a member of the 'Verband' until 1918. Contrary to wide belief, there were hardly any representatives of industry among the members (at least not until well into the war). Their influence was indirect, through economically oriented groups that attempted to influence German politics.
83. Fritz Fischer has pointed out that Caprivi oriented Germany's foreign policy more along Mitteleuropa lines, in so far as he tried to strengthen German relations with Austria and Turkey. Furthermore, he wanted to create a Central European customs bloc (which eventually failed) with Austria, Italy, Romania and Switzerland, excluding and directed against Russia. Caprivi's Mitteleuropa policy was based on his aversion to Russia rather than on a genuine interest in Central Europe. For Caprivi as well as Bismarck and Bethmann-Hollweg, Mitteleuropa was a means for securing the German–Prussian position at a historic crossroads. For Caprivi's Mitteleuropa orientation see Fischer, *Krieg der Illusionen*, especially ch. 9. After Bismarck's fall in 1896, Germany's position towards Mitteleuropa changed once again under its new Chancellor, von Hohenlohe, who was supposedly a friend of Russia.
84. The most obvious example is the Second Morocco Crisis of 1909, in which the Staatssekretär, Alfred von Kiderlen-Wächter, basically adopted the programme of the All-Germans. For a detailed account of the crisis as well as the relationship between the Association and Kiderlen-Wächter, see Fischer, *Krieg der Illusionen*, p. 118.
85. The most substantial demand of the Pan-Germans was unification with Austria as the second German heartland. The ongoing negotiations in the 1890s concerning the German–Austrian customs union were of central interest for the Association, which did not satisfy the Pan-Germans, who opted for unification. Here the Austrian section of the Association, under Georg Ritter von Schönerer, was even more radical in its demands. These were formulated in the so-called Linzer Programme. For the Austrian Pan-German section see Meyer, *Mitteleuropa in German Thought and Action*, pp. 39–43. For the plans on the customs union see Böhme, *Deutschlands Weg zur Großmacht*, p. 603; Rainer Eisfeld, *Mitteleuropa – Paneuropa. Der hegemoniale und der föderale Integrationsansatz im Zeichen der 'vierten Weltmacht'* (Bonn: Verlag

Europa Union, 1980), pp. 17–22; and Carl von Kresz, 'Die Bestrebungen nach einer Mitteleuropäischen Zollunion' (Heidelberg: dissertation, 1907), pp. 26–58.

86. Schönerer and his ideology also had a strong impact on the young Austrian Adolf Hitler, who explicitly mentions this in his *Mein Kampf*. See Hitler, *Mein Kampf* (New York: Reynal & Hitchock, 1940), pp. 85–162.
87. Around the turn of the century there was general frustration on the part of the Austrian-Germans concerning the declining interest in their problems on the part of the Reich-Germans. The latter were in fact quite satisfied with the 1871 Reich, and found new opportunities for their 'cultural missionary zeal' abroad (Meyer, *Mitteleuropa in German Thought and Action*, p. 50). In fact, several Reich-German associations, like the 'Allgemeiner deutscher Schulverein', which was founded to promote the establishment of German schools in Mitteleuropa as a base and haven of German culture, reoriented themselves in the second decade of the twentieth century towards overseas colonies. The 'Schulverein', for example, changed its name to 'Verein für das Deutschtum im Ausland'. The young Hermann Ullmann, later a Mitteleuropa enthusiast and advocate of the Bohemian-Germans' cause, succinctly described the Austrian-Germans' frustration when he wrote in 1914: 'How can we make the Reich-Germans understand us?' (quoted in Meyer, *Mitteleuropa in German Thought and Action*, p. 51).
88. In 1870 there were about twelve larger associations for industry and commerce, whereas in 1908 there were already 500 industrial interest groups. See Baumgart, *Deutschland im Zeitalter des Imperialismus*, p. 169.
89. For detailed figures, see Kennedy, *Rise and Fall of the Great Powers*, ch. 5.
90. For a detailed account of the 'Wirtschaftsverein' see the publication of one of its founders, Julius Wolf, *Materialien betreffend den mitteleuropäischen Wirtschaftsverein* (Berlin: Georg Reimer Verlag, 1904; 2nd edn).
91. See Baumgart, *Deutschland im Zeitalter des Imperialismus*, p. 171, for detailed numbers.
92. The most obvious indication of the dominance of heavy industry in the Verband is the fact that between 1893 and 1911 the Verband's leadership and that of the 'Association of German Iron and Steel Producers' were virtually identical.
93. After the defeat in the parliamentary election in 1910, the Hansabund demanded that the Socialist Party be incorporated into the system of parliamentary responsibility in order to create an effective government. This position was unacceptable to the Centralverband, which rejected any cooperation with the labour unions or the labour movement in general. The Verband's departure from politics weakened the Hansabund significantly and fragmented the political situation in Germany even more. See Baumgart, *Deutschland im Zeitalter des Imperialismus*, p. 172.
94. See Fritz Blaich, *Staat und Verbände in Deutschland zwischen 1871 und 1945* (Wiesbaden: Franz Steiner Verlag, 1979).
95. Ibid., p. 155.
96. Gustav Schmoller was a Reich-German economist and the founder of modern German economic history. His main works are the so-called *Schmollers Jahrbücher* [*Schmollers Jahrbuch für Gesetzgebung, Verwaltung und Volkswirtschaft im Deutschen Reiche* (Berlin: Duncker & Humblot, 1877–1891)],

published consecutively since 1877. In addition to Schmoller there was the economist Albert Schäffle, who was an advocate of Mitteleuropa and a supporter of the Wirtschaftverein. For Schäffle's work see Fischer, *Krieg der Illusionen*, pp. 25–8.

97. See R. Kaufmann, 'Der mitteleuropäische Zollverein', *Zeitschrift für die gesamte Staatswissenschaft*, 42 (1886): 530–84.
98. Gustav Schmoller, *Schmollers Jahrbuch*, vol. 15, 1890, p. 281.
99. The original Verein was established in 1904 in Germany. Soon thereafter, it became clear that groups in Germany's neighbouring states promoted the same goals. Thus the Verein expanded to Hungary (April 1905), Austria (December 1904), and Belgium (June 1909), exerting concerted pressure on the government in order to bring about economic harmonization. See Weimer, *Mitteleuropa als politisches Ordnungskonzept?*, p. 65.
100. Wolf, *Materialien betreffend den Mitteleuropäischen Wirtschaftsverein*, pp. 7–8.
101. The Verein deliberately kept its distance from the Pan-Germans, since it considered the latter to be too loud and politically too radical, hence counterproductive to an economic Mitteleuropa. For a good account of the influence of pressure groups and the relations among them see G. Schulz, 'Über Entstehung und Formen von Interessengruppen in Deutschland seit Beginn der Industrialisierung', in *Politische Vierteljahresschrift*, 2 (1961): 124–54; and T. Nipperdey, 'Interessenverbände und Parteien vor dem 1. Weltkrieg', ibid., pp. 262–80.
102. Meyer, *Mitteleuropa in German Thought and Action*, p. 64.
103. See Weimer, *Mitteleuropa als politisches Ordnungskonzept?*, p. 64.
104. Meyer, *Mitteleuropa in German Thought and Action*, p. 65.
105. Ibid., p. 64.

Notes to Chapter 4: The Imperial 'Mitteleuropa', 1914–1945

1. See Meyer, *Mitteleuropa in German Thought and Action 1815–1945* (The Hague: Martinus Nijhoff, 1955), p. 109.
2. As Christian Weimer has pointed out, during the First World War Mitteleuropa eventually failed because of the contradiction between the demand for an extended nation-state and the necessity to overcome such a nation-state in favour of a federal system. See Christian Weimer, *Mitteleuropa als politisches Ordnungskonzept?* (Würzburg: Universität Regensburg, 1992), p. 70.
3. Egbert Jahn, *Europa, Osteuropa und Mitteleuropa* (Frankfurt: Forschungsbericht 1/89 der Hessischen Stiftung Friedens- und Konfliktforschung, 1989), p. 425.
4. Of course, this is also true for Germany's Central European neighbours. However, as this work will show, the memory of the Central European states is somewhat longer than the Germans'. When writing about Mitteleuropa, several authors reach back to the time prior to 1914 to find similar concepts that link up with their Mitteleuropa visions today.
5. That the military was able to secure such an omnipotent position in Germany during the First World War was a result of the military's independence from the government. The officers were under the direct control

of the Emperor, but lacked civil control or subjugation. Prior to 1914, this led repeatedly to domestic conflict over the jurisdiction of the military and civilian units. One example is the Zabern incident in Alsace-Lorraine. In clear violation of the legal code, the military dispersed a mass demonstration and arrested twenty-eight persons. Following civilian protest regarding these arrests, the responsible officers were put on military trial and subsequently acquitted on very questionable grounds. The official legal system stood by, helpless (see Bruno Gebhart, *Handbüch der deutschen Geschichte* (Stuttgart: Union Verlag, 1973) vol. III, p. 306). This principle of a 'Staat im Staat' put the General Staff in an almost untouchable position.

6. See Klaus Hildebrandt, *German Foreign Policy from Bismarck to Adenauer* (Cambridge: Cambridge University Press, 1989), pp. 85–117.
7. In 1905, the Björkö Treaty was signed by Czar Nicolas and Emperor Wilhelm II. It was supposed to establish a continental alliance between Russia and Germany. It was not the first time that advances were made by the Emperor towards his cousin the Czar, but the Björkö Treaty constituted the only attempt that had a slim chance of success. The Treaty was primarily designed to relieve pressure on Germany's Eastern front and to weaken the Franco–Russian alliance. However, the Treaty never came into effect, since it was not only rejected by the German politicians but was incompatible with Russian obligations towards France. See Winfried Baumgart, *Deutschland im Zeitalter des Imperialismus 1890–1914* (Stuttgart: Verlag W. Kohlhammer, 1986), pp. 90–4.
8. For decades, the Habsburg monarchy had been convulsed by nationality conflicts. The 'irredenda', as it was called, had become a permanent condition in various parts of the Empire. By 1914, the situation with the Serbian minority and the agitation of 'The Black Hand' (Die Schwarze Hand) had become most annoying for the monarchy. But, even in the event of a locally limited war against Serbia, Austria wanted and needed German help, which Duke Berchtold, the Austrian Foreign Minister, pointed out to the German envoy in Vienna, Heinrich Leonard von Tschirschky and Bögendorff on 30 June 1914. See Michael Freund, *Die Deutsche Geschichte* (Berlin: Bertelsmann Lexicon Verlag, 1973), pp. 901–3.
9. See Meyer, *Mitteleuropa in German Thought and Action*, pp. 126 and following.
10. Among this group were such individuals as General Friedrich von Bernhardi (see Friedrich von Bernhardi, *Deutschland und der nächste Krieg* (Berlin: Gotta'sche Buchhandlung, 1912); and *Denkwürdigkeiten aus meinem Leben* (Berlin: Gotta'sche Buchhandlung, 1927)), the geographer and geopolitician Ernst Jäckh, the prominent historian Paul Rohrbach, and the former German Secretary of State (1906–07) Count von Tschirschky.
11. The two brochures were 'Von einem Deutschen', *Die Partei der Zukunft* (Leipzig: Dieterichsche Verlagshandlung, 1914), and one that Albert Ritter wrote under the pseudonym Karl von Winterstetten, *Berlin–Baghdad. Neue Ziele mitteleuropäischer Politik* (Munich: Fr. Lehmann's Verlag, 1915). However, these brochures led to his expulsion from the Verband.
12. Prince Ludwig of Bavaria, among others, held this view. See Richard v. Kralik, *Allgemeine Geschichte der neuesten Zeit von 1900–1913*, vol. 5 in *Allgemeince Geschichte der neuesten Zeit von 1815 bis zur Gegenwart*, ed.

Johann Baptist v. Weiss (Graz: Universitäts Buchdruck und Verlag Styria, 1922) for a more detailed account of the Triple Alliance as a Mitteleuropa concept.

13. The latter would become *the* advocate of Mitteleuropa. But while he argued for a moderate version of an economically united Mitteleuropa, he was deliberately misunderstood and misused by his contemporaries inside and outside of Germany. More on Naumann later in this chapter.
14. Jäckh to Naumann in August 1913. 'Jäckh Papers', Yale University, quoted in Meyer, *Mitteleuropa in German Thought and Action*, p. 108.
15. Fritz Fischer, *Krieg der Illusionen: Die deutsche Politik von 1911 bis 1914* (Düsseldorf: Droste Verlag, 1969), p. 641.
16. For a characterization of Bethmann-Hollweg see Baumgart, *Deutschland im Zeitalter des Imperialismus*, p. 106.
17. The Schlieffen Plan was developed by Duke Alfred von Schlieffen, Chief of the General Staff. In contrast to the elder Moltke, his predecessor, Schlieffen believed that the technological development of the previous thirty years would shorten the coming wars, since the decisive battles would be fought early on. Therefore, since 1897 he favoured a quick victory on the western front by way of marching through neutral Belgium (even at the price of engaging Britain in the war), in order to circumvent the French troops. By 1905, the plan was developed in detail and became the official military doctrine in the event of a continental European war.
18. Baumgart, *Deutschland im Zeitalter des Imperialismus*, p. 111.
19. Moltke only remained Chief of the General Staff until 14 September 1914. After losing the 'Marne Battle' and the subsequent failure of the Schlieffen Plan, Moltke was replaced.
20. See F. Fischer, 'Kontinuität des Irrtums. Zum Problem der deutschen Kriegszielpolitik im Ersten Weltkrieg', *Historische Zeitschrift*, 191 (1960): 83–100; also 'Deutsche Kriegsziele. Revolutionierung und Seperatfrieden im Osten 1914–1918', *Historische Zeitschrift*, 188 (1959): 248–310; and H. Herzfeld, 'Zur deutschen Politik im Ersten Weltkrieg. Kontinuität oder permanente Krise?', *Historische Zeitschrift*, 191 (1960): 67–82.
21. The programme was called the 'Hindenburg Programme' because Ludendorff, owing to his age, was technically serving under Hindenburg. This had been the case since his days as supreme commander on the Eastern Front. Hindenburg was placed in this role precisely because he would be willing to let Ludendorff command even though he was Ludendorff's superior. This arrangement, in the long run, paid off for Hindenburg. Eventually, Ludendorff had to take the blame for the loss of the war, and Hindenburg was able to launch his 'second career' as a politician.
22. See Paul Kennedy, *Rise and Fall of the Great Powers* (New York: Vintage Books, 1987), pp. 408ff; and Jochen Schmidt-Liebich, *Deutsche Geschichte in Daten* (Munich: Deutscher Taschenbuch Verlag, 1981), vol. 2.
23. It included the annexation of Luxembourg and parts of France, and in effect declared Belgium a German vassal state. See Fritz Fischer, *Griff nach der Weltmacht* (Dusseldorf: Droste Verlag, 1961), pp. 405ff.
24. Fischer, *Krieg der Illusionen*, p. 641.
25. See Alfred Kruck, *Die Geschichte des Alldeutschen Verbandes 1890–1939* (Wiesbaden: Franz Steiner Verlag, 1954). The Claß-Program was published in

1917 under the title *Zum deutschen Kriegsziel: eine Flugschrift* (Munich: Lehmann, 1917). See also Fischer, *Griff nach der Weltmacht*, pp. 113–14.

26. See Deutsches Zentralarchiv Potsdam, Reichskanzler, Großes Hauptquartier, Stammakte 21, Nr. 2476.
27. Ibid.
28. See Fischer, *Griff nach der Weltmacht*, p. 109.
29. Ibid.
30. Together with the Disconto-Society, the German Bank was the largest and most influential financial institution.
31. See Ulrich Cartarius (ed.), *Deutschland im Ersten Weltkrieg* (Munich: Deutscher Taschenbuch Verlag, 1982).
32. Quoted in Fischer, *Griff nach der Weltmacht*, pp. 110–11.
33. Rathenau was president of the electrical company AEG, and one of the leading figures in German business. Since August 1914, he had also been head of the War Resource Department (Kriegs-Rohstoff-Abteilung) in the War Ministry. Rathenau, in particular, had pushed the Chancellor to adopt an expansive Mitteleuropa concept. See E. Kollmann, 'Walther Rathenau and German Foreign Policy', 1 *Journal of Modern History*, 24 (1952): 127–42.
34. For a detailed account see also Fischer, *Griff nach der Weltmacht*, pp. 110–13.
35. See also Fischer, *Krieg der Illusionen*, pp. 740–74.
36. Quoted in Fischer, *Griff nach der Weltmacht*, p. 113.
37. See Fischer, 'Kontinuität des Irrtums. Zum Problem der deutschen Kriegszielpolitik im Ersten Weltkrieg', p. 94.
38. See W. Conze, 'Nationalstaat oder Mitteleuropa? Die Deutschen des Reichs und die Nationalitätenfragen Ostmitteleuropas im ersten Weltkrieg', in Werner Conze, *Deutschland und Europa*, pp. 201–32.
39. See P. R. Sweet, 'Leaders and Policies, Germany in the Winter of 1914/15', *Journal of Central European Affairs*, 16 (October 1956): 229–52.
40. The commercial societies' petition regarding the war aims in March 1915 has to be seen in connection with the government's ban on publicly discussing war aims. The societies combined their war aims petition with a petition on a public discussion of Germany's war goals. Knowing the public to be on their side, the societies hoped that a public discussion would give their demands more weight.
41. Aside from the Centralverband and the Bund, the Bund of Farmers, German Farmers' Union, Reichs German Middle Class and the Christian German Farmers' Union supported the petition.
42. Fischer, *Griff nach der Weltmacht*, p. 195.
43. Even though he was in agreement with the government regarding the ban on a public war-aim discussion, Naumann entered such a debate by issuing a memorandum to the government in November 1914 with the title 'What will become of Belgium?' See Friedrich Naumann, *Werke* (Opladen: Westdeutscher Verlag, 1964), vol. 4, pp. 446–9.
44. Although the German version is used primarily, here both the English and German editions are employed. Throughout, the particular version employed is indicated. Friedrich Naumann, *Mitteleuropa* (Berlin: Georg Reimer, 1916); *Central Europe* (London: P. S. King, 1917). Naumann, at the time, was a

member of parliament for the Liberal Party. For an extensive biography of Naumann see Theodor Heuß, *Friedrich Naumann. Der Mann, das Werk, die Zeit* (Stuttgart: Deutsche Verlagsanstalt, 1949).

45. Wolfgang Schieder, in the preface to Naumann's *Werke*, vol. 4, p. 375.
46. These thoughts clearly show the impact that List's writings had on Naumann. See Meyer, *Mitteleuropa in German Thought and Action*, p. 195.
47. Naumann, *Mitteleuropa*, p. 76.
48. Meyer, *Mittelturopa in German Thought and Action*, p. 199.
49. See R. Nürnberger, 'Imperialismus, Sozialismus und Christentum bei Friedrich Naumann', *Historische Zeitschrift*, 170 (1950): 525–48.
50. Naumann, *Werke*, vol. 2, p. 267.
51. See E. Eppler, 'Liberale und soziale Demokratie. Zum politischen Erbe Friedrich Naumanns', 30 *Die Neue Gesellschaft/Frankfurter Hefte*, 7 (1983): 628–37.
52. In arguing here for a corporatist state, Naumann, as in many other instances, was open to future adaptation and misuse by Hitler and others. For his view on national power and identity see W. O. Shanahan, 'Friedrich Naumann: A German View of Power and Nationalism', in Edward M. Earle, *Nationalism and Internationalism. Essays inscribed to Carlton J. H. Hayes* (New York: Columbia University Press, 1951), pp. 353–98.
53. Bethmann-Hollweg did not acknowledge the reception of the book before October 1916, and then did so only by means of a rather informal note. See Peter Theiner, *Sozialer Liberalismus und deutsche Weltpolitik. Friedrich Naumann im Wilhelminischen Deutschland* (Baden-Baden: Nomos, 1983). However, as indicated earlier, Naumann's work was published in France, Italy, Switzerland, Britain, and the US as early as 1916. The pan-German press reported in 1916 that Britain had given copies of the book to German prisoners of war, as anti-German propaganda (See Meyer, *Mitteleuropa in German Thought and Action*, p. 215). Whether or not this particular story is true, it is clear that, by mid-1916, high political circles in the Entente were convinced that Mitteleuropa had been a major objective for Germany when it started the war. As already stated, in Chapter 1, this thinking was one of the reasons for the United States' entry into the war in 1917. Therefore, it can be stated that, while Naumann's book had only a limited effect on the German government, it was perceived by Germany's enemies as a sort of semi-official revelation of Germany's war aims. To this extent, it had a significant effect on the Entente's policy. (See Weimer, *Mitteleuropa als politisches Ordnungskonzept?*, pp. 104–12; and Meyer, *Mitteleuropa in German Thought and Action*, pp. 215–17.)
54. For a detailed account of the military, economic and constitutional aspects of Naumann's *Mitteleuropa*, see Weimer, *Mitteleuropa als politisches Ordnungskonzept?*, pp. 82–97.
55. Formally, Falckenhayn had to resign as a result of Romania's entering the war. The truth is that he had to resign because of his political differences with the Chancellor. This is probably the last example during the war in which politicians trumped the military. Only a year later Bethmann-Hollweg had to go because he opposed the duo, Hindenburg–Ludendorff. See Fischer, *Griff nach der Weltmacht*, pp. 300–3.

56. Ibid., p. 403.
57. Ibid., pp. 820–56.
58. Meyer, *Mitteleuropa in German Thought and Action*, p. 291. Among the 'million men' was Hitler, whose vision of a 'gesamtdeutsches' Reich would shape German politics after 1933.
59. See Walter Görlitz (ed.), *Regierte der Kaiser? Kriegstagebücher, Aufzeichnungen und Briefe des Chefs des Marine-Kabinetts, Admiral Alexander von Müller, 1914–1918* (Göttingen: Musterschmidt, 1959), p. 421.
60. Michael Freund, *Deutsche Geschichte*, p. 1071.
61. For the factor of continuity regarding Mitteleuropa, see R. Berndt, 'Wirtschaftliche Mitteleuropapläne des Deutschen Imperialismus', in Gilbert Ziebura, *Grundfragen der Deutschen Aussenpolitik seit 1871* (Darmstadt: Wissenschaftliche Buchgesellschaft, 1975), pp. 305–36.
62. See K. D. Bracher, 'Demokratie und Machtergreifung: Der Weg zum 30. Januar 1933', in Karl Dietrich Bracher, Manfred Funke and Hans-Adolf Jacobsen, *Nationalsozialistische Diktatur 1933–1945. Eine Bilanz*, Schriftenreihe der Bundeszentrale für politische Bildung no. 192 (Bonn: 1983), p. 31 and following. The fragmentation of Central Europe into independent nation-states, according to Reinhard Frommelt, was only the end and highpoint of 'the pre-war tendency to dissolve supra-national entities such as the Habsburg or Osman Empire . . . that was guided by the principle of self-determination' (see Frommelt, *Paneuropa oder Mitteleuropa*, p. 7). However, this particularization was perceived in Germany partly as a chance to revive Großdeutsch concepts of the pre-Bismarck era.

    As a matter of fact, the newly established system of nation-states in Central Europe lent itself to German revisionist demands. The system was implemented hastily and half-heartedly by the victors. The borders were drawn rather randomly in various instances and the hypocritical use of ethnicity in the new democracies stirred the unrest and dissatisfaction of the (German) minorities in the new states and fed the call for revision among the Reich Germans.
63. See Andreas Hillgruber, *Die gescheiterte Großmacht: Eine Skizze des deutschen Reiches 1871–1945* (Düsseldorf: Droste Verlag, 1980), pp. 63–5.
64. Friedrich Meinecke's review of Bismarck's *Gedanken und Erinnerungen* (Stuttgart: Cotta, 1898), in *Historische Zeitschrift*, 82 (1899): 282–95, on p. 287; see also Friedrich Meinecke, *Werke*, vol. 6: *Ausgewählter Briefwechsel* (Stuttgart: Koehler, 1962), correspondence with Eugen Schiffer.
65. In *Deutsche Arbeit*, December 1918.
66. *Sozialistische Monatshefte* (1918): 993–1001; 1115–22.
67. Meyer, *Mitteleuropa in German Thought and Action*, pp. 293–5. For the view of Anschluß as a limitation of Mitteleuropa, see Heinrich Kanner, *Der mitteleuropäische Staatenbund. Ein Vorschlag zum Frieden* (Vienna: Braumüller, 1925); or Friedrich Funder, *Vom Gestern ins Heute. Aus dem Kaiserreich in die Republik* (Vienna: Herold Verlag, 1952).
68. Meyer, *Mitteleuropa in German Thought and Action*, p. 295.
69. For the survival of the Anschluß demand among the Reich-Germans, despite the Allies' intervention to forbid a public debate after 1920, see Friedrich Lange [Adriaticus], *Deutschlands gerechte Grenzen* (Berlin: Dietrich Reimer Verlag, 1924).

70. By 1926, however, Hitler's Nazi Party had revived großdeutsch plans again, but with different connotations and overtones from the ones in 1918.
71. In fact, the term 'gesamtdeutsch' (here translated as pan-German) was newly created after the First World War, in order to avoid 'alldeutsch' and its negative connotation.
72. Gustav Stresemann, *Reden und Schriften. Politik, Geschichte, Literatur 1897–1926* (Dresden: Karl Reissner Verlag, 1926), vol. 1, p. 237.
73. For a brief summary of the approaches towards a European union in the inter-war years see the series in *Europa Archiv*, 17 (1962) by Carl H. Pegg, 'Der Gedanke der europäischen Einigung während des Ersten Weltkrieges'; Carl H. Pegg, 'Vorstellungen und Pläne der Befürworter eines europäischen Staatenbundes in den Jahren 1925–1930'; Carl H. Pegg, 'Die wachsende Bedeutung der europäischen Einigungsbewegung in den zwanziger Jahren'.
74. See Weimer, *Mitteleuropa als politisches Ordnungskonzept?*, p. 121. There were also opponents to this interpretation of the war. The most prominent was Richard N. Coudenhove-Kalergi and his works *Kampf um Paneuropa*, vols 1–3 (Vienna: Braumüller, 1925–8). Coudenhove's vision is compared and contrasted with the pan-German vision in Frommelt, *Paneuropa oder Mitteleuropa?*.
75. Some of the organizations were the 'Ostmarken' societies, which concerned themselves with Silesia and East Prussia; the Verein for German folklore in foreign countries (Verein für das Deutschtum im Ausland); and the school societies (Schulgruppen).
76. For a summary of this period's publications, see P. Sweet, 'Recent German Literature on Mitteleuropa', *Journal of Central European Affairs*, 3 (1943): 1–24.
77. Meyer, *Mitteleuropa in German Thought and Action*, p. 299.
78. See Sweet, 'Recent German Literature', pp. 18–20.
79. Martin Spahn, in *Volk und Reich* (1925), quoted in Sweet, 'Recent German Literature', p. 3.
80. Ibid., p. 5.
81. Ibid., pp. 22–3.
82. See Friedrich Kleinwächter and Heinz von Paller, *Die Anschlußfrage in ihrer kulturellen, politischen und wirtschaftlichen Bedeutung* (Vienna: Braumüller, 1930).
83. Berndt, 'Wirtschaftliche Mitteleuropapläne des deutschen Imperialismus', p. 309.
84. Coudenhove's main works are cited above. This work does not deal with the Pan-Europe idea in detail because it lies beyond the scope of the paper. Pan-Europe basically suggested a confederate system in which all European powers would be integrated, much like the European Community after the Second World War. France and Germany were to be the keystone and heart of this system.
85. Richard Coudenhove-Kalergi, *Eine Idee erobert Europa: Meine Lebenserinnerungen* (Vienna: Desch, 1958), p. 159.
86. The Langnam Scociety was an economic group for the advancement of the common interests of the Rhineland and Westfalia, Germany's two heavy-industry states.

87. Berndt, 'Wirtschaftliche Mitteleuropapläne', p. 310.
88. See Frommelt, *Paneuropa oder Mitteleuropa?*, p. 23. The Hungarian economist Elemér Hantos tried to instrumentalize the Wirtschaftstag in order to create a union among Poland, Czechoslovakia, Austria, Hungary, Romania and Yugoslavia, while explicitly excluding Germany and France. Germany firmly rejected the idea since it was afraid that France could dominate this organization by way of the 'Little Entente'.
89. The individual institutes worked in specialized areas, for example, in Vienna on questions of currency and transportation problems, and in Budapest on agrarian questions.
90. Berndt, 'Wirtschaftliche Mitteleuropapläne', p. 321.
91. In fact, by 1930–31 Julius Wolf offered to re-establish the Wirtschaftsverein. However, the German foreign ministry, because of the Verein's past, decided that the Wirtschaftstag was the better tool for Germany's expansionist aspirations.
92. This is only true for the German side of the organization, since Hantos continuously wanted to limit the Germans' influence if not exclude them altogether.
93. Cited in Berndt, 'Wirtschaftliche Mitteleuropapläne', pp. 325–6.
94. Ibid., p. 327.
95. Subsequently, on 20 March 1931, Austria and Germany declared their intention to form a customs union.
96. It contained representatives of the heavy industries, the coal mining cartel of the Ruhr–Rhine region, the electro-industry, cigarette manufacturers, fabric and food industries, the major banks, and the influential IG Farben.
97. Berndt, 'Wirtschaftliche Mitteleuropapläne'.
98. See Frommelt, *Paneuropa oder Mitteleuropa?*, pp. 80–5.
99. Hillgruber, *Die gescheiterte Großmacht*, p. 73.
100. Ibid.
101. This is certainly not an attempt to lay out the Nazi ideology in *toto*. But these two aspects of it are most relevant to this work. Others, such as anti-semitism or anti-communism are of less interest here. To identify a clear Mitteleuropa concept during the Nazi regime is almost impossible. As with most political and ideological questions, Hitler also used and abused the idea of Mitteleuropa. In general, one can say that Hitler's ideological framework did not contain anything original or genuinely new. Mostly, it was a conglomeration of conservative, reactionary, social-Darwinist, and fascist thoughts, stirred together in a new 'revolutionary' fashion. (See H. James, *A German Identity 1770–1990*, New York: Routledge, 1989, pp. 136–61.) By mixing the economic and cultural aspects of Mitteleuropa with racial, gesamtdeutsch, and anti-communist crusade facets, he watered the term down to the point where it became a hollow propaganda phrase. Therefore, this work only briefly sketches the main parts of what may be called Hitler's Mitteleuropa.
102. Weimer, *Mitteleuropa als politisches Ordnungskonzept?*, pp. 134–5.
103. For the aspect of 'Volk' as a political ideology, see Kurt Sontheimer, *Antidemokratisches Denken in der Weimarer Republik. Die politischen Ideen des deutschen Nationalismus zwischen 1918 und 1933* (Munich: DTB, 1978).
104. See Gerhard Schulz, *Deutschland seit dem Ersten Weltkrieg 1918–1945*, 2nd

edn, Deutsche Geschichte, vol. 10, ed. Joachim Leuschner (Göttingen: Vandenhoeck und Ruprecht, 1982).

105. Moeller van den Bruck was a well-known nationalist political scientist and ideologue who founded the 'Nationale Hochschule für Politik', later renamed the 'Deutsche Hochschule für Politik', the only institute (aside from the geopolitical institute of Karl Haushofer) that pursued political science, although in a very tendentious form. See R. Eisfeld, '"Nationale" Politikwissenschaft von der Weimarer Republik zum Dritten Reich', 2 *Politische Vierteljahresschrift*, 31 (1990): 238–64.
106. Weimer, *Mitteleuropa als politisches Ordnungskonzept?*, p. 133.
107. Ibid., p. 133.
108. Wilhelm Schüssler, *Mitteleuropas Untergang und Wiedergeburt* (Berlin: Deutsche Verlags Anstalt, 1919), pp. 8–9.
109. Heinrich von Srbik, *Mitteleuropa. Das Problem und die Versuche seiner Lösung in der deutschen Geschichte* (Weimar: Hermann Böhlau, 1937), p. 16.
110. For a critical evaluation of the tendentious interpretation of the Reich idea and its relevance for Mitteleuropa concepts, see G. Ritter, 'Die Fälschung des deutschen Geschichtsbildes im Hitlerreich', 4 *Deutsche Rundschau*, 70 (1947): 11–20.
111. For a summary of these ideas see Geoffray Parker, *Western Political Thought in the 20th Century* (New York: St Martin's Press, 1985); Kjellén's main work is *Der Staat als Lebensform* (Leipzig: Hirtzel, 1917).
112. See Haushofer's work, *Weltpolitik von heute* (Berlin: Verlag- und Vertriebsgesellschaft, 1934).
113. Dan Diner, quoted in Weimer, *Mitteleuropa als politisches Ordnungskonzept?*, p. 135.
114. Heinz Brauweiler, *Berufstand und Staat* (Berlin: Ring Verlag, 1925), p. 249.
115. In order not to be misunderstood, the German Monroe Doctrine was not seriously pursued by Hitler. It was meant rather to disguise his true political motives and goals. For Hitler, 'Europe' or 'Mitteleuropa' was not a geographically or culturally defined term but rather an area defined by 'bloodlines' and 'racial value' (Weimer, *Mitteleuropa als politisches Ordnungskonzept?*, p. 141). However, it is as close as one can get to a Mitteleuropa conception between 1933 and 1941. Hitler's 'rassisch' motivated rage, which he pursued after 1939, his idea of a new European order organized according to his racial convictions, cannot be subsumed under the term 'Mitteleuropa'.
116. See Helmut Rumpf's essay 'Mitteleuropa. Zur Geschichte und Deutung eines politischen Begriffs', *Historische Zeitschrift*, 165 (1942): 510–27, in which he proclaimed that the term 'Mitteleuropa' (in 1942) had given way to the Großraum idea.
117. This conception of five world empires was the 'official' version until the beginning of the war and was intended to ease Great Britain's and Russia's worries. In the long run, only three empires would remain: Germany, the US and Japan.
118. For a legal discussion of why Hitler's analogy was false, see Lothar Gruchmann, *Nationalsozialistische Großraumordnung. Die Konstruktion eine 'deutschen Monroe-Doktrin'*, Schriftenreihe der Vierteljahreshefte für Zeitgeschichte, 4 (Stuttgart: Deutsche Verlagsanstalt, 1962), ch. IV.

119. See Gruchmann, *Nationalsozialistische Großraumordnung*, pp. 32–51.
120. See his main work in this area, Carl Schmitt, *Völkerrechtliche Großraumordnung und Interventionsverbot raumfremder Mächte. Ein Beitrag zum Reichsbegriff im Völkerrecht* (Berlin: Deutscher Rechtsverlag, 1939).
121. *Völkischer Beobachter*, 119 (29 April 1939): 5.
122. As expressed by Ribbentrop in a talk with the American Under-secretary of State, Sumner Welles, on 1 March 1940.
123. This view was firmly rejected by the racially oriented faction under Hitler, which would define the Großraum through Blut rather than Boden. The discussion among the various factions in the foreign ministry and the shadow ministry under von Ribbentrop contributed little to the theoretical development of the Hitler regime's Mitteleuropa foreign policy and are therefore disregarded here.
124. The Monroe Doctrine, Schmitt argues, united the area under the idea of independence from the European system. See Gruchmann, *Nationalsozialistische Großraumordnung*, p. 22.
125. Carl Schmitt, *Völkerrechtliche Großraumordnung mit Interventionsverbot für raumfremde Mächte*, p. 35.
126. Ibid., p. 45.
127. See Gruchmann, *Nationalsozialistische Großraumordnung*, ch. III.
128. Ibid., pp. 47 and following.

Notes to Chapter 5: 'Mitteleuropa' in the Adenauer Era, 1944–1963

1. Because of this *junctim* between the German and subsequent Central European division, this chapter in large part deals with the German question or 'Deutschlandpolitik'. However, after the Second World War, Deutschlandpolitik remained intertwined with Mitteleuropa.
2. The Goerdeler group basically came into existence in 1937, when Goerdeler resigned as mayor of Lübeck because of the decision to remove a bust of the (Jewish) composer Mendelssohn from the 'Gewandthaus'. The Kreisau Circle was largely comprised of former social democratic members of the Reichstag, such as Julius Leber. Helmut James von Moltke turned away from the Nazi ideology in 1939 and joined the group in 1941.

   Both groups operated independently until the offensive against Russia in 1941, whereafter they began to coordinate their efforts. There was also a communist resistance, which is disregarded in this work, since its dependence on Stalin's USSR and ideology make an independent analysis of its foreign-policy ideas impossible.
3. W. Vernohr, 'Das Vermächtnis des Deutschen Widerstands', in Wolfgang Vernohr (ed.), *Ein Deutschland wird es sein* (Erlangen: Straube Verlag, 1990), p. 21. Emphasis in the original. In many respects, Vernohr's book is rather dubious in argumentation and conclusion. However, it correctly points to the continuity between pre-Nazi foreign policy and the German resistance. Also W. Vernohr, 'Deutschlands Mittellage', 17 *Deutschland Archiv*, 8 (1984): 820–29.
4. Klaus Hildebrandt, *German Foreign Policy from Bismarck to Adenauer* (Cambridge, Mass.: Cambridge University Press, 1989), p. 171.

5. When one poses the question concerning what the resistance fought for one has to distinguish between the immediate goal of ending the war and the longer-term perspective of a post-war European order. Only the latter is relevant to this work and is presented here briefly.
6. Hans Rothfels, *Die deutsche Opposition gegen Hitler: Eine Würdigung* (Frankfurt: Fischer, 1969), p. 166.
7. Hildebrandt, *German Foreign Policy*, p. 172.
8. Quoted in Vernohr, 'Das Vermächtnis', p. 34.
9. See Ulrich von Hassel, *Vom anderen Deutschland: Aus den nachgelassenen Tagebüchern 1938–1944* (Zürich: Atlantis-Verlag, 1946), p. 324. The positions of the Goerdeler circle changed somewhat over the years. While, during the 1930s, it still advocated a Germany in the borders of 1914, and a European Großraum with Germany as its 'force for order' (Hildebrandt, *German Foreign Policy*, p. 174), that changed over the course of the war to the preservation of the smaller German Reich.
10. Gerhard Ritter, *Carl Goerdeler und die deutsche Widerstandsbewegung* (Stuttgart: Deutsche Verlags Anstalt, 1956), p. 312; also R. Breyer, 'Carl Goerdeler und die deutsche Ostgrenze', *Zeitschrift für Ostforschung* (1964): 198.
11. Hildebrandt, *German Foreign Policy*, p. 175.
12. Quoted in Wilhelm Ritter von Schramm, *Beck und Goerdeler: Gemeinschaftsdokumente für den Frieden 1941–1944* (Munich: Kindler Verlag, 1965), pp. 98–9.
13. Ritter, *Carl Goerdeler und die deutsche Widerstandsbewegung*, p. 329. These plans were not well received by the Allies. Because of the situation in Germany, they were not able to differentiate clearly between Hitler's Großraum and Goerdeler's suggestions.
14. Basically, they objected to nationalism in general.
15. Quoted in Ger van Roon, *Neuordnung im Widerstand: Der Kreisauer Kreis innerhalb der deutschen Widerstandsbewegung* (Munich: Oldenbourg Verlag, 1967), p. 452.
16. Hildebrandt, *German Foreign Policy*, p. 180.
17. In 1945, post-war Germany faced an entirely new situation. It had ceased to exist as a sovereign state. Therefore, one cannot rightfully speak of German foreign policy until 1949, when the Federal Republic regained a degree of external sovereignty from the Western Allies.
18. Hans-P. Schwarz, *Vom Reich zur Bundesrepublik: Deutschland im Widerstreit der außenpolitischen Konzeptionen in den Jahren der Besatzungsherrschaft 1945–1949* (Munich: Hermann Luchterhand, 1966), p. 18.
19. During the Cold War, some argued that the US, after defeating Germany, should have kept moving eastwards against the Soviet Union. However, since it was doubtful that such an endeavour would have resulted in military success, the US government would have been unable to justify such a military undertaking domestically.
20. Konrad Adenauer, *Erinnerungen 1953–1955* (Stuttgart: Deutsche Verlagsgesellschaft, 1966), vol. 2, p. 183.
21. Terence Prittie, *Konrad Adenauer: Vier Epochen deutscher Geschichte* (Stuttgart: Goverts, Krüger, Stahlberg Verlag, 1971; 2nd edn), pp. 332–6.
22. For that reason, he not only muted the discussion about alternative foreign

policies in his own party but also flatly rejected Stalin's offer of 1952, i.e., the so-called Stalin Note.

23. Helga Haftendorn, 'Adenauer und die europäische Sicherheit', in Dieter Blumenwitz (ed.), *Konrad Adenauer und seine Zeit: Politik und Persönlichkeit des ersten Bundeskanzlers* (Stuttgart: Deutsche Verlagsgesellschaft, 1976), vol. 2, p. 92.
24. Charles W. Thayer, *Die unruhigen Deutschen* (Stuttgart: Alfred Scherz Verlag, 1958), p. 140. See also F. Stern, 'Adenauer and a Crisis in Weimar Democracy', 1 *Political Science Quarterly*, LXXII (March, 1958): 1–23; in general, Arnulf Baring, *Außenpolitik in Adenauers Kanzlerdemokratie: Bonns Beitrag zur EVG* (Munich: R. Oldenbourg Verlag, 1969), pp. 48–61.
25. Adenauer, *Erinnerungen*, vol. 2, pp. 217–22.
26. Kurt Sontheimer, *Die Adenauer Ära: Grundlegung der Bundesrepublik* (Munich: DTV, 1991), p. 164.
27. See Paper of the CDU-Congress, *Deutschland und die Union: Die Berliner Tagung 1946, Reden und Aussprache* (Berlin, 1946), p. 17.
28. See especially the similarity in thinking to Trott von Stolz, earlier in this chapter.
29. Schwarz, *Vom Reich zur Bundesrepublik*, p. 306.
30. For Kaiser's appeal to Prussia see *Neue Zeit*, 13 July 1947.
31. Rainer Zitelmann, *Demokraten für Deutschland: Adenauers Gegner – Streiter für Deutschland* (Frankfurt: Ullstein-Buch, 1993), p. 32.
32. Kaiser's speech of 12 July 1947, in Christian Hacke (ed.), *Jacob Kaiser: Wir haben Brücke zu sein. Reden, Äußerungen und Aufsätze zur Deutschlandpolitik* (Cologne: Verlag Wissenschaft und Politik, 1988), p. 140.
33. See *Neue Zeit*, 17 April 1947.
34. Schwarz, *Vom Reich zur Bundesrepublik*, p. 303.
35. Kaiser defined socialism as the 'living folk tradition' (Volksgemeinschaft), in contrast to dogmatic Marxism. Ibid., p. 304.
36. Kaiser joined the first Adenauer cabinet in 1949 as minister for all-German questions. However, this was more an alibi move for Adenauer than an actual possibility for Kaiser to conduct an alternative policy to Adenauer's West integration. The tensions between the Chancellor and Kaiser became public with the dispute over Germany's accession to the European Council in 1949 and intensified until the Stalin Note in 1952. See A. Doering-Manteuffel, 'Konrad Adenauer – Jakob Kaiser – Gustav Heinemann: Deutschlandpolitische Positionen in der CDU', in Jürgen Weber, *Die Republik der fünfziger Jahre: Adenauers Deutschlandpolitik auf dem Prüfstand* (Munich: Olzog Verlag, 1989), p. 40. For Kaiser's relationship with Adenauer in general, see Zitelmann, *Demokraten für Deutschland*, pp. 24–47.
37. For a positive assessment see Tilmann Mayer, *Jacob Kaiser: Gewerkschafter und Patriot* (Cologne: Bund-Verlag, 1988). For the opposing view see Christian Hacke, *Weltmacht wider Willen: die Außenpolitik der Bundesrepublik Deuschland* (Stuttgart: Klett-Cotta, 1988).
38. See Schwarz, *Vom Reich zur Bundesrepublik*, pp. 481–522.
39. This theory was taken up by the Chancellor of the Grand Coalition, Kurt Georg Kiesinger, while the demand for an all-European security system remained a permanent topic in the SPD in the 1960s and 70s. See below, this chapter.

40. Schwarz, *Vom Reich zur Bundesrepublik.*
41. For Schumacher's anti-communism see Willy Albrecht, *Kurt Schumacher: Reden–Schriften–Korrespondenzen, 1945–1952* (Berlin: Dietz, 1985), pp. 938–53.
42. In Albrecht, *Kurt Schumacher*, p. 968.
43. In Arno Scholz and Günter Oschilewski (eds), *Kurt Schumacher: Reden und Schriften* (Berlin-Grunewald: arani-Verlag, 1962), p. 261.
44. Ibid., p. 379.
45. In Albrecht, *Kurt Schumacher*, p. 911.
46. For example, his demand for a more centralized federalism. The Allies originally wanted a strongly decentralized Germany, to which Schumacher objected. Eventually, the Allies followed Schumacher's suggestions.
47. Arnulf Baring, *Außenpolitik in Adenauers Kanzlerdemokratie* (Munich: Oldenbourg, 1969), pp. 48–75; and Dennis L. Bark and David R. Gress, *History of West Germany*, vol. I: *From Shadow to Substance 1945–1963*; vol. II: *Democracy and its Discontents 1963–1991* (Cambridge, Mass.: Blackwell, 1993), pp. 231–344.
48. While the SPD, especially its Berlin branch, had predicted the closure of the border since the late 1950s, the CDU government had disregarded that as political propaganda.
49. Brandt had in fact warned about such a possibility only a day before the actual closure, on 12 August 1961. Yet, he did not anticipate action so early. See Willy Brandt, *Begegnungen und Einsichten. Die Jahre 1960–1975* (Hamburg: Hoffmann und Campe, 1976), p. 18.
50. Before Brandt launched his 'Ostpolitik', the term did not really exist. For Chancellor Adenauer, there were Eastern politics and then there were German politics, which were intellectually and organizationally two different things, since they were also arranged in two departments in the government. Subsequently, researchers also split into GDR experts and East-European experts, who rarely overlapped. In Brandt's administration the two were joined under the new 'Ostpolitik', dealing with the GDR as part of the East, even though as a special unit. However, this work uses the term 'Ostpolitik' throughout as established during the Brandt era.
51. Peter Bender, *Neue Ostpolitik. Vom Mauerbau bis zum Moskauer Vertrag* (Munich: Deutscher Taschenbuch Verlag, 1986), p. 71.
52. Heinrich Krone, *Aufzeichnungen zur Deutschland- und Ostpolitik 1954–1969*; eds Rudolf Morsey and Konrad Repgen, Adenauer-Studien, vol. III (Mainz: Matthias-Grünewald Verlag, 1974), p. 148.
53. Ibid., p. 202.
54. Brandt, *Begegnungen und Einsichten*, pp. 64–5.
55. Bender, *Neue Ostpolitik*, p. 115.
56. The Doctrine not only isolated Germany in the Western Alliance but also hurt Germany economically since it created an additional hurdle for German exports to the East. That was already evident after Gerhard Schröder had become Foreign Minister in the last Adenauer cabinet. See William E. Griffith, *The Ostpolitik of the Federal Republic of Germany* (Cambridge, Mass.: MIT Press, 1978), p. 121.
57. Especially the latter became increasingly a burden under the new Kennedy administration. The more Adenauer's foreign policy towards Eastern Europe

relied on the US, the more it was jeopardized by a change of foreign-policy orientation within the US, which occurred under Kennedy. From the beginning, the differences between Adenauer and Kennedy were deep, partly as a result of a generational conflict between them.

58. Brandt, *Begegnungen und Einsichten*, p. 19; also Peter Bender, *Neue Ostpolitik*, p. 74. However, even though in the autumn election of 1961, when the CDU lost its absolute majority, the Wall did not strengthen the SPD as much as it had hoped, the CDU still remained the strongest political force. Yet, as Dennis Bark and David Gress point out 'the Berlin Wall crystallized the latent doubts that many West Germans held concerning the wisdom of the Hallstein Doctrine' (Bark, *From Shadow to Substance*, p. 479). Thus, even though the CDU took on the harder anti-Soviet stand, the Wall, in the long run, helped support the opposition's view that unification would not be brought about by Western action.

    After the election of 1961, Adenauer was forced to form a coalition with the FDP (the Liberal Party). As a result, Gerhard Schröder of the FDP became Foreign Minister. He was 'less pro-French, more pro-American, and more pro-activist Ostpolitik' than his predecessor Heinrich von Brentano. 'However, this did not mark the beginning of the new Ostpolitik. The new coalition's foreign policy was little changed.' Griffith, *The Ostpolitik*, p. 94.
59. Indubitably there was movement in Germany's policy towards Eastern Europe under the Erhard government and the Grand Coalition. Nevertheless, it did not constitute a fundamental change with regard to goals and means.
60. Charles W. Thayer, *Die unruhigen Deutschen* (Stuttgart: Alfred Scherz Verlag, 1958), p. 140. See also F. Stern, 'Adenauer and a Crisis in Weimar Democracy', 1 *Political Science Quaterly*, LXXII (March, 1958): 1–23; in general, Baring, *Außenpolitik in Adenauers Kanzlerdemokratie*, pp. 48–61.
61. For that reason this work does not give a summary of Adenauer's Ostpolitik, since it is a policy primarily directed towards the USSR with the singular goal of preventing the international acceptance of the GDR and subsequent German unification. Mitteleuropa, as an area of genuine German interest, did not exist for Adenauer and, therefore, is not relevant to this work.
62. Joachim J. Hesse and Thomas Ellwein, *Das Regierungssystem der Bundesrepublik Deutschland* (Opladen: Westdeutscher Verlag, 1992; 7th edn), p. 180.
63. Brandt, *Begegnungen und Einsichten*, p. 41.
64. Bender, *Neue Ostpolitik*, p. 125.
65. Ibid., p. 123.
66. The original German term was 'Wandel durch Annäherung'. The translation as 'rapprochement' or 'convergence' implies less than the original German term suggests.
67. Bender, *Neue Ostpolitik*, pp. 126–7. Even before the change of government, Berlin started to pursue the new policy in trying to come to terms with East Berlin on the question of lifting travel restrictions, which culminated in the 'travel-agreement' of 1963.
68. Peter Bender, *Die Ostpolitik Willy Brandts oder die Kunst des Selbstverständlichen* (Hamburg: Rowohlt Verlag, 1972), p. 125.
69. Bender, *Neue Ostpolitik*, p. 113.
70. Ibid., pp. 114–15.

71. See Wolfram Hanrieder, *Fragmente der Macht: Die Außenpolitik der Bundesrepublik* (Munich: Piper, 1981), pp. 40–56; also Griffith, *The Ostpolitik*, p. 131.
72. The core parts of the speech were drafted by Zbigniew Brzezinski, then with the Policy Planning Council of the State Department and a future key figure in American East–West relations. Ibid., p. 131.
73. Quoted in Bender, *Die Ostpolitik*, p. 34; translated by Griffith, *The Ostpolitik*, p. 133.
74. Quoted in Bark, *Democracy and its Discontents*, at p. 97.
75. Bundesministerium für gesamtdeutsche Fragen, Bonn (ed.), *Dokumente zur Deutschlandpolitik. 10. Juni 1963: Rede des Präsidenten Kennedy in der 'American University' in Washington* (Frankfurt: Alfred Metzner Verlag, 1978), series IV, vol. 9, pp. 382–8.
76. Griffith, *The Ostpolitik*, p. 134.
77. Brandt, interview in *Welt am Sonntag*, 7 January 1967, p. 3.
78. Bark, *Democracy and its Discontents*, p. 95.
79. Wolfram Hanrieder and Graeme P. Auton, *The Foreign Policies of West Germany, France and Britain* (Englewood Cliffs: Prentice-Hall, 1980), p. 62.
80. In August 1967, Germany opened a trade mission in Prague.
81. Hanrieder and Auton, *Foreign Policies*.
82. Ibid., p. 60.
83. Bark, *Democracy and its Discontents*, p. 40.
84. Kiesinger stated in February 1967 that Germany and the US were two different entities and that their policies and interests might coincide only in some areas. This was perceived as a heavy blow to the US and an attempt to improve Franco-German relations, since France, under de Gaulle, had become increasingly anti-American.
85. Bark, *Democracy and its Discontents*, p. 92.
86. Ibid. The 'traditional' liberals in German politics were true followers of the philosophy of enlightenment. In the Paul's Cathedral Assembly they took the position that individual, and consequently social, freedom for the people was more crucial than national unity without such freedom under a monarchy. The situation for the 'Werteliberale' in the FDP was similar concerning questions of unification and its conditions.
87. This turn brought an end to Erich Mende's chairmanship of the party and the beginning of a generational change within the party. Ibid., p. 94.
88. For a detailed account of the decision-making process leading to Ostpolitik, see Günther Schmid, *Entscheidung in Bonn: Die Entstehung der Ost- und Deutschlandpolitik 1969/1970* (Cologne: Verlag Wissenschaft und Politik, 1979).
89. Griffith, *The Ostpolitik*, p. 112.
90. The Foreign Minister under Adenauer–Erhard, Gerhard Schröder of the FDP, was a flexible Atlanticist, as were Brandt, Erler, and Helmut Schmidt among the SPD leaders. Schmidt remained an Atlanticist, even when the political climate within the SPD changed once more. This position eventually cost him his chancellorship in 1982.

    The inflexible conservatives in the CDU were mostly Catholics from the Rhineland and Bavaria, who were strong supporters of German–French ties and opposed to the American preference for Anglo-Soviet negotiations. German unification had priority and was to be achieved from a position of strength. See Griffith, *The Ostpolitik*, p. 115.

91. Jiri Dienstbier, *Träumen von Europa* (Berlin: Rowohlt, 1991).
92. Dienstbier, an intellectual and writer, was a dissident under the communist regime who was not allowed to publish and worked as a stoker instead. After the dismissal of the communists from power he became Czechoslovakia's Foreign Minister until the partition of the country.
93. Dienstbier, *Träumen von Europa*, Preface.
94. The resolution was actually instigated by Wenzel Jaksch, a Silesian-German within the SPD. See Timothy G. Ash, *Im Namen Europas: Deutschland und der geteilte Kontinent* (Munich: Carl Hanser Verlag, 1993), p. 30.
95. Ibid.
96. Quoted in Wolfram Hanrieder, *Germany, America, Europe: Forty Years of German Foreign Policy* (New Haven: Yale University Press, 1989), p. 195.
97. Timothy Ash points out that 'normalization' in the post-war situation had a very versatile meaning. On the one hand, German relations with their western neighbours, compared with the previous century, were much better than normal. On the other hand, establishing 'normality' with the Warsaw Pact states seemed to be impossible. Helmut Schmidt stated in 1978 that he wanted to achieve 'normalization' with the GDR, as it already existed in German relations with Poland. This demonstrates how widely and fuzzily the term was used.
98. Ash, *Im Namen Europas*, p. 32.
99. Quoted in ibid., p. 33.
100. See Ash, *Im Namen Europas*, pp. 37–9; also, Griffith, *The Ostpolitik*, pp. 228–33. To that extent this analysis seems accurate for all Central European states. The Central European people, in the period between 1949 and 1989, were in a permanent struggle for their independence and identity.
101. The new self-confidence of the SPD/FDP government with respect to Germany's role in international relations was exemplified when Brandt stated in his inaugural speech: 'I see myself as the Chancellor of a liberated, not a defeated, Germany. Our partners in the world will be dealing with a loyal government, but not always an easy one.' (quoted in Ash, *Im Namen Europas*, p. 149). See also Karl D. Bracher, Wolfgang Jäger and Werner Link, *Republik im Wandel 1969–1974: Die Ära Brandt*; vol 5/I of the series *Geschichte der Bundesrepublik Deutschland* (Stuttgart: Deutsche Verlagsanstalt, 1986).
102. Hanrieder, *Germany, America, Europe*, p. 202.
103. The legal difficulties of Germany's pursuit of its interests are not discussed in this work since they are not genuinely relevant. Basically, Germany had to clarify three questions. First, to what extent was Germany a sovereign state or, in other words, what did the phrase 'the Allied responsibility for all-German matters' mean in practical political terms? Secondly, how could the government solve the paradox of maintaining the demand for sole representation, while, at the same time, entering into negotiations with East Berlin? Thirdly, how could Germany accept the status quo without giving up claims to Germany's eastern territories? For a detailed account of these questions and subsequent considerations see Bender,

Neue Ostpolitik, pp. 167–70; Bark, *Democracy*, pp. 151–72; and Griffith, *The Ostpolitik*, pp. 177–81. For an American insider's view on this period see Henry Kissinger, *White House Years* (Boston: Little, Brown, 1979), pp. 502–30.

104. See Peter H. Merkl (ed.), *The Federal Republic at Forty* (New York: New York University Press, 1989), pp. 26–9.
105. Bender, *Neue Ostpolitik*, p. 173.
106. Text in Auswärtige Amt (ed.), *Die Auswärtige Politik der Bundesrepublik Deutschland* (Cologne: Verlag Wissenschaft und Politik, 1972), p. 762. Originally, the USSR wanted to use the term 'inviolable' instead of 'unchangeable'. This was a fine distinction that was generally overlooked in the emotional debate that began in Germany after the treaty was signed.
107. In fact, Brandt had already recognized the GDR in March 1970, when he met Willy Stoph, head of state of the GDR, in Erfurth, East Germany. This was the first visit of a West German official to the GDR and the first talk between the heads of state. In certain respects, the visit received more media attention than the subsequent talks with Moscow. See the special issue of *Der Spiegel*, 13 (1970).
108. See Griffith, *The Ostpolitik*, pp. 185–223.
109. Hanrieder, *Germany, America, Europe*, p. 205.
110. Demographic surveys support this statement. See Elisabeth Noelle-Neumann and Edgar Piel (eds), *Allensbacher Jahrbuch der Demoskopie 1978–1983* (Munich: K. G. Saur, 1983), pp. 595–8; 624–46. Over that period, one can observe a general decline in the acceptance of deterrence and security policies, as well as a growing anti-Americanism. Broken down by age, the surveys show that these tendencies are especially pronounced among the younger generation. For example, the perception of a Soviet threat (until the invasion of Afghanistan) between 1952 and 1980 declined from 66% to 35% (p. 626). Asked whether deterrence is the best security policy, the percentage disagreeing between 1976 and 1982 only rose by 2%, from 23% to 25%. However, when the figures are broken down by age, one sees an increase from 28% to 36% between 1979 and 1982 among 16–29-year-olds and an increase from 22% to 27% among 30–44-year-olds (p. 630).

    Furthermore, in 1961, 18% of the Germans believed that the Americans were hypocritical in defending world peace, and in fact wanted to secure their access to world markets. In 1981 this number rose to 27% (see p. 607). In terms of party affiliation that meant that in 1981, 10% of the CDU, 17% of the SPD, but 46% of the Green voters disagreed with America and its politics. This corresponds with the Green Party's election results and the thesis that overall dissatisfaction would eventually produce a change in voting behaviour. The Greens, as a melting pot for protest movements, have participated in state elections since 1978 with growing success, coming close to the 10% margin in some states, e.g., Hessen (1982), Hamburg (1982), Baden-Württemberg (1984). In federal elections they rose from 1.5% in 1980 to 5.6% only three years later. (Source, Wilhelm P. Bürklin, *Grüne Politik* (Opladen: Westdeutscher Verlag, 1984), appendix, table 1). This shows that dissatisfaction not only grew in the late 1970s and early 1980s, but also became organized.
111. Bark, *Democracy*, p. 118. As Bark states, 'the New Left itself was a disparate

combination of the leaders of published opinion, journalists, intellectuals, and academics' (ibid.). At the end of the 1960s, student revolutionaries joined ranks, thereby increasing the left's basis.

112. After Schmidt became Chancellor in 1972, his critics in the left wing of the SPD started to affiliate themselves with these movements.
113. The student revolt in Western countries in the late 1960s was also an important milestone in the establishment of the 'new left'. However, since this is not a chronology of the development of the intellectual left, the details of this process are omitted.
114. Jahn, *Europa, Osteuropa und Mitteleuropa*, p. 30.
115. Ronald Inglehart, *The Silent Revolution. Changing Values and Political Styles among Western Publics* (Princeton: Princeton University Press, 1977).
116. Egbert Jahn, *Europa, Osteuropa und Mitteleuropa*, Hessische Siftung für Friedens- und Konfliktforschung: Forschungsbericht 1/89 (Frankfurt, 1989), pp. 13–19.
117. For other dimensions, see the following chapter. For a brief summary of the security suggestions of that period and their relevance to Mitteleuropa see Christian Weimer, *Mitteleuropa als politisches Ordnungskonzept?*, pp. 276–88.
118. R. Jaworski, 'Die aktuelle Mitteleuropadiskussion in historischer Perspektive', *Historische Zeitschrift*, 247 (1988): 530.
119. It declined again later, not for political reasons, as it had previously during the Cold War, but for purely economic reasons such as saturated markets. See Bender, *Neue Ostpolitik*, p. 204.
120. Quoted in Bundesministerium für innerdeutsche Fragen, *Texte zur Deutschlandpolitik*, series II, vol. 3 (Bayreuth: Druckhaus Bayreuth, 1976), p. 165.
121. Ulrich Albrecht (ed.), *Europa, Atomwaffenfrei: Vorschläge, Pläne, Perspektiven* (Cologne: Pahl-Rugenstein, 1986), p. 45.
122. From the Germans' perspective this feeling of exclusion went from bad to worse under the Reagan administration. While the German government had had problems with Carter's approach to partnership, Helmut Schmidt and his government felt excluded under Reagan. See Helmut Schmidt, *Menschen und Mächte* (Berlin: Siedler Verlag, 1987); also Peter Merkl, 'The West German Peace Movement', in P. Merkl, *West German Foreign Policy: Dilemmas and Directions* (Chicago: The Chicago Council on Foreign Relations, 1982), pp. 78–89.
123. Bender, *Neue Ostpolitik*, p. 205.
124. Ash, *Im Namen Europas*, p. 457.
125. Ibid., p. 459.
126. Bahr had introduced a strategy paper to the SPD in 1970, in which he called for closer cooperation in Mitteleuropa regarding economic and military matters. He reformulated these ideas in 1980–81 as a member of the so-called Palme Commission of the CSCE. This commission and its widely read 1982 report became the platform for the German peace movement as well as the SPD faction in opposition to Schmidt's governmental politics.

    For a detailed, post-World War Two account of German and Central European initiatives for defence cooperation see Albrecht, *Europa Atomwaffenfrei*, pp. 57–242. For the Palme Report see ibid., pp. 180–5. For a general account of the idea of European detachment see the emotional and angrily written book by Peter Glotz, *Manifest für eine Neue Europäische Linke* (Berlin: Siedler Verlag, 1985), pp. 17–67; also Ash, *Im Namen Europas*, pp. 457–68.

127. M. Croan, 'Dilemmas of Ostpolitik', in Peter H. Merkl, *West German Foreign Policy*, p. 47.
128. For example, the so-called Bülow Paper, which opted for a withdrawal of the superpowers from Mitteleuropa by the year 2000; or Hermann Scheer, *Befreiung von der Bombe. Weltfrieden, europäischer Weg und die Zukunft der Deutschen* (Cologne: Bund Verlag, 1986); Oskar Lafontaine, *Angst vor den Freunden* (Hamburg: Spiegel Verlag, 1983).
129. The term was coined by Peter Bender, one of the original activists who supported the first Ostpolitik.
130. For organizational reasons this chapter separates the military-strategic debate of the 1970s and 1980s from the political and cultural one. However, when the term 'Mitteleuropa' reappeared in the mid-1980s it was by way of cultural concepts in Hungary and Czechoslovakia, which will be dealt with in the next chapter.
131. Bender, *Neue Ostpolitik*, pp. 214–16.
132. P. Glotz, 'Deutsch-böhmische Kleinigkeiten oder Abgerissene Gedanken über Mitteleuropa', *Neue Gesellschaft/Frankfurter Hefte*, 33 (1986): 585.

Notes to Chapter 6: The 'Mitteleuropa' Debate in the Mid-1980s

1. For the literature that sparked an interest among the intellectuals in this area see Chapter 1 of this work.
2. A. Nagorski, 'Are there 3 Europes? The Concept of Mitteleuropa is Staging a Dramatic Comeback', *Newsweek*, 109 (23 March 1987): 12; also A. Nagorski, 'The Rebirth of an Idea', *Newsweek*, 109 (30 March 1987): 38–40.
3. M. Kundera, 'Die Tragödie Zentraleuropas', *Kommune: Forum für Politik und Ökonomie*, 2 (1984): 43–52. This essay was first published in 1983 with the title 'Un occident kidnappé' in the French journal *Le Débat*. Subsequently, it appeared in the *New York Review of Books* before it was published in Germany in 1984. Here the German translation is used since that version inspired the subsequent debate in Germany. For critics of Kundera's view see the summarizing essay by A. Hampel, 'Vermittlung und Ausgleich sind geboten', *Politische Studien*, 36 (1985): 577–81.
4. Kundera, 'Die Tragödie', p. 45. This area is also roughly identical with the former Austrian dual monarchy.
5. The term 'Ordnungsmacht' may be best translated with hegemonic power or influence within a certain area. It provides a framework of formal or informal legal or procedural boundaries common to and binding on all participants in the area.
6. Kundera, 'Die Tragödie', p. 52.
7. Ibid., p. 49.
8. The difference between the Austrian-German influence as a common German bond and Reich-Germany's aspiration towards Germanization has been mentioned previously.
9. Kundera, 'Die Tragödie', p. 46. For a discussion of the role of Russia in

Europe see Christian Weimer, *Mitteleuropa als politisches Ordnungskonzept?*, (Würzburg: Universität Regensburg, 1992), p. 209.

10. This quote is a translation of a short version of Kundera's essay in Erhard Busek and Gerhard Wilfinger, *Aufbruch nach Mitteleuropa. Rekonstruktion eines versunkenen Kontinents* (Vienna: Wiener Journal, 1986), p. 143. This version is partly the better translation, which is why it is used here.
11. F. Bondy, 'Das Phantom Mitteleuropa und die politische Wirklichkeit. Nachdenken über die gemeinsame Kultur zwischen Ost und West', *Frankfurter Allgemeine Zeitung*, 21 December 1985, p. 3.
12. For a comparison of Kundera and Konrád, and specifically a discussion of Konrád's style and approach, see Timothy Garton Ash, *Ein Jahrhundert wird abgewählt. Aus den Zentren Mitteleuropas 1980–1990* (Munich: Hanser, 1990), p. 192.
13. György Konrád, *Antipolitik: Mitteleuropäische Meditationen* (Frankfurt: Luchterhand, 1985), p. 211.
14. Ibid., p. 211.
15. Ibid., p. 92.
16. Ibid., p. 19.
17. For a criticism of Konrád's thesis regarding Yalta as the epochal Fall, see Rudolf Jaworski, 'Die aktuelle Mitteleuropadiskussion in historischer Perspektive', *Historische Zeitschrift*, 247 (1988): 535–7.
18. György Konrád, *Stimmungsbericht* (Frankfurt: Suhrkamp, 1988).
19. Ibid., p. 65.
20. Ibid., p. 71.
21. Erhard Busek and Emil Brix, *Projekt Mitteleuropa* (Vienna: Ueberreuter, 1986); Erhard Busek, 'Besinnung auf Mitteleuropa', *Europäische Rundschau*, 13 (1985): 7–12.
22. E. Busek, 'Versuchsstation für Weltuntergänge – Hoffnung auf eine bessere Zeit?', in Sven Papcke and Werner Weidenfeld, *Traumland Mitteleuropa? Beiträge zur aktuellen Kontroverse* (Darmstadt: Wissenschaftliche Buchgesellschaft, 1988), p. 27.
23. Busek and Brix, *Projekt Mitteleuropa*, p. 94.
24. G. Wilfinger, 'Staatsnation und Kulturnation: Erinnerung an Mitteleuropa', in Busek and Wilfinger, *Aufbruch nach Mitteleuropa*, pp. 151–63.
25. See Günther Grass, *Deutscher Lastenausgleich, wider das dumpfe Einheitsgebot: Reden und Gespräche* (Frankfurt: Luchterhand, 1990).
26. E. Busek, 'Metropole Wien', in Busek and Wilfinger, *Aufbruch nach Mitteleuropa*, p. 9.
27. The 1980s was a decade of relative isolationism for Austria in Europe. This was partly a result of its geopolitical situation, and partly a result of its neutrality and pertinent refusal to join either the EC or NATO. Furthermore, the 1986 election of Kurt Waldheim as President became a burden. Not only was the rather shady figure of Waldheim and his role during the Nazi period a problem, but also Austria's refusal to deal adequately with its Anschluß of 1938 and subsequent role in Hitler's Nazi Germany. Waldheim merely became a symbol of Austria's hollow reiteration of its official version of Austria as Hitler's first victim. This led to a state of relative isolation concerning foreign affairs in the West that resulted in Austria's increased interest in the East, for example, in Mitteleuropa.

28. Jaworski,'Aktuelle Mitteleuropadiskusssion', p. 545. Otto von Habsburg, member of the EC parliament and grandson of the last Emperor, suggested that the constitution could also be a model for a constitution for the EC. He, as well as the Austrian proponents, disregarded in their harmonizing retrospective of Austrian history the 'often murderous hatered among the nationalities' and the 'awful antisemitism' which also formed a prominent part of the Double Monarchy. For a description and discussion of the problems of the K&K Constitution see 'Pankraz: Pankraz, Mitteleuropa und die Mokkazwerge', *Welt*, 22 September 1986.
29. For a short, but critical study of the political role that Mitteleuropa played in the East–West conflict see Z. Mlynar, 'Mitteleuropa im Ost-West-Konflikt', in Universität Innsbruck, *Symposium Mitteleuropa: Spuren der Vergangenheit – Perspektiven der Zukunft*, pp. 65–73.
30. This work has pointed out the importance of the erection of the Wall for Willy Brandt's political thinking and the subsequent development of the Ostpolitik.
31. Karl Schlögel, *Die Mitte liegt ostwärts. Die Deutschen, der verlorene Osten und Mitteleuropa* (Berlin: Siedler Verlag, 1986). Peter Glotz reiterates Schlögel's scheme in P. Glotz, 'Die Alleinherrschaft des Ost-West-Denkens gefährden', *Frankfurter Rundschau*, 25 May 1988.
32. Schlögel, *Die Mitte liegt ostwärts*, p. 7.
33. Nagorski stresses that point in Schlögel's argument. Nagorski, 'Are there 3 Europes?'
34. For a critical discussion of the cultural concept of Mitteleuropa and the establishing of a Mitteleuropa identity, especially concerning its potential results for East–West relations and the relationship of the Central European states with the Soviet Union, see J. Rovan, 'Mitteleuropa gegen Europa', in Papcke and Weidenfeld, *Traumland Mitteleuropa?*, pp. 1–14.
35. See K. Schlögel, 'Die blockierte Vergangenheit. Nachdenken über Mitteleuropa', *Frankfurter Allgemeine Zeitung*, 21 February 1987, Beilage 'Bilder und Zeiten'; K. Schlögel, 'Deutschland: Land der Mitte, Land ohne Mitte', in Rainer Zitelmann, Karlheinz Weißmann and Michael Großheim, *Westbindung: Chancen und Risiken für Deutschland* (Berlin: Propyläen, 1993); P. Glotz, 'Deutsch-böhmische Kleinigkeiten oder Abgerissene Gedanken über Mitteleuropa', *Neue Gesellschaft/Frankfurter Hefte*, 33 (1986): 584–5. For a critical discussion of this approach see F. Bondy, 'Viertraumland Mitteleuropa', in Papcke and Weidenfeld, *Traumland Europa?*, p. 39.
36. Examples of the positive German influence are, for Glotz and Schlögel, the eastward colonization, the history of the Hanse, and the foundation of German universities.
37. The term is used by Schlögel to describe the area in which most concentration camps were established as well as where most victims were rallied. Schlögel, 'Blockierte Vergangenheit'.
38. Glotz, 'Deutsch-böhmische Kleinigkeiten', p. 585.
39. Schlögel argues that, as a result of this 'loss of the East', the western states experienced 'the cutting in half of our perception of neighbourhood'. Schlögel, *Die Mitte liegt ostwärts*, at p. 121.
40. For this aspect of differentiating the Eastern Bloc, see Schlögel, *Die Mitte liegt ostwärts*, pp. 31–8; P. Glotz, 'Die Alleinherrschaft des Ost-West-Denkens

gefährden: Anmerkungen zu einer Idee des mitteleuropäischen Bewußtsein', *Frankfurter Rundschau*, 25 May 1988, p. 14; H. Bütler, 'Stichwort Mitteleuropa: Tatsachen, Ideen, Illusionen', *Neue Züricher Zeitung*, 6 July 1985, p. 43; F. Bondy, 'Das Phantom Mitteleuropa'; A. Khol, 'Mitteleuropa – Gefahren eines politischen Begriffs', in Andreas Khol, Günther Ofner and Alfred Stirnemann, *Österreichisches Jahrbuch für Politik 1986* (Munich: Oldenbourg, 1986), pp. 137–43.

41. Schlögel, *Die Mitte liegt ostwärts*, p. 17. Also Jaworski, 'Aktuelle Mitteleuropadiskussion', pp. 538–45.
42. Schlögel, *Die Mitte liegt ostwärts*, p. 17.
43. Ibid., p. 120.
44. Peter Glotz, *Manifest für eine Neue Europäische Linke* (Berlin: Siedler Verlag, 1985), p. 12. The previous chapter of this paper pointed out the connection between Mitteleuropa concepts, aspirations for detachment from the US, and the fear of US 'cultural imperialism'.
45. Schlögel, *Die Mitte liegt ostwärts*, p. 25.
46. Ibid., p. 120; and Glotz, *Manifest*, pp. 50–2.
47. See T. Assheuer, 'Repolitisierung? Zur Debatte um Mitteleuropa', *Frankfurter Rundschau*, 10 June 1988, p. 11.
48. For a discussion of the diffusion of methodology and content in the political Mitteleuropa debate, see T. G. Ash, 'Mitteleuropa?', *Daedalus*, 119 (1/1990): 1–22; S. Papcke, 'Diesseits oder jenseits der Freiheit? Die Deutschen suchen ihren Standort zwischen Ost und West', in Werner Weidenfeld, *Nachdenken über Deutschland: Materialien zur politischen Kultur der Deutschen Frage* (Cologne: Verlag Wissenschaft u. Politik, 1985), p. 105; Arnulf Baring, *Unser neuer Größenwahn: Deutschland zwischen Ost und West* (Stuttgart: Deutsche Verlagsantalt, 1988); Reinhard Opitz, 'Deutsche Frage und Mitteleuropa-Diskussion', *Marxistische Blätter*, 16 (6/1986): 21–30.
49. P. Bender, 'Mitteleuropa – Mode, Modell oder Motiv?', 34 *Neue Gesellschaft/Frankfurter Hefte* (1987): 297–304; also P. Bender 'Die Notgemeinschaft der Teilungsopfer', in Papcke and Weidenfeld, *Traumland Mitteleuropa?*, p. 86.
50. P. Glotz, 'Deutsch-böhmische Kleinigkeiten', p. 585. For a summary of this approach, see also W. von Bredow and Thomas Jäger, 'Niemannsland Mitteleuropa. Zur Wiederkehr eines diffusen Ordnungskonzepts', *Aus Politik und Zeitgeschichte*, 40/41 (1988): 42.
51. P. Glotz, 'Ein Instrument der Entspannung', *Rheinischer Merkur/Christ und Welt*, 31 October 1986.
52. Bender, 'Mitteleuropa – Mode, Modell oder Motiv?', p. 302.
53. See Glotz,'Deutsch-böhmische Kleinigkeiten', p. 585; Bender, 'Mitteleuropa', p. 300; and G. Heimann, 'Die europäische Mitte und die Zukunft Berlins', *Neue Gesellschaft/Frankfurter Hefte*, 33 (1986): 590–3.
54. For more information on the concept of 'Sicherheitspartnerschaft' see K. D. Voigt, 'Mitteleuropa – Ein Konzept mit unklarer politischer Substanz, ein Raum mit wechselnden Grenzen', in Papcke and Weidenfeld, *Traumland Mitteleuropa?*, pp. 96–103.
55. See 'Grundsätze für einen atomwaffenfreien Korridor in Mitteleuropa'. Gemeinsame Erklärung der Arbeitsgruppe SPD Bundestagsfraktion und SED. Hrsg. v. Vorstand der SPD, Abt. Presse und Information (Weimar: 1986).

56. Actually, in domestic affairs as well as foreign affairs these negotiations did not help the SPD at all to advance its position as the party of opposition. On the contrary, it drove the party even further into political isolation, especially with regard to the Western Allies. The main German ally, the United States, did not appreciate the advance since it ran counter to it's policy of strength, and domestically large parts of the electorate perceived it as an unjustified acknowledgement of the SED. The SPD's enthusiasm for these informal détente talks can only be explained by the shift in the party spectrum as a result of the establishment of the Green Party in Parliament. In turn, the left wing within the SPD gained power and moved the party to the left in order to win back some of the left-wing voters that had moved to the Greens. A substantial part of this move to the left was their assimilation with the Greens on questions of security policy and their adaptation of semi-pacifist positions regarding NATO, the armed forces, and detachment.
57. However, they also built their suggestions on the Bahr Paper of 1969.
58. Jochen Löser and Ulrike Schilling, *Neutralität für Mitteleuropa. Das Ende der Blöcke* (Munich: Bertelsmann, 1984), p. 9.
59. Ibid.
60. Ibid., pp. 107 and 170.
61. The 'Friedensbewegung' in Germany was developed in the mid-1970s as a result of the student revolts and an institutionalization of the 'Easter Marches'. The latter was an old tradition of the workers' movement and the labour unions: they marched for social welfare and world peace over a three-day period at Easter. The peace movement picked up on that tradition and tried to make people more conscious concerning the security situation and the irony of deterrence, which, in essence, holds one's own people as hostage. The movement gained a maximum momentum around the protests against the twin-track decision adopted by NATO in 1976 and implemented in 1982. The Green Party originally evolved in large part out of the peace movement.
62. Otto Schily, 'Rede über das eigene Land: Deutschland', in Rudolf Augstein, Otto Schily, Willy Brandt, Werner Herzog and Franz-Joseph Strauß, *Reden über das eigene Land: Deutschland* (Munich: Bertelsmann, 1984), p. 49.
63. Ibid., p. 50.
64. For a critical analysis of the 'German question' from a political sociologist's perspective see Ralf Dahrendorf, *Gesellschaft und Demokratie in Deutschland* (Munich: Piper, 1965).
65. For a brief summary of the Mitteleuropa debate in the tradition of Friedrich Naumann's *Mitteleuropa* and of his successors, see Markus Schubert's *Die Mitteleuropa-Konzeption Friedrich Naumanns und die Mitteleuropa-Debatte der 80er Jahre*, Libertas Papers, no. 3 (Sindelfingen, 1993).
66. Bernard Willms and Paul Kleinewefers, *Erneuerung aus der Mitte: Prag–Wie–Berlin. Diesseits von Ost und West* (Herford: Busse & Seewald, 1988). See also Heino Berg and Peter Burmeister, *Mitteleuropa und die deutsche Frage* (Bremen: Edition Temmen, 1990). Even though this is a more recent work, it summarizes the Mitteleuropa debate in Germany shortly before and around the time of unification and exemplifies the shift towards a more power-politics (machtpolitisch) oriented debate.
67. Willms and Kleinewefers, *Erneuerung aus der Mitte*, p. 32.
68. Ibid., pp. 187–288.

69. See R. Jaworski, 'Die aktuelle Mitteleuropadiskussion in historischer Perspektive', p. 535. One example is the above-mentioned Yalta assessment of Glotz and Schlögel that holds the Yalta agreement of the Allies mainly responsible for the developments in Central Europe. This view constitutes a segmentation of history that not only excludes the pre-war and war history of the states but also looks exclusively at exogenous factors – namely the policies of the Allies – to explain the development. This does not do justice to the more complex history of the times and the region.
70. W. Weidenfeld, 'Mitteleuropa – Traum oder Trauma von der Zukunft Europas', in Papcke and Weidenfeld, *Traumland Mitteleuropa?*, p. 91.
71. Of course the increase in national esteem in the international system for Austria meant an explicit exclusion of Germany from its Mitteleuropa views. In this constellation history repeats the similar situation of the mid-nineteenth century when Austria and Prussia were in a stalemate over the dominant influence in Mitteleuropa, one trying to exclude the other.
72. For critical discussion see Markus Schubert, *Die Mitteleuropa-Konzeption Friedrich Naumanns*, p. 48; also Christian Weimer, *Mitteleuropa als politisches Ordnungskonzept?*, p. 248.
73. See J. Rovan, 'Die Illusion des Westens. Zur Diskussion des Mitteleuropa-Gedankens', *Frankfurter Allgemeine Zeitung*, 4 April 1987, Beilage 'Bilder und Zeiten'. The most cited idea dealing with the adoption of an 'Austrian solution' for Germany ignored the political realities and the fundamental strategic difference between the two states. Neither in 1980 nor thirty years earlier had there been a chance for such an alternative of German neutrality (see Timothy Garton Ash, *Im Namen Europas*, p. 426). The 'Austrian way', ratified in the states treaty of 1955, was, at its core, identical with the agreement of the Allies' foreign ministers drafted at the Moscow conference in October 1943. The basis of that draft was the idea that Austria was Hitler's first victim and should be re-established in its pre-war borders, separated from Germany and neutral in its international orientation (see H. Bütler, 'Stichwort Mitteleuropa: Tatsachen, Ideen, Illusionen', *Neue Züricher Zeitung*, 6/7 July 1985). That the Soviet Empire under the rule of the Breshnev Doctrine would let individual Central European states break away from the Eastern bloc was utopian.
74. W. Weidenfeld, 'Mitteleuropa – ein alter Mythos stiftet Unruhe', *Rheinischer Merkur*, 3 October 1986, p. 3.

Notes to Chapter 7: Epilogue

1. This is true, since most concepts never went beyond the conceptual stage and were never translated into practical political action.
2. Eckhard Jesse, in his article 'Der "dritte Weg" vor und nach der Wiedervereinigung', in Rainer Zitelmann, Karlheinz Weißmann and Michael Großheim (eds), *Westbindung: Chancen und Risiken für Deutschland* (Frankfurt: Propyläen Verlag, 1993), pp. 215–43, points out that the discussion of the German Sonderweg in the decades before unification revolved around the triangular structure comprising unification, neutralism and

pacifism at each of its corners. These were the 1970s and 1980s equivalent of the nineteenth-century demand for a 'united, strong and safe' Germany. And, as in the preceding 140 years, there was no agreement among the participants in this discussion about the priority or compatibility of these goals.

3. As previously indicated, the exception to this pattern is the Adenauer era, in which Germany followed a clear Westbindung and abandoned Mitteleuropa.
4. Klaus Hildebrandt has pointed out that the term and the idea of a German 'Sonderweg' are part of a long European history. But, furthermore, the term 'Sonderweg' is Janus-faced. On one side, it bears a positive connotation when used by the Germans themselves; yet, when used as a verdict from abroad, it takes on a negative connotation. Even among the Germans, it does not contain exclusively positive sentiments. The one vision, as a positive self-image, 'involved the belief of a people that they were different from and better than their neighbors', The other side, as a negative self-image, 'arises within national frontiers, encouraged by feelings of national incompleteness, backwardness, or defectiveness' (Klaus Hildebrandt, *German Foreign Policy from Bismarck to Adenauer* (Cambridge, Mass.: Cambridge University Press, 1989), pp. 170–1). See also G. Nonnenmacher, 'Deutsche Einigung als "Sonderfall"', *Frankfurter Allgemeine Zeitung*, 13 April 1992, p. 8.
5. For the problems of nation-building and unification see S. Kinzer, 'As euphoria of unity fades, Eastern Germans feel scorned and excluded', *New York Times*, 18 April 1992, p. 3.
6. M. Stürmer, 'Mitten in Europa: Die deutsche Frage in Geschichte und Gegenwart', in Otmar Franz, *Europas Mitte* (Göttingen: Muster-Schmidt Verlag, 1987), p. 11; also Otmar Franz, 'Gibt es Mitteleuropa', *Frankfurter Allgemeine Zeitung*, 10 December 1986, p. 1.
7. For an extensive presentation of Michael Stürmer's discussion of the importance of Mitteleuropa for Germany and *vice versa*, see Christian Weimer, *Mitteleuropa als politisches Ordnungskonzept?*, pp. 292–300. In this context see also the publications of Werner Weidenfeld, *above*, Chapter 6; especially W. Weidenfeld and J. Janning, 'Die Zukunft des Kontinents. Perspektiven einer neuen Ordnung für Europa', *Frankfurter Allgemeine Zeitung*, 28 February 1990, p. 8.
8. See H. Magenheimer, 'Renaissance der Geopolitik', *Österreichische Militärische Zeitschrift* (2/1991): 131–9, at 137.
9. Nationality conflicts such as the Chechen war are ample proof of the continuous disintegration of the Russian Federation.
10. See the discussion below, in this chapter. Also R. Cohen, 'Continental Block Party or Exclusive Club?', *New York Times*, 10 May 1992, p. E5; also the interview with Bavaria's President, Edmund Stoiber, 'Es gab einmal eine europäische Bewegung . . .', *Süddeutsche Zeitung*, 2 November 1993, p. 14.
11. See Björn Hettne and Inotai András, *The New Regionalism* (United Nations University/WIDER, 1994), pp. 14–15.
12. Ibid., p. 14.
13. Hettne and András, *New Regionalism*, p. 12. Hettne properly observes that 'post-Maastricht Europe has lost speed as far as purposeful integration is concerned' (p. 15). Various problems that require joint management have

continued to accumulate over the last four years, i.e., 'security, environment, refugee migration and economic recession' (ibid.). Furthermore, the EU is increasingly divided on questions of enlargement, currency union, and payments. In light of the possible enlargement of the EU eastwards, a Europe of two speeds may actually turn into a Europe of three or four speeds.

14. Most notably Italy, but also France and Germany, experienced a political shift to the right.
15. Hettne and András, *New Regionalism*, p. 15.
16. Not only is Germany's position changing in Europe after the break-up of the Eastern Bloc but also all of Europe is in flux. Nevertheless, the German position in the European system is the focus of this work as well as being crucial for all-European development. See G. Nonnenmacher, 'Welche neue Rolle für den alten Kontinent', *Frankfurter Allgemeine Zeitung*, 19 March 1992, p. 14. On the double transformation crisis in Europe see Eckhart Lübkemeier, 'Globale Herausforderungen deutscher Sicherheit', in *Aus Politik und Zeitgeschichte* (B6, 1995): 27–36.
17. Margaret Thatcher's acid remarks about 'selling out Europe to Germany' in Maastricht and the statements in her memoirs regarding unification are quite explicit and shed light on the problem the West has with German unification. See Margaret Thatcher, *Downing Street No. 10: Erinnerungen* (Düsseldorf: Econ Verlag, 1993), pp. 1094–1106. After Thatcher's resignation in November 1990, Britain's position under John Major changed to the extent that it moved from total opposition to reserved cooperation.
18. See C. R. Whitney, 'Germany Focusses on German Unity: European Unity will Wait', *New York Times*, 13 May 1992, p. A12.
19. Since 1994, there have been tendencies in France towards distancing itself from the EU. Also the German-Franco relationship has been deteriorating since 1994. Thus further European integration may be endangered because this relationship has been considered the motor of European integration. If Chirac's statements before the election are more than just campaign rhetoric, the EU may become of even less importance in French politics.
20. See A. Riding, 'At East–West Crossroads, Western Europe hesitates', *New York Times,* 25 March 1992, p. A10; also M. Frank, 'Zwei Seiten eines ungeliebten Imperiums', *Süddeutsche Zeitung*, 18 March 1993, p. 3; also Hettne and András, *New Regionalism*, p. 13.
21. This is true not only for reasons of technology transfer but also for infrastructural and transit reasons. The latter partly accounts for the reason why the Alpe–Adria Initiative as well as the CEI, both currently excluding Germany in favour of Austria, have until now been largely ineffective. See *The Economist*, 305 (26 December 1987): 31–2; also 'Neue Ostpolitik', *Süddeutsche Zeitung*, 18 August 1993, p. 2.
22. Hans J. Morgenthau (ed.), *Germany and the Future of Europe* (Chicago: University of Chicago Press, 1951), p. 76.
23. The encouragement of the Clinton and Bush administrations for German leadership seems to suggest the opposite. More below, in this chapter.
24. See J. Tagliabue, 'In Germany, West plus East means policy shift', *New York Times,* 1 March 1992, p. E5.
25. V. Handl, 'Germany and Central Europe: "Mitteleuropa" restored?', *Perspectives: Review of Central European Affairs*, 1 (1993): 45–52, at 45.

26. George F. Kennan, *Memoirs 1925–1950* (Boston: Little, Brown, 1967), vol. 1, p. 417.
27. Bill Clinton, in an interview with the *Süddeutsche Zeitung*, 4 July 1994, p. 9; also 'Debate the Real European Issues', *New York Times*, 30 July 1992, p. A24.
28. The ongoing debate in and outside of Germany regarding its UN military involvement and the out-of-area discussion are more examples of this discrepancy.
29. Handl, '"Mitteleuropa" restored?', p. 49.
30. For an evaluation of the figures see above, Chapter 1. However, some German business representatives, such as Klaus Murmann, President of the German Association of Employers, claim that the United States has moved into the Eastern European market much faster than Germany and that German business is about to miss the boat, partly as a result of hesitant politics. For the development in trade see A. Pradetto and P. Sigmund, 'Deutschland und Osteuropa in der Ära des Postkommunismus', in Deutschland Archiv, 25, *Zeitschrift für das Vereinigte Deutschland*, 8 (1993): 890–904.
31. The way the asylum policy was presented to Germany's Central European neighbours caused a Polish member of parliament to speak out publicly about 'Germany's new attack on Poland'. See H. Prantl, 'Der neue Überfall auf Polen', *Süddeutsche Zeitung*, 1 March 1993, p. 3.
32. See U. Bergdoll, 'Anwalt der Balten', *Süddeutsche Zeitung*, 10 March 1994, p. 4.
33. See a report in the *Washington Post*, reprinted in the *Herald Tribune*, J. Hoagland, 'Germany and Russia are Getting Together', *Herald Tribune*, 17 May 1994, p. 6.
34. For example, Austria and Holland, partly in response to the new German law, also passed more restrictive laws and regulations.
35. See H. Suchocka, 'Desinteresse des Westens schürt Gefahren im Osten', *Süddeutsche Zeitung*, 26 February 1993, p. 9; also W. Koydl, 'Die Deutschen investieren, die anderen parieren', *Süddeutsche Zeitung*, 6/7 February 1993, p. 4.
36. See S. Kinzer, 'Triumph for Germany: Europe, backing Germans, accepts Yugoslav breakup', *New York Times*, 16 January 1992, p. A10; also, D. Binder, 'As Bonn talks louder, some in the US wince', *New York Times*, 7 January 1992, p. A2.
37. Handl points out that there were several other options for Germany to play an active role and use its influence in the region more constructively. For example, it could have pressed Croatia beforehand to meet the Serb minority halfway, or it could have stressed the EC's idea of a confederation rather than a total break-up. Handl, '"Mitteleuropa" restored?', p. 50.
38. Even though the recent decision of the German Supreme Court clarified the field for German out-of-area operations, the political debate continues. Another example of Germany's reluctance to act is its changing position on the question of a permanent seat in the Security Council.
39. The Baltic states traditionally have not been incorporated in German Mitteleuropa concepts, but are introduced here as an example of German foreign-policy approaches in the broader Central European region.
40. In general, one of the problems of Germany's reorientation in foreign

policy is that small countries traditionally take on a 'relatively low level of importance'. Germany has to refocus its view in order to understand fully the needs of the smaller Central European states. Handl, '"Mitteleuropa" restored?', p. 45.

41. J. Hoagland, 'Germany and Russia are Getting Together'.
42. Michael Stürmer, who was one of the main national-conservative Mitteleuropa advocates in the late 1980s, also stressed this. His warning of repeated Rapallo politics constitutes a moderation of his previous positions. The same is true for Werner Weidenfeld who, in light of the changed situation in Europe, now argues for German self-restraint within a European confederation. See M. Stürmer, 'Kein Wiedersehen in Rapallo', *Frankfurter Allgemeine Zeitung*, 16 April 1992, p. 5; and W. Weidenfeld and J. Janning, 'Schöpferische Vielfalt oder zerstörerischer Herrschaftswille', *Frankfurter Allgemeine Zeitung*, 15 April 1992, p. 8.
43. A further indication is the patchwork of cultural and military cooperation between Germany and Mitteleuropa. Germany offered military cooperation to Poland in the winter of 1992 with no practical consequences, yet denied the same to the Czech Republic, and instead opened a Goethe Institute in Prague. In April 1993 Germany again demanded military cooperation with all of Eastern Europe. See 'Tagung der Westeuropäische Union', *Frankfurter Allgemeine Zeitung*, 2 April 1992, p. 5.
44. Especially after the resignation of Foreign Secretary Genscher in 1992, German foreign policy became somewhat blurred. First, 'Genscherism' had been a factor of continuity in German foreign policy, even though Genscher had no coherent concept of how to deal with the changes of the post-Cold War era. Secondly, Genscher's successor, Klaus Kinkel, in reorienting German foreign policy, had to combat his predecessor's legacy not only abroad but also within his own party.
45. See Ohmae's article 'The Rise of the Region State', *Foreign Affairs* (Spring 1993): 78–87.
46. Hettne and András, *New Regionalism*, p. 15.
47. The same is valid for an expansion of NATO, which would lose credibility. It would hardly be credible deterrence at this point to state that any Western state would accept its own destruction to save, for example, Poland. While 'to many people "more Europe" is still the answer' to the existing problems in and around the EU, one may want to ask what is the question? See Hettne and András, *New Regionalism*, p. 16.
48. See here also Bernhard Schäfer (ed.), *Lebensverhältnisse und soziale Konflikte im neuen Europa* (Frankfurt: Campus Verlag, 1992).
49. Concerning the discussion of political concepts for Mitteleuropa and German foreign policy, see 40 *Die Neue Gesellschaft/Frankfurter Hefte*, 7 (July, 1993): 604–32.
50. See Peter Glotz, *Der Irrweg des Nationalstaates: Europäische Reden an ein deutsches Publikum* (Stuttgart: Deutsche Verlagsanstalt, 1990); also K. Ohmae, 'The Rise of the Region State', *Foreign Affairs* (Spring 1993): 78–87.
51. See the extensive suggestions for a regional European restructuring in Matthias Schulz, *Regionalismus und die Gestaltung Europas* (Hamburg: Verlag Dr Krämer, 1993).

52. See G. F. Treverton, 'Finding an Analogy for Tomorrow', 37 *Orbis*, 1 (Winter 1993): 1–19.
53. Before Maastricht in 1991 the EU 'foreign minister', Frans Andriessen, suggested a test membership for the Central European states in order to lead them into the union. At a closer glance, the suggestion really entails an associate status with the EU and membership within an independent regional organization. See the interview with the *Süddeutsche Zeitung*, 18 November 1991, p. 8.
54. Bruno Schoch has pointed out the importance of Germany's remaining a Western state for the stability of the region. See Bruno Schoch, *Deutschlands Einheit und Europas Zukunft* (Frankfurt: Suhrkamp, 1992), pp. 141–4.
55. Handl notes that 'Mitteleuropa can only come about as a consequence of homogenization of the region.' Handl, '"Mitteleuropa" restored?', p. 49.
56. See the German suggestion for a reorganization of NATO's relationship with the Central European states, 'Im deutschen Interesse: Sicherheitsgarantien für Oststaaten', *Süddeutsche Zeitung*, 5 July 1993, p. 2.
57. See Handl, '"Mitteleuropa" restored?', p. 49.
58. The two terms were coined by Hans-Peter Schwarz. For the context of Germany's distorted relationship to power see Gregor Schöllgen, *Angst vor der Macht: Die Deutschen und ihre Aussenpolitik* (Berlin: Ullstein, 1993).
59. Handl, '"Mitteleuropa" restored?', p. 50.
60. See J. Heilbrunn, 'Tomorrow's Germany', *National Interest*, 36 (Summer 1994): 44–52.

Bibliography

BOOKS AND DOCUMENTS

Adenauer, Konrad, *Erinnerungen*, 4 vols (Stuttgart: Deutsche Verlagsgesellschaft, 1966).

Albrecht, Ulrich (ed.), *Europa Atomwaffenfrei: Vorshläge, Pläne, Perspektiven* (Cologne: Pahl-Rugenstein, 1986).

Altmann, Rüdiger, *Das Erbe Adenauers* (Stuttgart: Seewald Verlag, 1960).

——, *Das deutsche Risiko: Außenpolitische Perspektive* (Stuttgart: Seewald Verlag, 1962).

Aretin, Freiherr von, *Deutschland und Europa in der Neuzeit* (Wiesbaden: Franz Steiner Verlag, 1988).

Art, Robert J. and Waltz, Kenneth N., *The Use of Force, International Politics and Foreign Policy* (Boston, Mass.: Little, Brown, 1971).

Ash, Timothy G., *Ein Jahrhundert wird abgewählt: Aus den Zentren Mitteleuropas 1980–1990* (Munich: Carl Hanser Verlag, 1990).

——, *Im Namen Europas: Deutschland und der geteilte Kontinent* (Munich: Carl Hanser Verlag, 1993).

Augstein, Rudolf, Schily, Otto, Brandt, Willy, Herzog, Werner, and Strauß, Franz-Joseph, *Reden über das eigene Land: Deutschland* (Munich: Bertelsmann, 1984).

Auswärtiges Amt, *Akten zur Deutschen Außenpolitik 1918–1945* (Baden-Baden: Imprimerie Nationale, 1950).

——, *100 Jahre Auswärtiges Amt, 1870–1970* (Bonn: Politische Archive im Auswärtigen Amt, 1970).

——, *Die Auswärtige Politik der Bundesrepublik Deutschland* (Cologne: Verlag Wissenschaft und Politik, 1972).

Baring, Arnulf, *Außenpolitik in Adenauers Kanzlerdemokratie: Bonns Beitrag zur EVG*, Schriften des Forschungsinstitutes der deutschen Geschichte für auswärtige Politik e.V., no. 28 (Munich: R. Oldenbourg Verlag, 1969).

——, *Unser neuer Größenwahn: Deutschland zwischen Ost und West* (Stuttgart: Deutsche Verlags-Anstalt, 1988).

Bark, Dennis L. and Gress, David R., *A History of West Germany*, vols 1 and 2 (Cambridge, Mass.: Basil Blackwell, 1993).

Baumgart, Winfried, *Deutsche Ostpolitik 1918: Von Brest-Litowsk bis zum Ende des 1. Weltkrieges* (Vienna: R. Oldenbourg Verlag, 1966).

——, *Vom Europäischen Konzert zum Völkerbund: Friedensschlüsse und Friedenssicherung von Wien bis Versailles* (Darmstadt: Wissenschaftliche Buchgesellschaft, 1974).

——, *Das Zeitalter des Imperialismus und des Ersten Weltkrieges (1871–1918)*, Quellenkunde zur deutschen Geschichte der Neuzeit, no. 5 (Darmstadt: Wissenschaftliche Buchgesellschaft, 1977).

——, *Deutschland im Zeitalter des Imperialismus 1890–1914* (Stuttgart: Verlag W. Kohlhammer, 1986).

Bender, Peter, *Die Ostpolitik Willy Brandts oder die Kunst des Selbstverständlichen* (Hamburg: Rowohlt Verlag, 1972).

——, *Neue Ostpolitik: Vom Mauerbau bis zum Moskauer Vertrag* (Munich: Deutscher Taschenbuchverlag, 1986).

Bernhardi, Friedrich von, *Deutschland und der nächste Krieg* (Berlin: J. F. Gotta'sche Buchhandlung, 1912).

——, *Denkwürdigkeiten aus meinem Leben* (Berlin: Gotta'sche Buchhandlung, 1927).

Besson, Waldemar, *Die Außenpolitik der Bundesrepublik: Erfahrungen und Maßstäbe* (Munich: R. Piper Verlag, 1970).

Bismarck, Otto von, *Gedanken und Erinnerungen* (Stuttgart: Cotta, 1898).

——, *Die gesammelten Werke*, critical edition by Georg Ritter and Rainer Stadelmann, 2nd rev. edn, 15 vols (Berlin: Deutsche Verlagsgesellschaft, 1924–35).

Blaich, Fritz, *Staat und Verbände in Deutschland zwischen 1871 und 1945* (Wiesbaden: Franz Steiner Verlag, 1979).

Blumenwitz, Dieter (ed.), *Konrad Adenauer und seine Zeit: Politik und Persönlichkeit des ersten Bundeskanzlers* (Stuttgart: Deutsche Verlagsgesellschaft, 1976).

Böhme, Helmut, *Deutschlands Weg zur Großmacht* (Cologne: Kiepenheuer & Witsch, 1966).

Borsody, Stephen, *The New Central Europe: Triumphs and Tragedies* (New York: Columbia University Press, 1993).

Bracher, Karl D., Funke, Manfred, and Jacobsen, Hans-Adolf, *Nationalsozialistische Diktatur, 1933–1945: Eine Bilanz*, Schriftenreihe der Bundeszentrale für politische Bildung, no. 192 (Bonn, 1983).

Bracher, Karl D., Jäger, Wolfgang, and Link, Werner, *Republik im Wandel 1969–1974: Die Ära Brandt*, no. 5/I, Geschichte der Bundesrepublik Deutschland (Stuttgart: Deutsche Verlags-Anstalt, 1986).

Brandt, Willy, *Außenpolitik, Deutschlandpolitik, Europapolitik* (Berlin: Berlin Verlag, 1968).

——, *Begegnungen und Einsichten. Die Jahre 1960–1975* (Hamburg: Hoffmann und Campe, 1976).

Brauweiler, Heinz, *Berufstand und Staat* (Berlin: Ring Verlag, 1925).

Brecher, Michael, *Crises in World Politics: Theory and Reality* (New York: Pergamon Press, 1993).

Bretano, Heinrich von, *Germany and Europe: Reflections on German Foreign Policy* (New York: Praeger, 1964).

Brill, Heinz, *Geopolitik heute: Deutschlands Chance?* (Berlin: Ullstein, 1994).

Brown, Seyom, *International Relations in a Changing Global System: Toward a Theory of the World Polity* (Boulder: Westview Press, 1992).

Buchner, Rudolf, *Geschichte im europäischen Rahmen: Darstellung und Betrachtungen* (Darmstadt: Wissenschaftliche Buchgesellschaft, 1975).

Bührer, Werner (ed.), *Die Adenauer-Ära: Dokumentation* (Munich: R. Piper Verlag, 1993).

Bürklin, Wilhelm P., *Grüne Politik* (Opladen: Westdeutscher Verlag, 1984).

Bundesministerium für gestamtdeutsche Fragen, Bonn (ed.), *Dokumente zur Deutschlandpolitik, 10 Juni 1963: Rede des Präsidenten Kennedy in der 'American University' in Washington*, series IV, vol. 9 (Frankfurt: Alfred Metzner Verlag, 1978).

Bundesministerium für innerdeutsche Fragen, Bonn (ed.), *Texte zur Deutschlandpolitik*, series II, vol. 3 (Bayreuth: Druckhaus Bayreuth, 1976).

Burmester, Hans-Peter, Boldt, Frank, and Mészáros, György (eds), *Mitteleuropa: Traum oder Trauma?* (Bremen: Edition Temmen, 1988).

Burmester, Hans-Peter and Berg, Heino, *Mitteleuropa und die deutsche Frage* (Bremen: Edition Temmen, 1990).

Busch, Erhald (ed.), *Aufbruch nach Mitteleuropa* (Vienna: Atelier Verlag, 1986).

Busek, Erhard and Brix, Emil, *Projekt Mitteleuropa* (Vienna: Ueberreuter, 1986).

Busek, Erhard and Wilflinger, Gerhard (eds), *Aufbruch nach Mitteleuropa: Rekonstruktion eines versunkenen Kontinents* (Vienna: Edition Atelier, Wiener Journal Zeitschriftenverlag, 1986).

Campbell, Edwina S., *Germany's Past and Europe's Future* (Washington: Pergamon-Brassey, 1989).

Cartarius, Urich (ed.), *Deutschland im Ersten Weltkrieg* (Munich: Deutscher Taschenbuch Verlag, 1982).

CDU-Congress, *Deutschland und die Union: Die Berliner Tagung 1946, Reden und Aussprache* (Berlin, 1946).

Charmatz, Richard, *Minister Freiherr v. Bruck: Der Vorkämpfer Mittel-Europas* (Leipzig: D. Hirzel Verlag, 1916).

Chéradame, André, *The Pangerman Plot Unmasked* (London, 1916).

——, *Le Française Réaliste* (Paris, 1929).

[Claß, Heinrich] Von einem Deutschen, *Die Partei der Zukunft* (Leipzig: Dieterichsche Verlagshandlung, 1914).

Claß, Heinrich, *Zum deutschen Kriegsziel: Eine Flugschrift* (Munich: Lehmann, 1917).

Conze, Werner, *Deutschland und Europa: Historische Studien zur Völker- und Staatenordnung des Abendlandes* (Düsseldorf: Droste Verlag, 1951).

——, *The Shaping of the German Nation* (London: George Prior, 1979).

Conze, Werner, Kosthorst, Erich, and Nebgen, Elfriede (eds), *Jacob Kaiser: Politiker zwischen Ost und West, 1945–49* (Stuttgart: W. Kohlhammer Verlag, 1969).

Coudenhove-Kalergi, Richard N., *Kampf um Paneuropa*, vols 1–3 (Vienna: Braumüller, 1925–8).

——, *Eine Idee erobert Europa: Meine Lebenserinnerungen* (Vienna: Desch, 1958).

Czempiel, Ernst-Otto, *Die Lehre von den internationalen Beziehungen* (Darmstadt: Wissenschaftliche Buchgesellschaft, 1969).

Dahrendorf, Ralf, *Gesellschaft und Demokratie in Deutschland* (Munich: R. Piper Verlag, 1965).

——, *Homo Sociologicus: Ein Versuch zur Geschichte, Bedeutung und Kritik der Kategorie der Sozialen Rolle*, 11th rev. edn (Opladen: Westdeutscher Verlag, 1972).

——, *Die Staatsräson der Bundesrepublik Deutschland*, Konstanzer Universitätsreden (Konstanz: Konstanzer Universitätsverlag, 1976).

Dann, Otto, *Nation und Nationalismus in Deutschland, 1770–1990*, Beck'sche Reihe 494 (Munich: C. H. Beck, 1993).

Deutsch, Karl W. and Lewis, Edinger, *Germany Rejoins the Powers* (Stanford: Stanford University Press, 1959).

Deutsches Liederbuch, 11th edn (Stuttgart: Deutsche Verlags-Anstalt, 1983).

Dienstbier, Jiri, *Träumen von Europa* (Berlin: Rowohlt, 1991).

Dönhoff, Marion Gräfin, *Die Bundesrepublik in der Ära Adenauer: Kritik und Perspektiven* (Hamburg: Rowohlt, 1963).

——, *Die Deutsche Ostpolitik* (Erlenbac-Zürich: Eugen Rentsch Verlag, 1968).

Duchacek, Ivo D., *Nations and Men: International Politics Today* (New York: Holt, Rinehart and Winston, 1966).
Earle, Edward M., *Nationalism and Internationalism: Essays Inscribed to Carlton J. H. Hayes* (New York: Columbia University Press, 1951).
Ehmer, Manfred and Frantz, Constantin, *Die politische Gedankenwelt eines Klassikers des Föderalismus* (Rheinfelden: Schäuble Verlag, 1988).
Eisfeld, Rainer, *Mitteleuropa – Paneuropa: Der Hegemoniale und der föderale Integrationsansatz im Zeichen der 'vierten Weltmacht'* (Bonn: Verlag Europa Union, 1980).
Erler, Fritz, *Demokratie in Deutschland* (Stuttgart: Seewald Verlag, 1965).
Eyck, Erich, *Geschichte der Weimarer Republik* (Stuttgart: Eugen Rentsch Verlag, 1954).
Fischer, Fritz, *Griff nach der Weltmacht: Die Kriegszielpolitik des kaiserlichen Deutschlands 1914/18* (Düsseldorf: Droste Verlag, 1961).
——, *Krieg der Illusionen: Die deutsche Politik von 1911 bis 1914* (Düsseldorf: Droste Verlag, 1969).
Foerster, Rolf H., *Europa: Geschichte einer politischen Idee* (Munich: Nymphenburger Verlagshandlung, 1967).
Funder, Friedrich, *Vom Gestern ins Heute. Aus dem Kaiserreich in die Republik* (Vienna: Herold Verlag, 1952).
Frantz, Constantin, 'Romantik und Realismus im Werk eines politischen Außenseiters' (dissertation, Groningen, 1879).
——, *Der Föderalismus als das leitende Prinzip für die sociale, staatliche und internationale Organisation, unter besonderer Bezugnahme auf Deutschland* (Mainz: Kirchheim, 1879).
——, *Die Weltpolitik unter besonderer Bezugnahme auf Deutschland*, 3 vols (Chemnitz: Schmeitzner, 1882–3).
Franz, Otmar, *Europas Mitte* (Göttingen: Musterschmidt Verlag, 1987).
Fraser, Lindley, *Germany between Two Wars* (London: Oxford University Press, 1945).
Freund, Gerald, *Germany between Two Worlds* (New York: Harcourt, Brace, 1961).
Freund, Michael, *Die Deutsche Geschichte* (Berlin: Bertelsmann Lexikon Verlag, 1973).
Frommelt, Reinhard, *Paneuropa oder Mitteleuropa? Einigungsbestrebungen im Kalkül deutscher Wirtschaft und Politik*, Schriftenreihe der Vierteljahreshefte für Zeitgeschichte, no. 34 (Stuttgart: Deutsche Verlags-Anstalt, 1977).
Fuller, Joseph Vincent, *Bismarck's Diplomacy at its Zenith* (Cambridge, Mass.: Harvard University Press, 1922).
Gebhardt, Bruno, *Handbuch der deutschen Geschichte*, vols 3 and 4, 6th rev. edn (Stuttgart: Union Verlag, 1973).
Gerlich, Peter and Glass, Krzysztof, *Wege aus der Krise: Mitteleuropäische Phantasmagorien* (Vienna: Böhlau Verlag, 1993).
Glotz, Peter, *Manifest für eine Neue Europäische Linke* (Berlin: Siedler Verlag, 1985).
——, *Der Irrweg des Nationalstaates: Europäische Reden an ein deutsches Publikum* (Stuttgart: Deutsche Verlagsanstalt, 1990).
Görlitz, Walter (ed.), *Regierte der Kaiser? Kriegstagebücher, Aufzeichnungen und Briefe des Chefs des Marine-Kabinetts, Admiral Alexander von Müller, 1914–1918* (Göttingen: Musterschmidt, 1959).

Göttinger Arbeitskreis (ed.), *Deutschland im weltpolitischen Umbruch*, Studien zur Deutschlandfrage, no. 11 (Berlin: Duncker & Humblot, 1993).

Grass, Günther, *Deutscher Lastenausgleich, wider das dumpfe Einheitsgebot: Reden und Gespräche* (Frankfurt: Luchterhand, 1990).

Graubard, Stephen R. (ed.), *Eastern Europe, Central Europe, Europe* (Boulder, Colorado: Westview Press, 1991).

Great Britain, Foreign Office, *British Documents on the Origins of the War, 1898–1914*, 11 vols, ed. G. P. Gooch and Harald Temperlay (London, 1927–38).

Grewe, Wilhelm G., *Deutsche Außenpolitik der Nachkriegszeit* (Stuttgart: Deutsche Verlags-Anstalt, 1960).

Griffith, William E., *The Ostpolitik of the Federal Republic of Germany* (Cambridge, Mass.: MIT Press, 1978).

Gruchmann, Lothar, *Nationalsozialistische Großraumordnung: Die Konstruktion einer 'deutschen Monroe-Doktrin'*, Schriftenreihe der Vierteljahreshefte für Zeitgeschichte, no. 4 (Stuttgart: Deutsche Verlags-Anstalt, 1962).

Guttenberg, Karl-Theodor Freiherr zu, *Die neue Ostpolitik: Wege und Irrwege* (Osnabrück: A. Fromm Verlag, 1971).

Hacke, Christian, *Weltmacht wider Willen: Die Außenpolitik der Bundesrepublik Deutschland* (Stuttgart: Klett-Cotta, 1988).

Hättich, Manfred, *Deutschland – eine zu späte Nation* (Mainz: von Hase & Koehler, 1990).

Haftendorn, Helga, *Theorie der internationalen Politik: Gegenstand und Methoden der internationalen Beziehungen* (Hamburg: Hoffmann und Campe, 1975).

Hahn, Herbert W., *Wirtschaftliche Integration im 19. Jahrhundert: Die hessischen Staaten und der Deutsche Zollverein* (Göttingen: Van der Hoeck & Ruprecht, 1982).

Halecki, Oskar, *Europa: Grenzen und Gliederung seiner Geschichte* (Darmstadt: Gentner Verlag, 1957).

Hanrieder, Wolfram F., *West German Foreign Policy, 1945–1963* (Stanford, CA: Stanford University Press, 1967).

—— (ed.), *Comparative Foreign Policy: Theoretical Essays* (New York: David McKay Company, 1971).

——, *Fragmente der Macht: Die Außenpolitik der Bundesrepublik* (Munich: R. Piper Verlag, 1981).

——, *Germany, America, Europe: Forty Years of German Foreign Policy* (New Haven, Conn.: Yale University Press, 1989).

Hanrieder, Wolfram F. and Auton, Graeme P., *The Foreign Policies of West Germany, France, and Britain* (Englewood Cliffs, NJ: Prentice-Hall, 1980).

Hanrieder, Wolfram F. and Rühle, Hans, *Im Spannungsfeld der Weltpolitik: 30 Jahre deutsche Außenpolitik (1949–1979)* (Stuttgart: Verlag Bonn Aktuell, 1981).

Hasse, Ernst, *Großdeutschland und Mitteleuropa um das Jahr 1950: Von einem Alldeutschen* (Berlin: Verlag Thormann et Goetsch, 1895).

——, *Deutsche Politik II: Deutsche Grenzpolitik* (Munich: J. F. Lehmann, 1905).

Hassel, Ulrich von, *Vom anderen Deutschland: Aus den nachgelassenen Tagebüchern, 1938–1944* (Zürich: Atlantis-Verlag, 1946).

Haushofer, Karl, *Weltpolitik von heute* (Berlin: Verlag- und Vertriebgesellschaft, 1934).

Hederman, Rea (ed.), *Writings on the East: Selected Essays on Eastern Europe for the New York Book Review* (New York: New York Review of Books, 1990).

Heine, Friedrich (ed.), *Dr Kurt Schumacher: Ein demokratischer Sozialist europäischer Prägung* (Göttingen: Musterschmidt, 1969).

Hesse, Joachim J. and Ellwein, Thomas, *Das Regierungssystem der Bundesrepublik Deutschland*, 7th edn (Opladen: Westdeutscher Verlag, 1992).

Hettne, Björn and Inotai, András, *The New Regionalism: Implications for Global Development and International Security* (UNU World Institute for Development Economics Research, Kirjapaino Oy, 1994).

Heuß, Theodor, *Friedrich Naumann. Der Mann, das Werk, die Zeit* (Stuttgart: Deutsche Verlagsanstalt, 1949).

Hildebrandt, Klaus, *Deutsche Außenpolitik, 1871–1918*, Enzyklopädie deutscher Geschichte, vol. 2 (Munich: R. Oldenbourg Verlag, 1989).

——, *German Foreign Policy from Bismarck to Adenauer* (Cambridge, Mass.: Cambridge University Press, 1989).

Hillgruber, Andreas, *Südost-Europa im 2. Weltkrieg*, Schriften der Bibliothek für Zeitgeschichte (Frankfurt: Bernard & Graefe Verlag, 1962).

——, *Deutsche Großmacht- und Weltpolitik im 19. und 20. Jahrhundert* (Düsseldorf: Droste Verlag, 1977).

——, *Die gescheiterte Großmacht: Eine Skizze des deutschen Reiches 1871–1945* (Düsseldorf: Droste Verlag, 1980).

——, *Die Last der Nation: Fünf Beiträge über Deutschland und die Deutschen* (Düsseldorf: Droste Verlag, 1984).

Hitler, Adolf, *Mein Kampf* (New York: Reynal & Hitchock, 1940).

Hubatsch, Walther (ed.), *Schicksalswege deutscher Vergangenheit: Beiträge zur geschichtlichen Deutung der letzten 150 Jahre* (Düsseldorf: Droste Verlag, 1950).

Inglehart, Ronald, *The Silent Revolution: Changing Values and Political Styles among Western Publics* (Princeton, NJ: Princeton University Press, 1977).

Jäckh, Ernst, *Der deutsche Krieg*, Politische Flugschriften, no. 22 (Stuttgart: Deutsche Verlagsanstalt, 1917).

Jahn, Egbert, *Europa, Osteuropa und Mitteleuropa*, Hessische Stiftung für Friedens- und Konfliktforschung: Forschungsbericht 1/89 (Frankfurt, 1989).

——, *Zur Zukunft Europas, Osteuropas und Mitteleuropas*, Hessische Stiftung für Friedens- und Konfliktforschung: Report 3/89 (Frankfurt, 1989).

Jahn, Egbert and Rittberger, Volker (eds), *Die Ostpolitik der Bundesrepublik: Triebkräfte, Widerstände, Konsequenzen* (Opladen: Westdeutscher Verlag, 1974).

James, Herold, *A German Identity, 1770–1990* (New York: Routledge, 1989).

Humboldt, Wilhelm von, *Eine Auswahl seiner politischen Schriften*, ed. Siegfried Kaehler, Klassiker der Politik, vol. 6 (Berlin: Hobbing, 1922).

Kaiser, Jacob, *Wir haben Brücke zu sein. Reden, Äußerungen und Aufsätze zur Deutschlandpolitik*, ed. Christian Hacke (Cologne: Verlag Wissenschaft und Politik, 1988).

Kaiser, Karl, *German Foreign Policy in Transition: Bonn between East and West* (London: Oxford University Press, 1968).

——, *Deutschlands Vereinigung: Die internationalen Aspekte* (Bergisch Gladbach: Bastei-Lübbe, 1991).

Kanner, Heinrich, *Der mitteleuropäische Staatenbund. Ein Vorschlag zum Frieden* (Vienna: Braumüller, 1925).

Kaplan, Morton A. (ed.), *New Approaches to International Relations* (New York: St Martin's Press, 1968).

Kehr, Eckart, *Der Primat der Innenpolitik*, ed. Hans U. Wehler (Berlin: de Gryter Verlag, 1976).

Kennan, George F., *Memoirs, 1925–1950*, vol. 1 (Boston: Little, Brown, 1967).

Kennedy, Paul, *Rise and Fall of the Great Powers* (New York: Vintage Books, 1987).

Keohane, Robert O. (ed.), *Neorealism and its Critics* (New York: Columbia University Press, 1986).

—— (ed.), *International Institutions and State Power: Essays in International Relations Theory* (Boulder, Colorado: Westview Press, 1989).

Khol, Andreas, Ofner, Günther, and Stirnemann, Alfred, *Österreichisches Jahrbuch für Politik 1986* (Munich: R. Oldenbourg Verlag, 1986).

Kindermann, Gottfried-Karl, *Grundelemente der Weltpolitik* (Munich: R. Piper Verlag, 1981).

Kissinger, Henry, *White House Years* (Boston: Little, Brown, 1979).

Kjellén, Rudolf, *Der Staat als Lebensform* (Leibzig: Hirtzel, 1917).

Kleinwächter, Friedrich F. G. and Paller, Heinz von (eds), *Die Anschlußfrage in ihrer kulturellen, politischen und wirtschaftlichen Bedeutung* (Vienna: Braumüller, 1930).

Knapp, Manfred and Krell, Gert, *Einführung in die Internationale Politik* (Munich: R. Oldenbourg Verlag, 1991).

Kolb, Eberhard, *Die Weimarer Republik* (Munich: R. Oldenbourg Verlag, 1984).

Konrád, György, *Antipolitik: Mitteleuropäische Meditationen* (Frankfurt: Luchterhand, 1985).

——, *Stimmungsbericht* (Frankfurt: Suhrkamp, 1988).

Kralik, Richard von, *Allgemeine Geschichte der neuesten Zeit von, 1900–1913*, in Johann Baptist von Weiss (ed.), Allgemeine Geschichte der neuesten Zeit von 1815 bis zur Gegenwart, no. 5 (Graz: Universitäts Buchdruck und Verlag Styria, 1922).

Krekeler, Norbert, *Revisionsanspruch und geheime Ostpolitik der Weimarer Republik* (Stuttgart: Deutsche Verlags-Anstalt, 1973).

Kresz, Carl von, 'Die Bestrebungen nach einer Mitteleuropäischen Zollunion' (PhD dissertation, University of Heidelberg, 1907).

Krippendorff, Ekkehart and Rittberger, Volker (eds), *The Foreign Policy of West Germany: Formation and Contents* (Beverly Hills, CA: Sage, 1980).

Krone, Heinrich, *Aufzeichnungen zur Deutschland- und Ostpolitik 1954–1969*, Adenauer Studien, no. 3, ed. Rudolf Morsey and Konrad Repgen (Mainz: Matthias-Grünewald-Verlag, 1974).

Kruck, Alfred, *Die Geschichte des Alldeutschen Verbandes, 1890–1939* (Wiesbaden: Franz Steiner Verlag, 1954).

Kutz, Martin, *Die Mitte Europas – Mitteleuropa: Ein Ideologem im Wandel, 1900–1992*, Beiträge zur Lehre und Forschung 1/93 (Hamburg: FÜAK, Fachgruppe Sozialwissenschaft, 1993).

Lafontaine, Oskar, *Angst vor den Freunden* (Hamburg: Spiegel Verlag, 1983).

de Lagarde, Paul, *Deutsche Schriften*, vol. 1 (Stuttgart: Alfred Kröner Verlag, 1933).

Lange, Friedrich [Adriaticus], *Deutschlands gerechte Grenzen* (Berlin: Dietrich Reimer Verlag, 1924).

Larousse du XXe Siècle, IV (Paris: Librairie Larousse, 1928–33).

Larrabee, Stephen (ed.), *The Two German States and European Security* (New York: St Martin's Press, 1989).

Lemberg, Hans, *Osteuropa, Mitteleuropa, Europa: Formen und Probleme der*

'Rückkehr nach Europa', Historische Mitteilungen der Ranke Gesellschaft, no. 4 (Stuttgart: Franz Steiner Verlag, 1993).

List, Friedrich, *National System of Political Economy* (Philadelphia: J. B. Lippincott, 1856).

——, *Schriften, Reden, Briefe*, 10 vols, ed. Eduard von Beckenrath et al. (Berlin: R. Hobbing Verlag, 1935).

Löser, Jochen and Schilling, Ulrike, *Neutralität für Mitteleuropa: Das Ende der Blöcke* (Munich: Bertelsmann, 1984).

Macridis, Roy C. (ed.), *Foreign Policy in World Politics*, 8th rev. edn (Englewood Cliffs, NJ: Prentice-Hall, 1992).

Majonica, Ernst, *Deutsche Außenpolitik* (Stuttgart: W. Kohlhammer Verlag, 1965).

Mansbach, Richard W. and Vasquez, John A., *In Search of Theory: A New Paradigm for Global Politics* (New York: Columbia University Press, 1981).

Marsh, David, *The Germans: A People at the Crossroads* (New York: St Martin's Press, 1990).

Matthée, Ulrich, 'Die Wiedergeburt der Europäischen Mitte und die Grenzen des Abendlandes', mimeograph (Kiel: Hermann-Ehlers-Akademie, 18 January 1992).

Mattox, Gale and Shingleton, A. Bradley, *Germany at the Crossroads: Foreign and Domestic Policy Issues* (Boulder, Colorado: Westview Press, 1992).

Mayer, Tilmann, *Jacob Kaiser: Gewerkschafter und Patriot* (Cologne: Bund-Verlag, 1988).

Mehnert, Klaus, *Der deutsche Standort* (Stuttgart: Deutsche Verlags-Anstalt, 1967).

Meier, David A., 'Managing the West Germans: The Occupation Statute of 1949 from Gestation to Burial' (PhD dissertation, University of Wisconsin, 1990).

Meinecke, Friedrich, *Werke*, vol. 6 (Stuttgart: Koehler, 1962).

Meissner, Boris (ed.), *Die deutsche Ostpolitik, 1961–1970* (Cologne: Verlag Wissenschaft und Politik, 1970).

Melville, Ralph and Schröder, Hans-Jürgen (eds), *Der Berliner Kongreß von 1878: Die Politik der Großmächte und die Probleme der Modernisierung in Südosteuropa in der zweiten Hälfte des 19. Jahrhunderts* (Wiesbaden: Franz Steiner Verlag, 1982).

Menges, Constantine C., *The Future of Germany and the Atlantic Alliance* (Washington, DC: AEI Press, 1991).

Merkl, Peter H., *German Foreign Policies, West and East* (Santa Barbara, CA: ABC-Clio, 1974).

——, *West German Foreign Policy: Dilemmas and Directions* (Chicago: Chicago Council on Foreign Relations, 1982).

—— (ed.), *The Federal Republic of Germany at Forty* (New York: New York University Press, 1989).

Meyer, Henry C., *Mitteleuropa in German Thought and Action, 1815–1945* (The Hague: Martinus Nijhoff, 1955).

——, *Germany from Empire to Ruin, 1913–1945* (London: Macmillan, 1973).

Meyers, Reinhard, *Die Lehre von den internationalen Beziehungen: Ein entwicklungsgeschichtlicher Überblick* (Düsseldorf: Droste Verlag, 1981).

Michaelis, Herbert, Schraepler, Ernst, and Scheel, Günter (eds), *Ursachen und Folgen: Vom deutschen Zusammenbruch 1918 und 1945 bis zur staatlichen Neuordnung* (Berlin: Dokumenten-Verlag Dr Herbert Wendler, 1961).

Möller, Heidrun von, *Großdeutsch und Kleindeutsch: Die Entstehung der Worte in den Jahren 1848–49* (Berlin: Ebering Verlag, 1937).

Morell, Renate and Steger, Hans-Albert (eds), *Ein Gespenst geht um . . . : Mitteleuropa*, Dokumentation der internationalen Tagung 'Grenzen und Horizonte' in Regensburg, 1986 (Munich: Theo Eberhard Verlag, 1987).

Morgenthau, Hans J. (ed.), *Germany and the Future of Europe* (Chicago: University of Chicago Press, 1951).

Müller-Armack, Alfred, *Religion und Wirtschaft* (Stuttgart: W. Kohlhammer Verlag, 1959).

Namier, Landon, *1848: The Revolution of the Intellectuals* (London: The Raleigh Lecture, 1946).

Naumann, Friedrich, *Mitteleuropa* (Berlin: Georg Reimer, 1916).

——, *Central Europe* (London: P. S. King, 1917).

——, *Werke*, vol. 4 (Opladen: Westdeutscher Verlag, 1964).

Nitzschke, Heinrich, *Die Geschichtsphilosophie Lorenz von Stein*, Historische Zeitschrift, Beiheft 26 (Munich: R. Oldenbourg Verlag, 1932).

Noack, Ulrich, *Bismarcks Friedenspolitik und das Problem des Deutschen Machtverfalls* (Leipzig: Quelle & Meyer, 1928).

Noelle-Neumann, Elisabeth and Piel, Edgar (eds), *Allensbacher Jahrbuch der Demoskopie, 1978–1983* (Munich: K. G. Saur, 1983).

Olson, William C. (ed.), *The Theory and Practice of International Relations*, 7th edn (Englewood Cliffs, NJ: Prentice-Hall, 1987).

Oncken, Hermann, *Das alte und das neue Mitteleuropa: Historisch-politische Betrachtungen über deutsche Bündnispolitik im Zeitalter Bismarcks und im Zeitalter des Weltkrieges* (Gotha: Friedrich Andreas Perthes Verlag, 1917).

Papcke, Sven and Weidenfeld, Werner, *Traumland Mitteleuropa? Beiträge zur aktuellen Kontroverse* (Darmstadt: Wissenschaftliche Buchgesellschaft, 1988).

Parker, Geoffray, *Western Political Thought in the 20th Century* (New York: St Martin's Press, 1985).

Paterson, William E. and Wallace, William (eds), *Foreign Policy Making in Western Europe: A Comparative Approach* (New York: Praeger, 1978).

Peckert, Joachim, *Zeitwende zum Frieden* (Herford: Busse Seewald, 1990).

Pelinka, Anton, *Zur österreichischen Identität: Zwischen deutscher Vereinigung und Mitteleuropa* (Vienna: Ueberreuter, 1990).

Pfetsch, Frank R., *Die Außenpolitik der Bundesrepublik 1949–1980* (Munich: UTB, Wilhelm Fink Verlag, 1981).

——, *Einführung in die Außenpolitik der Bundesrepublik Deutschland* (Opladen: Westdeutscher Verlag, 1981).

——, *West Germany: Internal Structures and External Relations* (New York: Praeger, 1988).

Pfizer, Paul A., *Briefwechsel zweier Deutschen* (Stuttgart: Cotta Verlag, 1832).

Pribersky, Andreas (ed.), *Europa und Mitteleuropa? Eine Umschreibung Österreichs* (Vienna: Sonderzahl Verlag, 1991).

Planck, Charles R., *The Changing Status of German Reunification in Western Diplomay, 1955–1966* (Baltimore, NJ: Johns Hopkins University Press, 1967).

Plessner, Helmuth, *Die verspätete Nation* (Frankfurt: Suhrkamp, TB Wissenschaft, 1974).

Plutynski, Anton, *We are 115 Millions* (London: Eyre & Spottiswoode, 1944).

Prittie, Terence, *Konrad Adenauer: Vier Epochen deutscher Geschichte*, 2nd edn (Stuttgart: Goverts, Krüger, Stahlberg Verlag, 1971).

Ratliff, William G., *Faithful to the Fatherland: Julius Curtius and Weimar Foreign Policy, 1920–1932* (Texas: Texas Technical University, 1988).

Rautenberg, Hans-Werner, *Traum oder Trauma? Der polnische Beitrag zur Mitteleuropa-Diskussion, 1985–1990* (Marburg: Johann Gottfried Herder Institut, 1991).

Riemeck, Renate, *Mitteleuropa: Bilanz eines Jahrhunderts*, 4th rev. edn (Potsdam: Edition Babelturm, 1990).

Ripka, Hubert, *A Federation of Central Europe* (New York: Macmillan, 1953).

Ritter, Albert [Winterstetten, Karl von], *Berlin-Baghdad. Neue Ziele mitteleuropäischer Politik* (Munich: Fr. Lehmann's Verlag, 1915).

Ritter, Gerhard, *Carl Goerdeler und die deutsche Widerstandsbewegung* (Stuttgart: Deutsche Verlags-Anstalt, 1956).

Rochau, Ludwig A., *Grundsätze der Realpolitik angewendet auf die staatlichen Zustände Deutschlands* (Stuttgart: Göpel Verlag, 1853; 2nd rev. edn, Heidelberg: J. C. B. Mohr Verlag, 1869).

Rohrbach, Paul, *Deutschland unter den Weltvölkern*, 2nd rev. edn (Berlin-Schöneberg: Buchverlag der 'Hilfe', 1908).

Roon, Ger van, *Neuordnung im Widerstand: Der Kreisauer Kreis innerhalb der deutschen Widerstandsbewegung* (Munich: R. Oldenbourg Verlag, 1967).

Rosenau, James N., *Domestic Sources of Foreign Policy* (New York: Free Press, 1967).

——, *International Politics and Foreign Policy: A Reader in Research and Theory* (New York: Free Press, 1969).

——, *The Scientific Study of Foreign Policy* (New York: Free Press, 1971).

——, *Turbulence in World Politics: A Theory of Change and Continuity* (Princeton, NJ: Princeton University Press, 1990).

Rosenau, James N., Davis, Vincent and East, Maurice A., *The Analysis of International Politics* (New York: Free Press, 1972).

Rosenau, James N., Thompson, Kenneth W. and Boyd, Gavin, *World Politics: An Introduction* (London: Free Press, 1976).

Roskin, Michael G., *The Rebirth of East Europe* (Englewood Cliffs, NJ: Prentice-Hall, 1991).

Rotfeld, Adam D., and Stützle, Walter, *Germany and Europe in Transition* (New York: Oxford University Press, 1991).

Roth, Reinhold, *Parteiensystem und Außenpolitik: Zur Bedeutung des Parteiensystems für außenpolitische Entscheidungsprozesse. Bundesrepublik Deutschland* (Meisenheim am Glan: Verlag Anton Hain, 1973).

Rothfels, Hans, *Bismarck und der Osten* (Leipzig: Hinrichs Verlag, 1934).

——, *Bismarck Briefe* (Göttingen: Vandenhoeck & Ruprecht, 1955).

——, *Bismarck, der Osten und das Reich* (Darmstadt: Wissenschaftliche Buchgesellschaft, 1960).

——, *Die deutsche Opposition gegen Hitler: Eine Würdigung* (Frankfurt: Fischer, 1969).

Rüstow, Alexander, *Ortsbestimmung der Gegenwart*, vols 1–3 (Zürich: Eugen Rentsch Verlag, 1963).

Russett, Bruce, *Grasping the Democratic Peace: Principles for the Post-Cold War World* (Princeton: Princeton University Press, 1993).

Schapiro, Jacob S., *Modern and Contemporary European History, 1815–1952* (Boston, Mass.: Houghton Mifflin, 1953).

Schäfer, Bernhard (ed.), *Lebensverhältnisse und soziale Konflikte im neuen Europa* (Frankfurt: Campus Verlag, 1992).

Schäffle, Albert, *Aus meinem Leben*, vols 1 and 2 (Berlin: Hofmann, 1905).

Scheer, Hermann, *Befreiung von der Bombe. Weltfrieden, europäischer Weg und die Zukunft der Deutschen* (Cologne: Bund-Verlag, 1986).

Schlögel, Karl, *Die Mitte liegt ostwärts: Die Deutschen, der verlorene Osten und Mitteleuropa* (Berlin: Corso bei Siedler, 1986).

Schmid, Günther, *Entscheidung in Bonn: Die Entstehung der Ost- und Deutschlandpolitik 1969/70* (Cologne: Verlag Wissenschaft und Politik, 1979).

Schmidt, Helmut, *Menschen und Mächte* (Berlin: Siedler Verlag, 1987).

Schmidt-Liebich, Jochen, *Deutsche Geschichte in Daten*, vol. 2 (Munich: Deutscher Taschenbuch Verlag, 1981).

Schmitt, Carl, *Völkerrechtliche Großraumordnung und Interventionsverbot raumfremder Mächte: Ein Beitrag zum Reichsbegriff im Völkerrecht* (Berlin: Deutscher Rechtsverlag, 1939).

Schmoller, Gustav, *Schmollers Jahrbuch für Gesetzgebung, Verwaltung und Volkswirtschaft im Deutschen Reiche*, 18 vols (Berlin: Duncker & Humblot, 1877–92).

Schoch, Bruno, *Nach Straßburg oder nach Sarajewo? Nationalismus in postkommunistischen Gesellschaften*, Hessische Stiftung für Friedens- und Konfliktforschung: Forschungsbericht 1/92 (Frankfurt, 1992).

——, *Deutschlands Einheit und Europas Zukunft* (Frankfurt: Suhrkamp, 1992).

Schöllgen, Gregor, *Angst vor der Macht: Die Deutschen und ihre Außenpolitik* (Berlin: Ullstein, 1993).

Scholz, Arno and Oschilewski, Günter (eds), *Kurt Schumacher: Reden und Schriften* (Berlin-Grunewald: arani-Verlag, 1962).

Schramm, Wilhelm Ritter von, *Beck und Goerdeler: Gemeinschaftsdokumente für den Frieden, 1941–1944* (Munich: Kindler Verlag, 1965).

Schubert, Markus, *Die Mitteleuropa-Konzeption Friedrich Naumanns und die Mitteleuropa-Debatte der 80er Jahre*, Libertas Paper, no. 3 (Sindelfingen: 1993).

Schüssler, Wilhelm, *Mitteleuropas Untergang und Wiedergeburt* (Berlin: Deutsche Verlags-Anstalt, 1919).

Schulz, Gerhard, *Deutschland seit dem Ersten Weltkrieg 1918–1945*, Deutsche Geschichte, vol. 10, 2nd edn, ed. Joachim Leuschner (Göttingen: Vandenhoeck und Ruprecht, 1982).

Schulz, Matthias, *Regionalismus und die Gestaltung Europas: Die konstitutionelle Bedeutung der Region im europäischen Drama zwischen Integration und Desintegration* (Hamburg: Krämer, 1993).

Schumacher, Kurt, *Reden, Schriften, Korrespondenzen, 1945–1952*, ed. Willy Albrecht (Berlin: J. H. Dietz, 1985).

Schwarz, Hans-Peter, *Vom Reich zur Bundesrepublik: Deutschland im Widerstreit der außenpolitischen Konzeptionen in den Jahren der Besatzungsherrschaft, 1945–49* (Berlin: Hermann Luchterhand Verlag, 1966).

——, *Handbuch der deutschen Außenpolitik* (Munich: R. Piper Verlag, 1975).

——, *Die Zentralmacht Europas: Deutschlands Rückkehr auf die Weltbühne* (Berlin: Siedler Verlag, 1994).

Schweigler, Gebhard, *West German Foreign Policy: The Domestic Setting*, The Washington Papers, no. 106 (New York: Praeger, 1984).

Snyder, Richard C., Bruck, H. W. and Sapin, Burton, *Foreign Policy Decision-Making: An Approach to the Study of International Politics* (New York: Free Press of Glencoe, 1962).

Sontheimer, Kurt, *Antidemokratisches Denken in der Weimarer Republik. Die*

politischen Ideen des deutschen Nationalismus zwischen 1918 und 1933 (Munich: Deutscher Taschenbuch Verlag, 1978).
——, *Die Adenauer-Ära: Grundlegung der Bundesrepublik* (Munich: Deutscher Taschenbuch Verlag, 1991).
Speier, Hans, *Force and Folly: Essays on Foreign Affairs and the History of Ideas* (Cambridge, Mass.: MIT Press, 1969).
Speier, Hans and Davison, Philip (eds), *West German Leadership and Foreign Policy* (New York: Row, Peterson, 1957).
Srbik, Heinrich von, *Mitteleuropa: Das Problem und die Versuche seiner Lösung in der deutschen Geschichte* (Weimar: Hermann Böhlau, 1937).
Staatslexikon: Recht, Wirtschaft, Gesellschaft, 5 vols (Freiburg: Görres Gesellschaft, 1987).
Stadelmann, Marcus, A., 'The Adenauer Era Revisited: German Foreign Policy 1949–1963' (MA thesis, University of California, Riverside, 1987).
——, 'The Dependent Ally: A Historical-Sociological Analysis of Postwar German Foreign Policy' (PhD dissertation, University of California, Riverside, 1990).
Stein, Heinrich F. K. Freiherr vom, *Briefwechsel, Denkschriften und Aufzeichnungen*, ed. Emil Botzenhart, 4 vols (Berlin: C. Heimann, 1933).
Stresemann, Gustav, *Reden und Schriften: Politik, Geschichte, Literatur 1897–1926*, vol. 1 (Dresden: Karl Reissner Verlag, 1926).
Ströhm, Gustaf C. and Daschitschew, Wjatscheslaw (eds), *Die Neuordnung Mitteleuropas* (Studienzentrum Weikersheim e.V. Mainz: von Hase & Koehler, 1991).
Thatcher, Margaret, *Downing Street No. 10: Erinnerungen* (Düsseldorf: Econ Verlag, 1993).
Thayer, Charles W., *Die unruhigen Deutschen* (Stuttgart: Alfred Scherz Verlag, 1958).
Theiner, Peter, *Sozialer Liberalismus und deutsche Weltpolitik: Friedrich Naumann im Wilhelminischen Deutschland* (Baden-Baden: Nomos, 1983).
de Tocqueville, Alexis, *De la démocratie en Amérique*, 2 vols (Brussels: L. Haumann, 1835–40).
Tönnis, Ferdinand, *Gemeinschaft und Gesellschaft* (Berlin: Verlag Curtious, 1922).
Treitschke, Heinrich von, *Politik: Vorlesungen gehalten an der Universität zu Berlin* (Leipzig: Hirzel, 1900).
Treverton, Gregory F., *America, Germany, and the Future of Europe* (Princeton, NJ: Princeton University Press, 1992).
——, *The Shape of the New Europe* (New York: Council on Foreign Relations Press, 1992).
Turner, Edward R., *Europe since 1789* (New York: Doubleday Page, 1924).
University of Innsbruck, *Symposium Mitteleuropa: Spuren der Vergangenheit – Perspektiven der Zukunft*, Veröffentlichungen der Universität Innsbruck, no. 160 (Innsbruck: Wagner'sche Universitäts Buchhandlung, 1987).
Verheyen, Theodorus F., 'Foreign Policy Culture: Germany and the United States in Historical and Comparative Perspective' (University of California, PhD thesis, 1988).
Vermeil, Edmond, *Germany's Three Reichs* (London: Dakers, 1945).
Vernohr, Wolfgang, *Ein Deutschland wird es sein* (Erlangen: Dietmar Straube Verlag, 1990).
Viotti, Paul R. and Kauppi, Mark V., *International Relations: Theory, Realism, Pluralism, Globalism*, 2nd rev. edn (New York: Macmillan, 1993).

Vorstand der SPD (ed.): Presse und Information, *Grundsätze für einen atomwaffenfreien Korridor in Mitteleuropa* (Weimar, 1986).

Waltz, Kenneth N., *Theory of International Politics* (Reading: Addison-Wesley, 1979).

Ward, Barbara, *Hitler's Route to Baghdad* (London: George Allen & Unwin, 1939).

Weber, Jürgen, *Die Republik der fünfziger Jahre: Adenauers Deutschlandpolitik auf dem Prüfstand* (Munich: Olzog Verlag, 1989).

Weidenfeld, Werner, *Konrad Adenauer und Europa: Geistige Grundlagen der westeuropäischen Integrationspolitik* (Bonn: Europa Union Verlag, 1976).

——, *Nachdenken über Deutschland: Materialien zur politischen Kultur der Deutschen Frage* (Cologne: Verlag Wissenschaft und Politik, 1985).

Weimer, Christian, 'Mitteleuropa als politisches Ordnungskonzept? Darstellung und Analyse der historischen Ideen und Pläne sowie der aktuellen Diskussionsmodelle' (PhD dissertation, University of Regensburg, 1992).

Weinberg, Gerhard L., *The Foreign Policy of Hitler's Germany*, vols 1 and 2 (Chicago: University of Chicago Press, 1970).

Willms, Bernard and Kleinewefers, Paul, *Erneuerung aus der Mitte: Prag–Wien–Berlin. Diesseits von Ost und West* (Herford: Busse & Seewald, 1988).

Windsor, Philip, *Germany and the Management of Détente*, Studies in International Security, no. 15 (New York: Praeger Publishers, 1971).

Winiewicz, Josef M., *Aims and Failures of the German New Order* (London: Polish Research Centre, 1943).

Wirsing, Giselher, *Zwischeneuropa und die deutsche Zukunft* (Jena: E. Diederichs Verlag, 1932).

Wolf, Julius, *Materialien betreffend den mitteleuropäischen Wirtschaftsverein*, 2nd edn (Berlin: Georg Reimer Verlag, 1904).

Wolffsohn, Michael, *West-Germany's Foreign Policy in the Era of Brandt and Schmidt, 1969–1982* (Frankfurt: Peter Lang, 1986).

Woyke, Wichard (ed.), *Handwörterbuch Internationale Politik*, 3rd rev. edn (Opladen: Leske und Budrich, 1986).

Ziebura, Gilbert (ed.), *Grundfragen der deutschen Außenpolitik seit 1871* (Darmstadt: Wissenschaftliche Buchgesellschaft, 1975).

Ziebura, Gilbert, Ansprenger, Franz, and Kiersch, Gerhard, *Bestimmungsfaktoren der Außenpolitik in der 2. Hälfte des 20. Jahrhunderts*, Schriftenreihe des Fachbereichs Politische Wissenschaft der Freien Universität Berlin, no. 4 (Berlin: Universität Berlin, 1974).

Zitelmann, Rainer, *Adenauers Gegner: Streiter für die Einheit* (Erlangen: Straube, 1991).

——, *Demokraten für Deutschland: Adenauers Gegner – Streiter für Deutschland* (Frankfurt: Ullstein, 1993).

Zitelmann, Rainer, Weißmann, Karlheinz, and Großheim, Michael, *Westbindung: Chancen und Risiken für Deutschland* (Berlin: Propyläen, 1993).

ARTICLES

Albright, Madeleine, 'The Role of the US in Central Europe', *Proceedings of the Academy of Political Science*, no. 1 (1991), pp. 71–84.

Altmann, Rüdiger, 'Den Kopf über dem Nebel. Constantin Frantz – ein vergessener deutscher Klassiker des Föderalismus', *Frankfurter Allgemeine Zeitung*, 2 May 1991, p. N3.

Andriessen, Frans, interview in *Süddeutsche Zeitung*, 18 November 1991, p. 8.

Ash, Timothy G., 'Mitteleuropa?', *Daedalus*, no. 1 (1990), pp. 1–22.

Asmus, Ronald D., 'East and West Germany: Continuity and Change', *The World Today*, 40 (1984): 142–51.

Assheuer, Thomas, 'Repolitisierung? Zur Debatte um Mitteleuropa', *Frankfurter Rundschau*, 10 June 1988, p. 11.

Baker, James and Genscher, Hans-Dietrich, 'US–German Views on the New European and Trans-Atlantic Architecture', *US Department of State Dispatch*, 13 May 1991, pp. 345–7.

Bender, Peter, 'Mitteleuropa – Mode, Modell oder Motiv?', *Neue Gesellschaft/ Frankfurter Hefte*, 34 (1987): 297–304.

Bergdoll, Udo, 'Anwalt der Balten', *Süddeutsche Zeitung*, 10 March 1994, p. 4.

Besançon, Alain, 'What Troubles Germany', *Atlantic Community Quarterly*, 25 (1987): 253–5.

Binder, David, 'As Bonn Talks Louder, Some in the US Wince', *New York Times*, 7 January 1992, p. A2.

Bondy, François, 'Das Phantom Mitteleuropa und die politische Wirklichkeit. Nachdenken über die gemeinsame Kultur zwischen Ost und West', *Frankfurter Allgemeine Zeitung*, 21 December 1985, p. 3.

Brandt, Willy, interview in *Welt am Sonntag*, 7 January 1967, p. 3.

Bredow, Wilfried von, and Jäger, Thomas, 'Niemannsland Mitteleuropa. Zur Wiederkehr eines diffusen Ordnungskonzepts', *Aus Politik und Zeitgeschichte*, Beilage der Zeitung 'Das Parlament', 40/41 (1988): 42.

Breyer, Richard, 'Carl Goerdeler und die deutsche Ostgrenze', *Zeitschrift für Ostforschung*, no. 1/2 (1964), pp. 198–208.

Bütler, Hugo, 'Stichwort Mitteleuropa: Tatsachen, Ideen, Illusionen', *Neue Züricher Zeitung*, 6 July 1985, p. 43.

Burley, Anne-Marie, 'The Once and Future German Question', *Foreign Affairs*, no. 5 (1989/90), pp. 65–84.

Busek, Erhard, 'Besinnung auf Mitteleuropa', *Europäische Rundschau*, 13 (1985): 7–12.

'Can Mitteleuropa Find Itself?', *The Economist*, 16 September 1989, pp. 117–18.

'Central Europe: The Empire Strikes Back', *The Economist*, 25 August 1990, pp. 17–19.

Cohen, Roger, 'Continental Block Party or Exclusive Club?', *New York Times*, 10 May 1992, p. E5.

Coker, Christopher, 'At the Birth of the Fourth Reich? The British Reaction', *Political Quarterly*, July 1990, pp. 278–84.

Dahrendorf, Ralf, 'Wanted: A new Vision of Europe', *World Press Review*, January 1990, p. 24.

'Debate the Real European Issues', *New York Times*, 30 July 1992, p. A24.

Dormann, Manfred, 'Faktoren der außenpolitischen Entscheidung', *Politische Vierteljahreszeitschrift*, no. 1 (1971), pp. 14–28.

'East is East and West is West, and What is in the Middle?', *The Economist*, 26 December 1987, pp. 31–2.

Eisfeld, Rainer, '"Nationale" Politikwissenschaft von der Weimarer Republik zum Dritten Reich', *Politische Vierteljahresschrift*, no. 2 (1990), pp. 238–64.

Eppler, Erhard, 'Liberale und soziale Demokratie. Zum politischen Erbe Friedrich Naumanns', *Neue Gesellschaft/Frankfurter Hefte*, 7 (1983): 628–37.

Falin, Valentin, 'A Soviet View of Reunification', *World Press Review*, April 1990, pp. 26–8.

Fischer, Fritz, 'Deutsche Kriegsziele. Revolutionierung und Separatfrieden im Osten 1914–1918', *Historische Zeitschrift*, 188 (1959): 248–310.

——, 'Kontinuität des Irrtums. Zum Problem der deutschen Kriegszielpolitik im Ersten Weltkrieg', *Historische Zeitschrift*, 191 (1960): 83–100.

Fontaine, André, 'Imperialist Threat or European Anchor?', *World Press Review*, July 1990, pp. 26–7.

Frank, Michaeal, 'Zwei Seiten eines ungeliebten Imperiums', *Süddeutsche Zeitung*, 18 March 1993, p. 3.

Franz, Otmar, 'Gibt es Mitteleuropa', *Frankfurter Allgemeine Zeitung*, 10 December 1986, p. 1.

Gati, Charles, 'East-Central Europe: The Morning After', *Foreign Affairs*, no. 5 (1990/91), pp. 129–45.

'Germanies in Confusion', *The Economist*, 7 October 1989, pp. 27–8.

Glotz, Peter, 'Deutsch-Böhmische Kleinigkeiten oder Abgerissene Gedanken über Mitteleuropa', *Neue Gesellschaft/Frankfurter Hefte*, 33 (1986): 584–5.

——, 'Die Alleinherrschaft des Ost-West-Denkens gefährden: Anmerkungen zu einer Idee des mitteleuropäischen Bewußtseins', *Frankfurter Rundschau*, 25 May 1988, p. 14.

Görlich, Ernst, 'Großmitteleuropäisch und kleinmitteleuropäisch um die Mitte des 19. Jahrhunderts', *Welt als Geschichte*, 7 (1941): 259–66.

Gress, David, 'What the West should Know about German Neutralism', *Commentary*, no. 1 (1983), pp. 26–31.

Habermas, Jürgen, 'Historical Consciousness and Post-Traditional Identity: Remarks on the Federal Republic's Orientation to the West', *Acta Sociologica*, 31 (1988): 3–13.

Hampel, Adolf, 'Vermittlung und Ausgleich sind geboten', *Politische Studien*, 36 (1985): 577–81.

Handl, Vladimir, 'Germany and Central Europe: "Mitteleuropa" Restored?', *Perspectives: Review of Central European Affairs*, no. 1 (1993), pp. 45–52.

Havel, Václav, 'The Future of Central Europe', *The New York Review of Books*, 29 March 1990, pp. 18–19.

Heilbrunn, Jacob, 'Tomorrow's Germany', *National Interest*, Summer 1994, pp. 44–52.

Heimann, Gerhard, 'Die europäische Mitte und die Zukunft Berlins', *Neue Gesellschaft/Frankfurter Hefte*, 33 (1986): 590–3.

Herzfeld, Hans, 'Zur deutschen Politik im Ersten Weltkrieg. Kontinuität oder permanente Krise?', *Historische Zeitschrift*, 191 (1960): 67–82.

Hitchens, Christopher, 'Washington's Kohl Front: Embracing a Chancellor, Eschewing Debate', *Harper's*, no. 1685 (1990), pp. 74–82.

Hoagland, Jim, 'Germany and Russia are Getting Together', *Herald Tribune*, 17 May 1994, p. 6.

Hrbek, Rudolf, 'The EC and the Changes in Central and Eastern Europe', *Intereconomics*, 25 (1990): 131–9.

Jahn, Egbert, 'Ein Kontinent wird vermessen: Mitteleuropa Rekonstruktion im Überblick', *Blätter für deutsche und internationale Politik*, no. 1 (1989), pp. 1322–9.

Jaworski, Rudolf, 'Die aktueel Mitteleuropadiskusion in historischer Perspektive', *Historische Zeitschrift*, 247 (1988), pp. 529–50.

Johnson, R. W., 'L'Europe c'est moi: Fear of German Power Remains the Key to French Policy', *New Statesman and Society*, no. 106 (1990), pp. 20–2.

Kádár, Béla, 'Central Europe Once Again', *New Hungarian Quarterly*, no. 121 (1991), pp. 3–18.

Kaltefleiter, Werner, 'Außenpolitische Willensbildung in der Gegenwart', *Geschichte und Gegenwart*, September 1982, pp. 19–29.

Kaufmann, Richard von, 'Der mitteleuropäische Zollverein', *Zeitschrift für die gesamte Staatswissenschaft*, 42 (1886), pp. 530–84.

Kinzer, Stephen, 'Triumph for Germany: Europe, Backing Germans, Accepts Yugoslav Breakup', *New York Times*, 16 January 1992, p. A10.

——, 'As Euphoria of Unity Fades, Eastern Germans Feel Scorned and Excluded', *New York Times*, 18 April 1992, p. 3.

Kissinger, Henry A., 'A Plan for Europe', *Newsweek*, 18 June 1990, pp. 32–7.

Kofmann, Jan, 'Economic Nationalism in Eastern and Central Europe in the Interwar Period', *Oeconomica Polona*, 15 (1988), pp. 103–11.

Kohák, Erazim, 'Can there be a Central Europa?', *Dissent*, 37 (1990), pp. 194–7.

Kollmann, Eric C., 'Walther Rathenau and German Foreign Policy', *Journal of Modern History*, 24 (1952), pp. 127–42.

Koydl, Wolfgang, 'Die Deutschen investieren, die anderen parieren', *Süddeutsche Zeitung*, 6/7 February 1993, p. 4.

Krippendorf, Ekkehardt, 'Ist Außenpolitik Außenpolitik?', *Politische Vierteljahresschrift*, no. 3 (1963), pp. 243–66.

Kundera, Milan and Konrád, György, 'Die Tragödie Zentraleuropas', *Kommune: Forum für Politik und Ökonomie*, July 1984, pp. 43–52.

Löwenthal, Richard, 'The German Question Transformed', *Foreign Affairs*, no. 2 (1984/85), pp. 303–15.

Magenheimer, Heinz, 'Renaissance der Geopolitik: Deutschland und Mitteleuropa 1890–1990', *Österreichische Militärische Zeitschrift*, no. 2 (1991), pp. 131–9.

'Make Way for the Germans', *The Economist*, 14 October 1989, pp. 13–14.

Meinecke, Friedrich, 'Gedanken und Erinnerungen', *Historische Zeitschrift*, 82 (1899), pp. 282–95.

Meyer, Michael, 'Bonn's Ostpolitik for the '90s', *Newsweek*, 15 May 1989, p. 24.

Molnar, Thomas, 'Recentralizing Europe', *National Review*, 24 November 1989, pp. 34–6.

Moreton, Edwina, 'All Quiet on the German Front? Germany in the Post-Detente Era', *Government and Opposition*, no. 4 (1984), pp. 438–50.

Münkler, Herfried, 'Europa als politische Idee', *Leviathan*, 19 (1991), pp. 521–41.

Nagorski, Andrew, 'Are there 3 Europes? The Concept of Mitteleuropa is Staging a Dramatic Comeback', *Newsweek*, 23 March 1987, p. 12.

——, 'The Rebirth of an Idea', *Newsweek*, 30 March 1987, pp. 38–40.

Neue Gesellschaft/Frankfurter Hefte, 40 (1993), pp. 604–32.

'Neue Ostpolitik', *Süddeutsche Zeitung*, 18 August 1993, p. 2.

Nipperdey, Thomas, 'Interessenverbände und Parteien in Deutschland: Vor dem Ersten Weltkrieg', *Politische Vierteljahresschrift*, no. 3 (1961), pp. 262–80.

Nonnenmacher, Günther, 'Welche neue Rolle für den alten Kontinent?', *Frankfurter Allgemeine Zeitung*, 19 March 1992, p. 14.
——, 'Deutsche Einigung als "Sonderfall"', *Frankfurter Allgemeine Zeitung*, 13 April 1992, p. 14.
Novak, Josef, 'Europe: All of Nothing at All', *World Press Review*, November 1988, p. 23.
Novotny, Alexander, 'Der Berliner Kongreß und das Problem einer europäischen Politik', *Historische Zeitschrift*, 186 (1958), pp. 285–307.
Nürnberger, Richard, 'Imperialismus, Sozialismus und Christentum bei Friedrich Naumann', *Historische Zeitschrift*, 170 (1950), pp. 525–48.
Odom, William E., 'Top of the Agenda: Germany's Future', *US News and World Report*, 22 January 1990, p. 36.
Ohmae, Kenichi, 'The Rise of the Region State', *Foreign Affairs*, Spring 1993, pp. 78–87.
'On the Eve. A Survey of West Germany', *The Economist*, 28 October 1989, after p. 64.
Opitz, Reinhard, 'Deutsche Frage und Mitteleuropa-Diskussion', *Marxistische Blätter*, no. 6 (1986), pp. 21–30.
Owen, David, 'The Politics of Central Europe', *Atlantic Community Quarterly*, 21 (1983): 10–16.
Pascal, Richard, 'The Frankfurt Parliament, 1848, and the Drang nach Osten', *Journal of Modern History*, 18 (1946), pp. 108–9.
Pegg, Carl H., 'Der Gedanke der europäischen Einigung während des Ersten Weltkrieges und zu Beginn der zwanziger Jahre', *Europa Archiv*, 17 (1962), pp. 749–58.
——, 'Vorstellungen und Pläne der Befürworter eines europäischen Staatenbundes in den Jahren 1925–1930', *Europa Archiv*, 17 (1962), pp. 783–90.
——, 'Die wachsende Bedeutung der europäischen Einigungsbewegung in den zwanziger Jahren', *Europa Archiv*, 17 (1962), pp. 865–74.
Pradetto, August and Sigmund, Petra, 'Deutschland und Osteuropa in der Ära des Postkommunismus', *Deutschland Archiv*, no. 8 (1993), pp. 890–904.
Prantl, Heribert, 'Der neue Überfall auf Polen', *Süddeutsche Zeitung*, 1 March 1993, p. 3.
Riding, Alan, 'At East–West Crossroads, Western Europe Hesitates', *New York Times*, 25 March 1992, p. A10.
Ritter, Gerhard, 'Die Fälschung des deutschen Geschichtsbildes im Hitlerreich', *Deutsche Rundschau*, no. 4 (1947), pp. 11–20.
Robejsek, Peter, 'Deutschland und Osteuropa', *Rissener Jahrbuch*, (1991/92), pp. 57–62.
Rovan, Joseph, 'Die Illusion des Westens: Zur Diskussion des Mitteleuropa-Gedankens', *Frankfurter Allgemeine Zeitung*, 4 April 1987, Beilage 'Bilder und Zeiten'.
Rumpf, Helmut, 'Mitteleuropa: Zur Geschichte und Deutung eines politischen Begriffs', *Historische Zeitschrift*, 165 (1942), pp. 510–27.
Rupnik, Jacques, 'Borders of the Mind', *New Republic*, 9 March 1987, pp. 17–19.
Sanders, Ivan, 'The Quest for Central Europe', *Wilson Quarterly*, no. 2 (1990), pp. 26–36.
Schieder, Theodor, 'Idee und Gestalt des übernationalen Staates seit dem 19. Jahrhundert', *Historische Zeitschrift*, 184 (1957), pp. 336–66.

Schlögel, Karl, 'Die blockierte Vergangenheit. Nachdenken über Mitteleuropa', *Frankfurter Allgemeine Zeitung*, 21 February 1987, Beilage 'Bilder und Zeiten'.

Schmidt, Helmut, 'Deutschlands Rolle im neuen Europa', *Europa Archiv*, 46 (1991), pp. 611–24.

Schulz, Gerhard, 'Über Entstehung und Formen von Interessengruppen in Deutschland seit Beginn der Industrialisierung', *Politische Vierteljahresschrift*, no. 2 (1961), pp. 124–54.

Seiffert, Wolfgang, 'Deutschland – Eine Vormacht in Osteuropa? Chancen, Risiken und neue Verantwortung', *Rissener Jahrbuch*, (1991/1992), pp. 470–2.

Shouzheng, Yin, 'A Look at Helmut Kohl's Foreign Policy', *Beijing Review*, 7 May 1990, pp. 15–18.

Sinnhuber, Karl A., 'Central Europe – Mitteleuropa – Europe Centrale', *Transactions and Papers 1954. Institute of British Geographers*, no. 20 (1954), pp. 15–39.

Stanglin, Douglas, 'But Bonn Widens its World Reach', *US News and World Report*, 11 April 1988, p. 37.

Stent, Angela, 'The One Germany', *Foreign Policy*, Winter 1990/91, pp. 53–70.

Stern, Fritz, 'Adenauer and a Crisis in Weimar Democracy', *Political Science Quarterly*, March 1958, pp. 1–23.

Stobbe, Dietrich, 'Der Traum von der Wiederherstellung der Europäischen Mitte', *Neue Gesellschaft/Frankfurter Hefte*, 33 (1986), pp. 586–7.

Stoiber, Edmund, 'Es gab einmal eine europäische Bewegung . . .', *Süddeutsche Zeitung*, 2 November 1993, p. 14.

Stürmer, Michael, 'Kein Wiedersehen in Rapallo', *Frankfurter Allgemeine Zeitung*, 16 April 1992, p. 5.

Suchocka, Hanna, 'Desinteresse des Westens schürt Gefahren im Osten', *Süddeutsche Zeitung*, 26 February 1993, p. 9.

Sullivan, Scott, 'The Resurrection of the Greater Reich?', *Newsweek*, 13 November 1989, p. 56.

Sweet, Paul, 'Recent German Literature on Mitteleuropa', *Journal of Central European Affairs*, no. 1 (1943), pp. 1–24.

——, 'Leaders and Policies: Germany in the Winter of 1914–15', *Journal of Central European Affairs*, no. 3 (1956), pp. 229–52.

Szabo, Stephen, 'The New Germany', *Journal of Democracy*, January 1992, pp. 97–108.

Tagliabue, John, 'In Germany, West Plus East Means Policy Shift', *New York Times*, 1 March 1992, p. E5.

Thalberg, Hans, 'Zentraleuropa: Die Kunst des Möglichen', *Europäische Rundschau*, 14 (1986), pp. 3–8.

'The Triumphs and Harrumphs of Genscherism', *The Economist*, 16 January 1988, pp. 41–2.

Ties, Jochen, 'West Germany: The Risks ahead', *The World Today*, May 1989, pp. 76–9.

Treverton, George F., 'Finding an Analogy for Tomorrow', *Orbis*, no. 1 (1993), pp. 1–19.

Turnock, David, 'Europe Reintegrates', *Geographical Magazine*, May 1990, pp. 14–18.

Tütsch, Hans E., 'From Nostalgia to Utopia', *The American Scholar*, Winter 1987, pp. 94–8.

Vernohr, Wolfgang, 'Deutschlands Mittellage: Betrachtungen zur ungelösten deutschen Frage', *Deutschland Archiv*, no. 8 (1984), pp. 820–9.

Waever, Ole, 'Three Competing Europes: German, French, Russian', *International Affairs*, no. 3 (1990), pp. 477–94.

Walter, Helga, 'Appeasement in our Time', *National Review*, 2 June 1989, pp. 26–31.

Waltz, Kenneth N., 'The Emerging Structure of International Politics', *International Security*, no. 2 (1993), pp. 44–79.

Weige, Zhu, 'Federal Germany's Policy towards the East', *Beijing Review*, October 1989, pp. 14–18.

Weidenfeld, Werner, 'Mitteleuropa – ein alter Mythos stiftet Unruhe', *Rheinischer Merkur*, 3 October 1986, p. 3.

——, 'Die Zukunft des Kontinents. Perspektiven einer neuen Ordnung für Europa', *Frankfurter Allgemeine Zeitung*, 28 February 1990, p. 8.

Weidenfeld, Werner and Janning, Josef, 'Schöpferische Vielfalt oder zerstörter Herrschaftswille', *Frankfurter Allgemeine Zeitung*, 15 April 1992, p. 8.

Whitney, Craig R., 'Germany Focusses on German Unity: European Unity will Wait', *New York Times*, 13 May 1992, p. A12.

Witte, Barthold C., 'Alte Bindungen und neue Wege nach Mittel- und Osteuropa', *Europa Archiv*, 46 (1991), pp. 201–10.

Index